THE LIFE AND RECOLLECTIONS

OF

E. M. DAVENPORT

MAJOR, H. M. 66th REGIMENT

WRITTEN BY HIMSELF

"Notes on what I have seen and done."

FROM 1835 to 1850

The Rifles Wardrobe and Museum Trust
The Wardrobe, 58 The Close, Salisbury, SP1 2EX
www.thewardrobe.org.uk

2011

First published by the Author for private circulation in 1869

The rights of the author, Major Ernest Montagu Davenport of the 66th Regiment, his heirs and successors are recognised.

Apart from any fair dealing for the purposes of research or private study, or criticism or review, as permitted under the Copyright Designs and Patents Act 1988, this publication may only be reproduced, stored or transmitted, in any form or by any means, with the prior permission in writing of the publisher or, in the case of reprographic reproduction, in accordance with the terms of licences issued by the Copyright Licensing Agency.

Copyright in this printing © 2011 The Rifles Berkshire and Wiltshire Wardrobe and Museum Trust

The publisher makes no representation, express or implied, with regard to the accuracy of the information contained within this book and cannot accept any legal responsibility or liability for any errors or omissions that may be made.

ISBN 978-1-908076-30-4

Introduction

The Rifles (Berkshire and Wiltshire) Wardrobe and Museum Trust holds the collection and archives of the former 66th (Berkshire) Regiment, later the 2nd Battalion Royal Berkshire Regiment. This re-publication of Davenport's book provides an insight into the life of an infantry officer in the British Army from 1835 to 1850; his attitude to people, places and animals.

Davenport was born in 1817 and commissioned into the 66th (Berkshire) Regiment in 1835. His service was both in the Regiment at home and abroad and in its Depot, which remained in Great Britain and Ireland. He remained with the Regiment until 1858. The variety of places where he served is evident from the Contents.

Michael Cornwell
Lieutenant Colonel
(Retired)
Manager/Curator
February 2011

Contents

Voyage From Plymouth To Cork	11
Bandon	13
Kinsale	19
Cork	20
Voyage To Canada	21
Quebec	24
Sorel	33
St. Denis	37
St. Ours	41
Sorel	44
Colonel Wetherall's Expedition	47
Richelieu	49
St. Hillaire	53
St. Charles	54
Chambly And St. John's	56
Sorel	57
Niagara	59
State Of New York	61
Syracuse To Utica	62
New York	63
Philadelphia	65
Montreal	66
Richelieu	67
Boucherville	68
Beltil	69
St. John's	71
La Prairie	72
Sorel	74
La Prairie	75
The Bush	77
Montreal	79
Chateauguy	81
Montreal	90
Voyage To England	92
Portsmouth	95
Winchester	99
Route To Manchester	101
Davenport	103
Glasgow	106
Fort William	110
Edinburgh	129

Belfast	132
Dublin	143
Scotland	144
London	147
Dublin	150
Philipstown	153
Birr	156
Athlone	158
Killaloe	166
Clare Castle	171
Ennis	173
Templemore	176
Thurles	179
Fermoy	183
Castletown Roach	186
Fermoy	188
Kinsale	195
Killarney	207
Kinsale	217
Newcastle	220
Tralee And Shooting At Tralee	225
Voyage To The West Indies	233
Barbadoes	236
Voyage: Barbadoes To Demerara	240
Demerara	242
A Trip Up The Essiquibo River	254
Georgetown, Demerara	264
Voyage To St. Vincent	273
St. Vincent	276
Trip To The Soufriere	285

LIFE AND RECOLLECTIONS OF

E. M. DAVENPORT.

I was just seventeen years old, my father got my name put down upon Lord Hill's private list for a Commission in the army, through a great friend of both parties, Colonel Gatacre of Gatacre, Colonel in the Shropshire Militia. My name had been entered on the list about three months when it was thought expedient that I should call upon Lord Hill and ask what chance I had of getting a Commission. I rode over to Hawkestone accordingly, with Mr. Harris of Benthal, and found his Lordship at home. We first of all discussed luncheon, and then talked about business, He told me he was very glad I had called upon him as he now *saw* that I was fit for a Commission. He said that he, had then, on his own private list, no fewer than five hundred names of gentlemen anxious to get into the army; that my name came very low down amongst them, and therefore that I need not expect an immediate appointment. However, Lord Hill said he would do what he could for me and we parted.

Three months after my interview with him, I received my Commission in the 66th Regiment, dated 24th of April, 1835, and I know that my calling upon his Lordship and letting him see my long, and even then, not very lanky body, accelerated my appointment very much. The authorities did not give me much leave on appointment, for I was ordered to join the depot, quartered at Plymouth Citadel, on the 20th of May. I therefore bade adieu to Davenport House, and arrived at Plymouth, on the 19th. I went up to the Citadel and reported my arrival to the renowned John Daniell, Major, commanding the depot, who at that moment was at his favourite amusement of teaching the sword-exercise to the officers and non-commissioned officers in the barrack square. I was, as may be supposed, very green, a regular Johnny Raw but I found amongst the officers, one to whom I shall be ever grateful for his kindness in taking me by the hand, and giving me always his advice, and that was George Maxwell, then a Lieutenant. He really was as good as a father to me, and as I felt so much his kindness at the time, it has always caused me to look after youngsters on joining in the same way, and to give them a little friendly advice whenever I saw they required it.

From what I now recollect of Plymouth, I found it a very pleasant quarter. Our depot was the favourite one of the garrison, and we were, some of us, out almost every night. Although I went to Plymouth without a single introduction, yet in a very short time I was well acquainted with many families. Mr. Strode, of Newnham Park soon called on me, and from him I received a great deal of hospitality, as well as from the Scobells and many others. Last, though not least, were the Major-General Sir Willoughby Cotton, and the Admiral Hargood, from both of whom I received my share of kindness. On Sir W. Cotton's hearing that Ensign Davenport had joined the 66th depot, he immediately sent me an invitation to dinner, which I of course accepted. After shaking me cordially by the hand, Sir W. Cotton said, well Davenport, how are all your friends in Cheshire? I have no doubt they are all well Sir Willoughby, but although they *are* related to us, I don't know any of them. Mine is the *Shropshire* branch, and I believe a great uncle of mine had a quarrel with the Cheshire stock, since which we have not known each other."

"Oh, I thought you were a *Cheshire* man! however, dinner is ready, so let us proceed."

Sir W. Cotton was somehow related to the Cheshire family, and thought I was his cousin. As he did not take a dislike to me for not being one of his Cheshire friends I dined there often and met pleasant people. Sir W. Cotton was one day talking to his son Corbett, who was his A.D.C., and on mentioning the 32nd depot, who were quartered there, he said, "By-the-bye Corbett, is there not a Captain in that depot of the name of Brooke?"

"Oh, yes! a very good fellow."

"Ha! ask the Captain to dinner, and we will give him a cutlet. And Dixon; there is an Ensign of that name, is there not?"

"Yes, sir, there is."

"Ha! ask him to dinner also, and we will give the Ensign a bone."

This story was repeated, and went the rounds, not of the garrison of Plymouth alone, but I have heard it in almost every place that I have been quartered at.

Sir Willoughby Cotton took, I think, an interest in me, (goodness only knows why,) for he would sometimes catch me by the arm, and walk away down the streets with me; and, upon one occasion, he asked me if I did not want leave to go and see my friends? I replied that I should like it much; but was afraid the Major would not yet recommend me for any, as I scarcely knew my drill. "Oh," he said, "I have no doubt the Major will make it all right; and certainly, about a fortnight afterwards, Major Daniell told me that if I wished it, I might go away for a fortnight, which was quite unexpected by me; so away I went home.

We had a very nice garrison at Plymouth and Devonport. We had in the citadel with us, the 75th depot, who were afterwards relieved by the 37th depot; and at Devonport were the 32nd, 56th, 58th, and 98th depots; also for a short time the 10th.

The 66th were invited to dine with the 98th one Saturday at Mount Wise Barracks, where we met some other officers of the different depots quartered there. We sat rather late, and just when the devilled bones, etc., were being brought up, Major B—, 98th, got up to make a speech, and said it was a most pleasant evening, and that he only wished he could meet the same party

3

oftener; when some one of the guests exclaimed, That might easily be done if he wished it; upon which the Major, who was decidedly cracked,' and went by the name of "The Mad Major," took the hint, and said, he would be delighted if *the whole of* the guests present would dine with him there on the following Saturday.

We of course, out of common courtesy, could not refuse, and assembled at the time appointed.

Upon this occasion we sat still later than the time before. Three of the 36th had to go to their Barracks the same way that I and McCarthy were to go to Plymouth; one of the 98th, a strapping fellow, accompanying us. We had not proceeded far along the street, when we were met by some blackguard civilians, who, in some way, insulted Whyate, 36th; and he immediately knocked one of then down. This commenced a row, shouting began, some fighting, watchmen's rattles going; till the opposing party numbered about twenty watchmen and forty civilians. We all closed up, and walked down the street in battle array, and had not gone far, when the civilian who had been floored wanted us all to be taken to the watch-house, which, of course, we could not think of consenting to. The row began again, and the fighting began again, but I did not embroil myself and kept McCarthy, who was but a weak stripling, out of it. However, presently a fellow came up to me with a complaint of the usage he got, (seeing me standing quietly looking on.) I told him he only got what he deserved, when he grew furious, telling me I was as bad as the rest, and he would give me a — good hiding. He at once commenced to take off his coat, which I did not object to, but when he pinioned his own arms behind his back in his coat sleeves, I could not resist the temptation, and knocked him head over heels. I saw no more of *him*. At that moment I saw Gibson, 36th, being carried away by four watchmen to their lock-up. I immediately rushed up to them, floored the two right and left that had hold of his legs, and gave the whole weight of my body to the other two, who went asunder as if they had been shot. Gibson got on his legs, we put ourselves back to back, and walked out of the mob, no one daring to lay hold of us, though several blows were aimed at us, and the watchmen stood as though paralyzed. We then got into the 36th barracks till the mob dispersed, and McCarthy and I betook ourselves home to the Citadel at about five o'clock. The battle was bloody, for £5 was offered for Gibson's shirt, as an evidence of the fury of the onslaught; but his washing-woman refused to show it. The affair came to the General's ears, but he said he would take no notice of it if not officially reported, which it never was.

The garrison were constantly getting into rows of that sort, being composed chiefly of young boys, just let loose from their mothers' apron-strings, who, of course, must let out their young hot blood, and sow their wild oats. I certainly was in a few myself, but not in so many as some of my friends. At one of these dinners with the 98th depot, were one or two Yankees, who, having been obliged to put into Plymouth, had to stop some time to repair their ship. They enjoyed themselves very much, drank deeply, and got to their hotel *somehow*. However, the following morning, one of them called on the 98th, and said he was sure he had insulted some of them the previous night, and that he came for the express purpose of giving "satisfaction" to the officer he had offended. He was told he had offended no one, and that nothing extraordinary had occurred, but this would not satisfy him, for he called to mind a few of the names of the officers, declaring that he had insulted first one and then the other, and, as a "gentleman," he was bound to give that satisfaction which was due on such occasions. It was with great difficulty they got rid of this Yankee rifleman, and, I believe, made up their minds not to ask any more of that I kidney' to their mess.

As for the sporting about Plymouth, I cannot say much. I joined in the summer, and, of course, fishing was the first thing I thought of, being very fond of that amusement. The rivers at Ivy Bridge and Earne Bridge are talked of as very good; but, for my own part, I pronounce them both to be bad, for though I am not a bad fisherman by any means, I never saw any trout caught there longer than one's finger.

There is no shooting at all to be had about Plymouth, excepting some snipe upon Dartmoor, eleven miles off. Lord. Cochrane, who was in the 66th, used to drive out there very often, and, although a capital shot, he seldom brought back more than two couple.

The hunting, I believe, was not first-rate. I was not mounted myself, so can only speak from hearsay. The country is very hilly, and the fences large embankments, with hedges on the tops of them; therefore, it required a very clever horse and one trained to that particular country, or else one imported from Ireland, to get over it at all. When the 66th depot went there first, they arrived from Cork, and took several Irish horses over with them, and the cry always was, when out hunting, "Oh, let the Irish horses go first, and clear the way!"

The scenery round Plymouth is very pretty. The most of Devonshire is beautiful; but Mount Edgecumbe is particularly so, and many are the picnics perpetrated there during the summer.

Our quarters in the citadel were very good, each of us having a bed-room, sitting-room, and kitchen underneath, and there was a beautiful walk round the ramparts, with a fine view of the sea. Lloyd's Station - was on the saluting-battery; we could see the flagstaff from all the front quarters, and, by an arrangement we made with his men, there were certain signals hoisted for different kinds of shipping, either coming in or going out of the offing, so that we always could tell when our telescopes were of use, without the trouble of keeping a look-out for ourselves. The breakwater is a very remarkable structure at the harbour's mouth, and well worth a visit. It is in view from the citadel, distance about three miles.

One morning I was aroused from my slumbers by Daniell, one of our subs, coming into my room, (where I had given Ditmas a "shake down,") saying that the citadel was on fire. He told us to get up immediately, but as he was always playing tricks, we thought that this was one of them, so we bundled him downstairs by throwing our boots at him. Immediately afterwards up came Johnny Vivian with the same story; this also we said was "humbug," so we dismissed him with the boot-jack and slippers. I, however, lay quiet a few minutes listening, and fancied I heard a strange concourse of voices in the square below, and what should I see but the *remains* of the men's barracks, in rear of the governor's house, still burning, and a double line of men handing up and returning buckets to and from the sally-port. There were three depots from Devonport, our own and the 75th hard at work, and had been since four o'clock, a.m., besides the crews of two ships which were in the harbour, and a lot of the marines. There were Ditmas and I! sleeping through the whole of it, although the flames, they said, reached my windows at one time. My Company's rooms were burnt, as well as the poor old Fort-Major Watson and his two daughters, in their quarters; they, poor people, were afterwards found all clung together, one mass of ashes! The poor old man was at one time seen at one of the windows endeavouring to escape, and was entreated by our men to throw himself out, and they would break his fall, there being no ladder available at the moment; why he did not, God only knows, for at that moment he disappeared, and was no more seen, till picked out of the ruins, a burnt cinder. The magazine had a narrow escape, as the fire was driven by the wind right over it; however, they kept throwing water on the blankets with which they covered the roof, and it escaped. The fire originated in the Fort-Major's house, from the servant's having put some chips of wood near the fire to dry; these became ignited, and set fire to the flooring of the room—hence the conflagration. The fire was not extinguished till late in the day, when it was considered quite out; however, at about eleven o'clock that night, the wind was blowing fresh, when it burst out again. The "turn-out" was sounded, and it was soon extinguished. The Fort-Major's two sons were in the house at the time; the one, a blind one, managed to make his escape himself; the other did so also, but lost everything belonging to himself and the whole family, which I dare say was not much. A subscription was set on foot, and enough was scraped together to establish him in some way in Newfoundland.

There is always a regatta in the Sound, both for sailing and rowing. We had a boat entered for one, in which she won a silver goblet. However, one day she was swamped about a mile from shore, between Drake's Island and "The Hoe." One of our men, (Steward,) who was on detachment on the island, seeing the accident, jumped into the sea, and swam off to the rescue, which was a very gallant thing to do; but other boats came up in time, and all were saved. This gallant fellow (for he did other equally fine actions) was drummed out of the regiment at Glasgow in 1842, for constantly thieving in a small way. He certainly was the handsomest man in the regiment.

There is, at Saltash, (a village about twelve miles up the river from Devonport,) a stout set of women who always row up to market and back again every week. They enter their boats in the races against the men, and what is most extraordinary, they always win the matches. There were also races set apart for the women alone to pull for.

We had a detachment at Drake's Island of one subaltern and about twenty men. Ensign Carey was at this time quartered there; but he fell in love, so away he went to Gretna Green, got spliced, and returned, all in a few days, when nobody missed him. He was under orders to join the Service Companies in Canada, and thereupon embarked with his wife, when it occurred to them both that milk (*fresh*) would be a very nice thing to have every morning for breakfast, so it was agreed between them that he should go on shore instanter, and buy a goat at "The Hoe," where there were numbers of them grazing. He got the Captain's boat, and away he went in a terrible hurry. When he landed, he saw, as he thought, the finest goat that ever was, so nothing would suit him but this goat, which, after a lot of bargaining and bating, he purchased, and, crowing over his good fortune in obtaining such a fine one, he returned to the ship with his prize. Nothing was talked of the whole evening but the fresh hot milk they were to enjoy so much, and all went smoothly till breakfast-time next morning, when the "slavey" was sent to milk the goat. Oh, horror! the animal was a billy-goat, instead of a nanny!

There were races held on Lord Morley's grounds every year, and very good flat races I have seen; but they do not get up steeple-chases.

I mounted my first guard with poor McCarthy in the magazine, and a jolly night we made of it. We both came to the conclusion the following morning, that though there were a good many empty bottles and butt ends of cigars lying about, we went to sleep quite sober and correct. As was the custom in those days, I paid my guinea to the men of the guard on dismounting; being my first. They were the 58th.

At one of Sir John Cameron's Inspections of the Depot under Major Daniell, Sir John was very cross, and made up his mind to be displeased with everything, and at last he said, "Major Daniell, take your men home, sir, and drill them, and when they are fit for a General Officer's Inspection, I will see them;" upon which, the Major, who was rather hot-tempered, and sometimes bellowed like a bull if put out, roared out, "They are *perfectly* drilled now, and fit for *anyone's* Inspection. I have drilled them myself. I am the best drill in the army, and the Horse Guards know it." And he marched away in disgust. He was very much disliked by many, owing to his bullying propensities; but he was a first-rate officer, an excellent drill, and the best swordsman in the army. Although he was so disliked, and pretended not to be fond of many, yet, when he got into the post-chaise to leave us, (having gone on half-pay,) I really was very sorry, and I saw the tears trickle down his face as he drove off.

VOYAGE FROM PLYMOUTH TO CORK

WE left Plymouth in the Athole troop-ship in July, 1836, in very rough weather. We expected to reach Cork in three days at the farthest; but as the wind was dead ahead, we were just seven days. Luckily we had laid in provisions sufficient for the emergency. One night during the voyage, the gale increased, and about twelve o'clock, just as I was going into my cabin after my watch on deck was finished, I heard a tremendous thump. Upon inquiry, I found this was occasioned by John Clarke, our commanding officer, then a captain, having been rolled against the side of his berth by a lurch of the ship with such force that it gave way, and down he went, a drop of about five feet, on the floor, with his bed on the top of him. About the third day of our voyage, we reached the Scilly Islands, and as we had been much longer at sea than the captain intended, he resolved to tack the ship between the islands and the "Seven Stones," (which lie between the Scilly Isles and Cornwall.) However, the ship "missed stays," and was within a few feet of going slap upon the rocks of one of the islands. The captain was in a great stew about it; but providentially they got her round without her striking at all. If she had struck, no doubt many lives would have been lost. After getting out of this difficulty, we proceeded with villanous weather, but without any accident, till we were tacking into Cove Harbour, when, just as the captain wanted to put the ship about under Camden Fort, from some unaccountable reason the tiller-rope got twisted, and we were going eight knots an hour on to the rocks. The captain was furious; he stamped and danced on deck, swore at everybody, and the women in particular, as he said it must have been some of their infernal clothes that had got round the tiller 'down below.' However, Providence again assisted us, and we got in all right, and anchored on the seventh day from Plymouth. That evening I went ashore with one of the navy officers, and ordered dinner at the hotel at Cove.

They were some time in bringing up dinner, so what should my friend Mr. E— do, but set to work to carve up the table-cloth, which he called a "spree" but I did not see any fun in it at all myself. He of course paid willingly for the damage he had committed.

The next day we went up the river, (a most beautiful sail, with Glanmire and all its villas and woods on the right, and a host of places on the left,) disembarked, and marched up to the barracks on the 26th July, 1836. We were put into the most filthy rooms I ever was in. I complained of mine to the barrack sergeant, who gave it over to me, as having a horrible smell in it. His reply was, "Why sir, they are not very clean, for there have been in these rooms, parts of *thirty-six different regiments this year!*" The men's rooms were equally bad, and so full of fleas was the bedding, and so dirty, that it was obliged to be changed immediately.

I saw but little of Cork at that time, for I was ordered on detachment with Captain Jenner and about forty men, to march to Bandon, on the 1st of August.

BANDON

THE barracks at Bandon were in a very ruinous state. How they kept together I know not. I could see through the floor of my bedroom into the archway which led out of the Barrack Square. On my arrival there, the family at the castle, Lord and Lady Bandon, and Lord and Lady Bernard, were all in England; but soon returned, and I received the greatest kindness from them. Lady Bernard had been Miss Whitmore, of Apley, in Shropshire, and had been our near neighbour: that is, our property and the Whitmores' joined, and we had lived within four miles of each other for years. I found them very nice people: Lady Bandon a *very nice* old lady, and Lady Bernard a most delightful person. I very soon had the whole of the fishing to myself; also permission to shoot in the park, where there was very good rabbit and, in the winter, first-rate woodcock shooting. My horse got laid up from an accident, and I happened to mention this one day I was dining at the castle, when both Lord and Lady Bernard, in the kindest way possible, said that I was perfectly welcome to any of the horses in their stable, and begged that when I wanted a horse, I would, without ceremony, send up for one. I did not send up, as I never wanted a horse, except to hunt, and did not like to hunt a friend's horse, for fear of accidents; so another day I was asked why I did not use their horses; to which I replied, that I was much obliged for their kindness, but that I seldom went out riding.

From that time, I found a groom and horse at the barrack gate, every day at twelve o'clock, waiting to know if I should like to go out to ride.

The shooting about Bandon is very good. There are bogs for snipe in all directions; but the best beat is north of the town, in the direction of Crookstown or Macroom, and a little on the Bandon side of that place is first-rate ground, where a good shot ought to kill from fifteen to twenty-five couple a day. It was on this ground that

Captains Lindsey and Chetwode, of the 8th Hussars, made up a bag of thirty-five couple of snipe, besides a few other things, in one day, (from Ballincollig,) in 1847; but they were both capital shots. Chetwode seldom missed a snipe at all. I never shot in the park, except with Captain Bernard, a brother of Lord Bandon's, as he, being *a sportsman*, I did not like to disturb the ground he shot over before him. When shooting with him there, I have seen as many as forty couple of woodcocks in a morning. I *once* went out partridge-shooting with Mr. Swanston, the Duke of Devonshire's agent, Captain Jenner, and young Rogers. We were up at sun-rise, walked all day till nearly six o'clock, and saw about half a dozen birds. If I recollect right, we bagged *one brace*! I have invariably since found that the partridge-shooting in Ireland is the same, and the more they talk of having coveys on their land, the less likelihood is there of ever seeing them. I think it was on Christmas night, I and my Captain Jenner were dining at Mr. Lane's, and it being a very hard frost, I happened to say, "there would be wild ducks to be shot on the river the following morning, and that I should go and look after them"; upon which, I got bets of five shillings all round the table that I would not kill a couple. They all laughed at me, and recommended that I should go at once, and sit in a barrel all night, (as they said,) with my *eye* through the bung-hole. I was up at six o'clock the following morning, walked quietly up the river, and, before nine o'clock, had got three couple of ducks in my pocket. I then returned to breakfast, and to laugh at my friends of the night before. It was a bitterly cold morning, and as I had to wade into the water to pick up - my birds, my trousers froze as stiff as boards up to my knees; but I cared not for that, I had my sport. Captain Jenner had a rather nice pointer here, but not trained. I undertook to break him, which I did very shortly, and he was a good dog; but he always expected to have his game killed. One day Jenner went out *snipeing* with him, and missed half a dozen shots. He lost his temper, and scolded the dog, when Mr. Don dropped his stern, and trotted off to the barracks, leaving his master in a bog by himself, five miles from home, very much disgusted at his bad shooting. He afterwards sold the dog to me for £4. I found him a good dog when in the bog; but he had a disinclination to leave the barracks, consequently I always had to lead him out. On one or two occasions, he left me before I got to my shooting-ground, so on the last, I pronounced sentence of death upon him, as he was more trouble than he was worth; and I *"put him out of the way"* on my return by shooting him; which is the most merciful way of destroying any animal, for he never feels the least pain, nor does he even hear the report of the gun that kills him, and is quite unconscious of his end.

The fishing I found was bad; the river was so very much poached, even in the "park." Since that time, it has been preserved, and there are a few salmon in it; but it is so unmercifully flogged by everyone, that there is but little chance of getting even a rise. I have fished it at the best of times, and at all times, and never got a *single rise* from a salmon. The banks of the river, from Bandon to Innishannon, used to be lined with poachers, who took the fish with a "stroke-haul," which is a rod about twenty feet long, a whipcord line, at the end of which is attached a triangle of three large hooks, with a weight about a foot above them. These men know "the lie" of every salmon, and as sure as there is one in a pool, they will have him out with this "infernal machine," which they throw across the pool, and then jerk it towards them, working it in this way till the hooks stick fast in the back or side of the salmon, when very short work is made about landing him. These men used constantly to be taken up, and sent to Cork Jail for this offence, for two months at a time; but no sooner clear of its walls, than they were at their old tricks again. It must have paid them well, or they never would have run the risk they did. They scarcely let a salmon escape them.

The hunting about Bandon was not good, though

occasionally we had a tolerable run with Mr. Beecher's hounds, of Rockcastle, about four miles below Bandon. One great fault was, that he hunted *both* hares and foxes: the consequences may be easily conceived.

I had a wild mare that it was hard to manage. I bought her from a farmer, and understood afterwards he could do no good with her, and was obliged to part with her in consequence. She invariably reared as soon as one's foot was put in the stirrup to mount, and often has she fallen back; but I was always lucky enough to get out of 'the way in the fall. She injured one groom I had by falling back on him, and he was discharged the service in consequence. Another, belonging to the 3rd Dragoon Guards, who looked after her, she laid up in hospital for a long time. She also had a great objection to the saddle being put upon her, if it had not been on every day. One day she was saddled in the stables, not having had it on for the three previous days, and immediately it was girthed, she kicked till she kicked it off! She was thoroughbred, but the wildest devil I ever saw. There was no tiring her: I never saw her tired after the longest day's hunting in England afterwards. When at Bandon, I was obliged to get Desmond (a celebrated jockey) to break her in for me, which he did; but she caught a bad sore throat, and was laid up for a fortnight, after which she was as wild and intractable as ever. He had her for another week or fortnight, and then pronounced her quiet. I had her then clipped, and the fool of a man, when he went to singe her after the clipping, rubbed spirits of wine on her coat, and then set fire to it! (instead of having a proper singeing-machine,) which of course blistered the poor brute dreadfully in many places. In consequence of this, she was not able to be used for a week, after which rest there was no mounting her, and Desmond was obliged to take her again. During all these misfortunes, Lord and Lady Bernard were good enough to *send* me a horse every day for my use, if I wanted one. Whilst I was looking out of the window one day, Desmond passed, riding my mare. At the Barrack-gate is the corner of a wall, the boundary of a field which comes to a point between two roads. Mr. Desmond being drunk, as usual, ran the mare at this, and she cleared it beautifully backwards and forwards twice, before I could stop him. I measured the height of the wall, and found it to be five feet six inches, and coped with slates put up on the edge! I took her to England when I went on leave, and had some good sport hunting. She carried me beautifully; but my father, seeing her rear with me and fall back, one morning when going out, got frightened, and persuaded me to leave her at Davenport to be sold when my leave was up. She was then covered with blemishes from her own evil tricks.

The Rev. Dr. Newman was the clergyman at Kilbrogan, (which one half of Bandon is called.) He was a most devout and religious man, and when he called upon us, we generally underwent some sort of lecture from him. One day I was returning a visit at his house,- and during the conversation, he remarked that the following Monday would be St. Stephen's Day. I put in a rejoinder unluckily, saying, "Oh, yes! so it is! the hounds meet at Kilcoleman." The poor man was taken quite aback at my heathenish remark, and replied, -I was not thinking about hounds and horses; it is only *scampering people* delight in such amusements. I was going to say that there would be service in this church on that day, that you might attend if you were so inclined."

Once or twice I had baskets of game sent to me from Shropshire, in which were, amongst other things, some pheasants. I sent a brace of these to a friend in the town, (a brace of cock birds; they certainly were very large ones, and fat,) which he kept as long as they *would* keep, as a show for the benefit of his neighbours. I believe one half of them never saw a pheasant before.

Bandon was a quarter where there was very little duty of any sort to be done, and being out of the line of the main thoroughfares of Ireland, the escort duty was light. During the six months I was there, I only had to go with one batch of prisoners to Cork. One half of them, I recollect, were women, who were more trouble and made more noise than three times the number of men would have done. Some had friends about there, and in consequence, a great crowd was collected; in fact, the town was full of people from the country, and there were some symptoms of a desire to rescue, though no attempt was made. I was not sorry to see the crowd diminishing by degrees, as we got farther away from the town. We got to Cork all right, and I delivered over "*the bodies*," as they are called, to the gaoler. The next day, I returned from Cork with my escort of seventeen men, and marched the twenty miles in five and a half hours, including half an hour's halt at the half-way house. Not bad going!

KINSALE

ON the 9th January, 1837, I left Bandon with Captain Jenner and our detachment, and marched to Kinsale to rejoin the depot.

> "Sligo is the divil's place,
> And Mullingar is worse;
> Longford is a shocking hole,
> To Boyle I give my c—e;
> But of all the towns I e'er was in,
> Bad luck to ould Kinsale."

The above lines I found scratched on a pane of glass in the mess-room window, describing somebody's disgust at being quartered at "ould Kinsale." It certainly was not a lively place, and very little society to be had. There were a few small tea-parties, but I never patronized that sort of entertainment.

The town itself is an old Spanish-built place, and at one time was occupied by Spaniards. The streets are very narrow, the main street in particular, in many places of which, two cars could not pass each other. The filth of the place is beyond that of most Irish towns. Kinsale used to be the principal sea-port on the south coast, and it boasted a dockyard; but this has for many years been done away with. It is also celebrated for its class of fishing-vessels, called "hookers." They are built in a very peculiar way, and though open, will stand any weather. It is an odd thing that they will not sail nearly so well if half or whole decked, as when quite open.

On 14th February, I obtained two months' leave of absence, went over to Davenport with my wild mare, and had some hunting. Returned to Kinsale 14th of April, and on the 24th of May we marched to Cork. I had charge of the baggage-guard, and was given half an hour's start of the depot. Notwithstanding that one of my carts broke down, and many of the carmen got drunk, by dint of *thrashing* them, I got into Cork more than half an hour before the depot.

CORK

MAY 24th, 1837, we marched into Cork barracks, and uncommonly dirty barracks they were.

The draft to go out to Canada was formed here; consisting of Captain Dames, myself, and Ensign Trench, with sixty rank and file, who remained at Cork, and the depot marched on to Fermoy. We were made honorary members of the 78th Highlanders' mess, and remained there till the 8th of June, when we embarked on board the Rajah freight-ship at Cove.

VOYAGE TO CANADA

ON board the Rajah, we found a draft of the 32nd depot, (our old friends from Plymouth,) under Captain Browne. The following day being Friday, of course the captain did not like to sail, from the superstitious fear all sailors have of that day. However, we told Captain Fergusson that he *was* superstitious, which he denied, and said, to prove it, he would start the next morning. The day was very wet, and the wind blowing half a gale; however, the captain was as good as his word, for sail we did; but, after buffeting about outside the harbour for three hours, and having got only three miles, we were obliged to run back for shelter, which I was not at all sorry for, being very sick when out. On the 10th, it still blew great guns, with lots of rain, and we got news of the Stakesby transport, with a detachment of the 43rd regiment on board, being on shore near the Old Head of Kinsale. We sailed again at about two o'clock, the pilot expressing his doubts at the same time of our being able to get clear out of the harbour. However, we got out all right, and I was very ill for three days.

Our amusement was generally backgammon or *écarté* when not reading, and when we got a little fine weather, I got my gun, and shot at gulls and Mother Carey's chickens, which followed in the wake of the ship, to pick up anything that was thrown overboard. We had, on the whole, a very rough time of it, the wind chopping round very frequently, and sometimes blowing almost a hurricane. At one time, the sea was "in mountains rolling." I used to amuse myself with watching these mountains come rolling down as if to overwhelm the ship, and then, as if by magic, disappearing astern of us; for I was then so accustomed to the rolling of the ship, that I did not feel it rising over the waves.

One sea did strike the ship on the starboard quarter, and carry away a lot of things from off the deck, and nearly half filled the cabin. Our greatest annoyance was

Mrs. D—s' child, which was ill, and never ceased crying all the voyage, besides having *pap* made, and all other things necessary for infants, in the mess-cabin. I used often to say,' Well, I hope I shall never be obliged to go on a voyage again with a lady and child."

The 1st of July was as cold as the beginning of March; the 2nd was colder; indeed so cold, that we could not have prayers read to the men. I put on winter clothing, and two pairs of socks. On the 3rd, we passed a field of ice, that somewhat accounted for the cold. On the 5th, we were on the banks of Newfoundland, which, as usual, were enveloped in a thick fog. We were obliged to take in sail in consequence, for fear of running down some fishing vessel. The fishermen there, in general when in a fog, keep a bell ringing to avoid being run into by passing ships; a precaution very necessary, for we ran close to several without knowing it, until we had almost passed them. We spoke a Yankee fishing schooner, and bartered two bottles of brandy and seven pieces of pork for a few cod fish, which, when we got them, were so flabby and soft, that they were not good; but we found that by salting for two or three days, they got firmer, and were very good.

On the 8th, we passed an iceberg, about forty feet above the water, therefore, about eighty feet below it. As the wind had been blowing from the direction of the berg, it accounted for the excessive coldness that we had experienced for the few days previously. About this time we saw several large whales spouting up the water to an immense height; one of them came very close to our vessel.

We got into the Gulf of Saint Lawrence about the 14th of July, and as the weather had moderated a good deal, I shot away at Mother Carey's chickens, which the superstitious sailors think most unlucky. These said chickens are very difficult birds to hit, and it requires long practice to become a good shot at them. We were now about thirty miles from land, and could smell the pine-wood *quite strongly*!

At about half-past two o'clock on the morning of the 16th July, I was awoke by a most tremendous thunderstorm. I immediately got up to see it, for I think nothing is so awfully grand. I never recollect seeing such lightning before. Some of it was so vivid that it blinded all who were out for some seconds. The captain was dreadfully afraid of the forked lightning striking the ship. A thunderbolt did fall close to us. The storm lasted about an hour, the rain falling in torrents, and, strange to say, the sea was very smooth. However, at four o'clock the wind got up, and it blew a heavy gale till half-past seven, during which time we were drifting away to the eastward, under only a close-reefed fore topsail, and drifted twenty-seven miles in that short time. The captain did not know well where he was, and was in great fear lest he should lose the ship, for he had been wrecked in the two last vessels he had commanded, and they were totally lost.

On the 26th of July, we got up to Quebec, after seven weeks' voyage, and disembarked the same day. Just before I landed, I went to the steward, and asked him for some luncheon, when he told me that there was not a bit of anything to eat on board: not a bit of bread, flour, biscuit, or anything of the sort. I was aware, when we entered the Gulf of Saint Lawrence, that we were very short of provisions, but it was not known to anyone else except Captains Browne and Dames, so we kept it a secret, and, as it turned out, we had just sufficient to carry us up the river.

The cause of the thunder-storm we experienced in the gulf was attributed by the captain, (who was *not* superstitious!) and by the crew, to my shooting the Carey chickens!

QUEBEC

ON the 26th July, 1837, I disembarked with the draft at Quebec, and joined the head-quarters of the 66th regiment, under the command of an excellent old man, Colonel Baird, who always carried on the duty in a quiet way, giving as little trouble to anyone as he could possibly do. We were in the St. Lewis' Street barracks, with the 15th regiment. The 83rd, under Colonel Dundas, were quartered in the citadel.

Our mess-room and that of the 15th regiment were close together, and we pulled together as one regiment: whichever mess broke up first, some of the members invariably went over to the other. The consequence was, that often we did not get to bed till three or four o'clock in the morning. On one of these occasions, I, with Lord Cochrane, 66th, and Captain B—, were taking a walk down the street, smoking our cigars, when we were suddenly challenged by a party at the bottom of the street. The party consisted of seven men, who, after calling to us several times, came up, and began a row. I stood quite still, until I saw Lord Cochrane nearly knocked down, upon which I floored a couple right and left, and Lord Cochrane laid about him right well with a good walking-stick I had lent him, and which he broke over one of the fellows' heads. Our third man, Captain B—, left us in the lurch to contend with these seven ruffians. However, the two that I knocked down, not liking the joke, disappeared as suddenly as our friend B—, so that we had *only* five left. Three of them came sparring and hopping round me, showing all their science in the art of fighting. I, not having any of the art, let them know that "a little knowledge is a dangerous thing," by going in straight at a brace of them, and sending them spinning across the street. The other rascal threw a half-brick at me, which cut my hat, and staggered me considerably. However, I recovered my legs, and just at this moment they all took to their heels, with the two that Lord Cochrane had been engaged with. We gave chase, and ran two of them into a yard, from which there was no outlet. One of them I discovered in a place that shall be nameless. I delivered him over to my companion, who, after giving him a good drubbing, let him go. The other fellow disappeared in some very ignominious way. Whilst we were looking for the walking-stick that had been dropped in this scuffle in the yard, we heard a mob coming down the street, collected no doubt by some of the fellows we had been engaged with. Luckily for us, some married men of the 15th regiment were lodging in a house adjoining this yard, and finding who we were, and seeing the mob coming down upon us, threatening to murder us if they got hold of us, they let us into the house for shelter. We instantly barricaded the doors and windows, when the mob made a furious attack upon the house, and every moment we expected the door to give way. I accordingly ordered everyone in the house to go upstairs, and having picked up a small iron bar, not so thick as my little finger, remained on the stairs to defend them to the last, and had Cochrane and two or three other men at my back. At last we heard a tremendous crash, and we all thought it was the door that had given way. Immediately I *heard* a man rush up the stairs, for it was pitch dark. I stood my ground, and challenged him, but getting no answer, struck at and staggered him—still no answer, but a second rush. I struck again, when the fellow groaned out, "Oh God, you've killed me!" Immediately he spoke, the other men recognised him as one of themselves! We picked him up, and laid him on a bed, when he guided my hand to the wound on his forehead, and I shall not forget how my finger slipped into a bloody gash, which seemed to me to be an inch deep. We applied a cold wet towel to the wound, and then thought how we could get a doctor, for although the door had not given way, still the mob were there, swearing they would murder us. Lord Cochrane, however, got through a back window on to the top of the next house at the back, and thence down a *fire-safety ladder* into the yard, and gained admittance into the house. He

25

called to me through the stove-pipe which runs through both houses, to follow his example, and make a rush for the Artillery Barracks, which were only across the street. I did follow his example, and just as we were about to make our rush, the Artillery Guard turned out, and dispersed the mob. We instantly knocked up Dr. Seaton, R.A., and took him to my wounded man, whom he pronounced to be in no danger, but who would probably be quite well and fit for duty in a fortnight, so we sent him off to the hospital, with, I think, about fifteen dollars for a plaster. The doctor then examined me, and found a deep cut in my head from the brick, and I was a mass of congealed blood from my head to my middle. However, mine did me no harm, though I felt a little lightheaded afterwards from the loss of blood. Lord Cochrane got a cut or scratch from a knife in the struggle. This same party of seven men, it appeared, had been to the theatre, and had a row there with some others, who had escaped them, and they fancied that we were the party they were in search of. They attacked a veterinary surgeon that night in the street, and stabbed him in the breast. He could only extricate himself from the grasp of the ruffian who had him down, by drawing his own knife, which he ran through the fellow's arm.

Lord Gosford was then Governor-General of Lower Canada, and the seat of government was Quebec. He was a most good-natured warm-hearted man. He used sometimes to meet some friend in the street, and say, "Come and cut your mutton with me to-day!" instead of sending a formal invitation to dinner. The officer of the Castle Guard always dined with him. After dinner, it was his rule to play one game at billiards with the officer of the guard, (if he could play,) and then sit down to his game of whist, after which, at about eleven o'clock, he used to retire to bed, begging the company not to disturb themselves on his account. He generally had eight or ten at dinner every day.

The weather when we landed was very hot, though not

so hot as it became about the 22nd of August. At that time, I took a trip with Colonel Dundas, 83rd, Horrocks and Capel, 15th Regiment, and a few others, up to the Montreal Races. A West Indian whom I saw there, told me it was as hot as in the West Indies.

On our arrival in the steamer at Montreal, we were met by the mess butlers of the 1st Royals and the 32nd regiment, who always attended the boats to pick up *any officers* who might arrive, and to conduct them to their messes. On this occasion, the 32nd got hold of us, and we lived at their mess during the race-week; and a capital mess it was—without exception, the best I ever saw.

The weather soon changed, for whilst at Quebec in October, I have found the sheets of my bed frozen with my breath, on awaking in the morning. I have also known it frequently that, while shaving with hot water, the soap on the brush would be frozen before it was required for a second lather. On stirring the water in the tumbler with the tooth-brush, it would turn to ice, (like pounded ice,) and this in a room where there was a large open stove, well piled up with wood the previous night, and with double windows. The snow round Quebec lies from five to eight feet deep in winter; also in the woods where there is no drift; consequently all the fences disappear, and the country is one sheet of unbroken snow.

The quantity of shipping at Quebec is enormous. I recollect seeing, *at one tide*, seventy vessels floating up the river, and as there was no breeze, the damage amongst them was very great, by their coming in contact with one another. The river St. Lawrence at Quebec is about two miles wide, but it is narrower higher up, and in some places not more than a mile, though in others it spreads out into lakes of from nine to fifteen miles across.

Quebec being the seat of government, a good many people were living there, and we had a little society, though not much. Picnics to the different lions about, were the chief amusement: to the Falls of Montmorency,

Falls of La Chaudière, and the Indian village of Lorette. The Falls of Montmorency are two hundred and forty feet high, which is much higher than Niagara, or any waterfall in Canada, and is the chief attraction near Quebec, being only about nine miles distant.

One very hot day, I visited these falls with Lord Cochrane and some one else; we determined to descend to the bottom, and bathe in the basin underneath. I was the first undressed, and went in head first, but did not attempt to make a dive, as I did not know but that I might strike a rock; and very lucky it was for me that I did not, for as it was, I had the greatest difficulty in getting to the surface of the water again, as I was being sucked- underneath by an undercurrent. As soon as I did come up, I cautioned my friends, or they might have come off worse than I did. I afterwards 'discovered that the main body of the water which comes over the fall empties itself into the St. Lawrence, *underneath* the rocks. There are several under-currents in the St. Lawrence, and if a man does happen to fall in from a ship or boat, it is seldom or ever he is saved, being invariably carried away when under water.

* * * * * * * * * *

I was walking down Quebec one day with Captain B—, 15th, and on my remarking two very pretty girls on the opposite side of the street, he said, "Should you like to be introduced to them?"

"Oh, very much! Do you know who they are?"

"Not exactly, but I will introduce you."

"All right, come along!"

Accordingly we crossed the street. Captain B— took off his hat and said, "Good morning to you, will you allow me to introduce my friend, Mr. Davenport?"

No answer was elicited.

I thought then we were in for a scrape, but B— was not to be done, for he pretended not to see the slight, but went on talking, and at last they seemed to enjoy the affair. We walked and talked with them for some time, till at last they said they were near home, and hoped we would go no further. We accordingly sheered off, and I saw no more of them till we were quartered at St. John's, (some 200 miles from Quebec,) in 1838, when I went to a ball, and on entering the room, where I fancied I should meet no one I knew, I discovered two pretty faces on the sofa that I thought I had met somewhere, but for the life of me, could not tell where. I immediately went tip and renewed our acquaintance, remarking at the time, "I really forget where we last met."— "Oh, I believe it was in Quebec, (the one said with an arch smile,) and I don't think I should have recollected you so long a time but for your extreme impudence when there."

We immediately became great friends, and had a long talk, when I found out that my introduction at Quebec was not the first time we had met. I had met them and danced with them only a fortnight before at a picnic at Montmorency, but they said I appeared to have forgotten them, therefore they did not acknowledge me when walking with Captain B—.

I received a good deal of kindness from Colonel and Mrs. Gore, at Marchmont. He was then quartermaster general. Mrs. Gore was very fond of archery, and I, as a boy, used also to have a liking that way. I was always asked by them to attend all the archery meetings and club meetings also. The second day I went there, happened to be one of the club meetings, and I, as a friend of the Gores, was made to shoot in the match for a prize of a dozen arrows. We shot away till luncheon time, when the score was added up, and, to my utter surprise, I was named the winner, and carried off the arrows, although I had nothing to do with the club. Colonel Gore was very fond of shooting pigeon matches, and for the purpose of keeping the birds, he had a stable fitted up for them, and fed them with wild berries. He had at one time seven or eight dozen of these birds, which had been netted by the

Canadians, and brought in at four shillings per dozen. We at last finished up the stock, and the stable was left open; the next day one of these wild pigeons returned to the stable, having escaped his shot, and took up his quarters there. Lieutenant Parker, Lord Cochrane and I got four dozen pigeons to shoot at, and out of the forty-eight only five escaped. They are not so large as the English pigeon, but about the size and colour of the dove, and with a long tail, nearly as long as a magpie's.

There is some shooting to be had in August and September in the Bijou swamp, about a mile and a half out of Quebec, but the musquitos are the *very devil* there. At Chateau Richi, twenty or twenty-five miles below Quebec, on the left shore of the river, and where the spring-tides overflow, the snipe shooting is beyond anything a person can conceive. There, one gun could easily bag fifteen to thirty couple. There is some tolerable trout and other fishing in the St. Charles River, and some above the Falls of Montmorency. The best salmon fishing within distance is at Jacartier, twenty miles from Quebec, but by going down for a fortnight to Mall Bay or the River Sagunay, there will be got the best fishing in the world. Above the Falls of La Chaudière also is good trouting. On the 9th of October I took a trip down to St. Anne's to see the waterfalls, found there a very comfortable little inn for a night, and was much gratified with the Fall of St. Ferriol, over which comes an immense body of water. The Consecutive Falls, of which there are five or six, tumbling one into the other, are also very fine, and much higher than the St. Ferriol. Then there is La Rose Fall, which is exceedingly high, but has not a great deal of water in it; I should think this pretty fall must be above two hundred feet high. The La Puse Fall is also another well worth seeing.

"The Bush," or forest all about this country, abounds with wild animals. The moose deer, caraboo, and common red deer have been driven back some twenty miles into the woods, but there are bears in abundance, wolves, and a kind of tiger cat. I recollect a child at Beaufort being attacked by one of these animals, which would have carried it off, had it not been for some people who came to the child's assistance.

The citadel at Quebec is situated on the highest point of land, or rather rock, which is called Cape Diamond, I believe, from the quantity of small diamonds that are seen glittering there on a sunny day: some exceedingly good ones have been picked up and set.

Having bought a horse from our adjutant, and a sleigh from a very worthy friend of mine, and of every one's who knew him, Captain Dickson, I considered myself set up for the winter.

Mr. Papineau, the Speaker of the House of Assembly, having thought fit to stir up the people to rebel (which he was rather more successful in doing than he intended,) I was ordered to go to Sorel with two Companies, to join one that was there already. We went up on the 5th of November in the steamer, (about one hundred and fort), miles,) up the river. I was appointed acting adjutant and quarter-master, by which I got forage allowance for my horse, although no extra pay. Our detachment consisted of Captain Crompton, Lieutenant Rainsford, Lieutenant Lord Cochrane, myself, and Dr. Auglin. Just at this time, our Paymaster Ross, a very good fellow, had been dining at the mess in St. Lewis Street, Quebec, and on returning to his house, which was about a quarter of a mile from the works, he was met at the St. Lewis Gate by three men, who not only robbed him of his watch, snuff-box, and epaulettes, but actually took his cloak and boots, and then left him to go home to his wife and family nearly naked. We often joked him about it, telling him that if he wore straps, he would not so easily have lost his boots, but he had a great aversion to straps, and rather a liking to short-legged trowsers.

It was now getting rather late for shooting, as at the beginning of November, the snipe and ducks leave that part of Canada. However, I went down to Lake St. Peter two or three times with Lord Cochrane, but it was very cold work, and we had but little sport, the ducks being very wild, and not easily got at. On one of these occasions we had a canoe each, took our own directions round the different islands and creeks, and met in the evening at the house where we had left the horse and cart, and which belonged to Chaterau, the man who always went with me in the canoe. It was so cold, and freezing so hard, that each time the paddle was dipped it became encrusted with a fresh coat of ice. I killed very little, but Lord Cochrane had four or five couple of ducks. We were both half frozen, and drove back to Sorel (nine miles) to mess. The next day I felt the consequences, for I was laid up with fever, and was very ill. Dr. Skey, the P. M. O. who happened to be there, attended me, and got me round in a few days. He said he saw the previous night at mess that I should be attacked, for I came in very cold, ate a large dinner, and drank a quantity of wine.

SOREL

JUST at this time the country was in a state of ferment. There had been a long course of factious and turbulent opposition manifested by the House of Assembly of the Lower Province towards the Government and institutions of Great Britain, and at last the legitimate control of the mother country was scornfully set aside. Public meetings were held in every parish and county of the province, and were harangued by the leaders of the House of Assembly in the most inflammatory terms. At several places on the Richelieu river, the tri-coloured flag was hoisted, and the people warned to arm themselves.

On the 23rd of October, the "cap of liberty" was erected at St. Charles, and solemn oaths taken under it to be faithful to the principles of which it was the emblem. It was resolved at this meeting that the authority of Great Britain over the Canadas should not continue, but that Canada should govern itself. The state of affairs became so alarming, that it was necessary to issue warrants for the apprehension of twenty-six individuals charged with high treason. Two of these rebels were at St. John's and St. Athanase, and were taken prisoners by a party of the Volunteer Cavalry of Montreal, who, when returning to Montreal with them, were attacked by the armed "habitans," fired upon, and the prisoners rescued.

Sir John Colborne, Commander of the Forces, now ordered Colonel Wetherall to march with the Royals to Chambly, to reinforce that garrison. Colonel Wetherall was ordered to assist the civil power in arresting the offenders, and in case of any resistance or firing upon the troops, to destroy any house they might fire from.

All the way from Longueil to Chambly, the houses were closed or barricaded, but the inhabitants had fled. There were a few shots exchanged between Colonel Wetherall's skirmishers and some men in the woods, but without result on either side. The prisoners were taken with arms in their hands, ammunition having been distributed the previous night at a large meeting at Chambly. About three hundred rebels had taken up a position at the bridge of that place, for the purpose of resisting the cavalry, but on the approach of the advanced guard of "The Royals," they fled in all directions. The whole country was in arms, though evidently panic-struck. Two days after this occurrence, it was reported that T. S. Brown, an ironmonger in Montreal, styling himself *General*, had collected a large force of insurgents at St. Charles, on the river Richelieu, which place he was trying to fortify, and that Papineau (the Speaker of the House of Assembly,) O'Callaghan, and Dr. Walfred Nelson was doing the same at St. Denis, six miles from St. Charles. Against all these *leaders (?)* warrants had been issued. The mails and every communication through the country had been stopped by the rebels.

Whilst all this was going on, we at Sorel were daily expecting an order to march somewhere. Captain Crompton, who commanded our two companies at Sorel, therefore got his men into fine marching condition, for which purpose we marched out into the country about three days a week. The bayonets of the Light Company (his own) he had *sharpened*, the consequence was, the men cut their fingers with them in returning them to their scabbards! He had a hint from good authority that we might be suddenly called on; therefore, we were on the look-out for squalls. However, on the night of the 22nd November, 1837, we were quietly sipping our wine after dinner, at about eight o'clock, when Leggate, of the Commissariat Department, rushed into the room with the words, "You are pretty fellows to be sitting here while troops from Montreal are marching into your barracks." Of course everyone jumped up in astonishment. The fact was, Colonel Gore, the quartermaster-general, in obedience to orders from Sir John Colborne, left Montreal with the flank companies of the 24th regiment, (Captains Harris and Maitland), under command of

Lieut.-Colonel Hughes, the Light Company, (Captain Markham and Jack Inglis,) of the 32nd, one twelve-pound howitzer, and a party of the Montreal Cavalry, on board the St. George steamer, and disembarked at Sorel the same evening, at eight p.m. Our two companies, (Light and No. 1,) were then ordered to be supplied with sixty rounds of ammunition and three days' cooked provisions, and to be ready to march at ten o'clock that night, with the force just landed. Accordingly, we were on parade at half-past nine p.m., and marched off at ten o'clock. Whilst I was examining the men and their accoutrements previous to marching, a very large bird, (what it was I could not tell,) swept just over us, scarcely clearing the men's heads, which aroused the superstition of many of them, for I heard it whispered, "What bird was that? It is to be hoped not one of ill omen." Altogether, the force amounted to two, hundred and eighty men, and one gun. The whole division proceeded on the back road to St. Denis, which Colonel Gore had been directed to carry, and then moved rapidly on to assist Lieut.-Colonel Wetherall in his attack on St. Charles. Colonel Gore was accompanied by the deputy-sheriff, who was charged with warrants for the apprehension of the leaders mentioned. St. Denis is only eighteen miles from Sorel by the front road, but twenty-four by the back concession, which latter Colonel Gore took to avoid disturbing St. Ours, a village twelve miles on the road to St. Denis; thereby alarming the country, and giving notice to the rebel leaders of our approach. This was quite unnecessary, for they had a mounted spy on the wharf when the troops landed, and he communicated his news to them before we left Sorel. However, we left so quietly, that not a soul knew that the march had taken place, till daylight the following morning. The night was so pitch-dark, that I actually could not see my hand before my face, and being in the rear of the division with the spare ammunition, and the baggage of Colonel Gore, my party separated, and lost for a time the main body. The rain fell in torrents, and the roads were knee-deep in

35

mud and water.

At about two o'clock in the morning of the 23rd, the rain changed to sleet and snow, and it became a little lighter, but up to that time, we distinguished nothing but the white blanket which was strapped on the outside of the men's knapsacks. I then discovered that the men were straggling, and picked up several of them separately on my horse, and brought them up to the body of troops in front. I then galloped on to report the men were straggling, and knocked up, and asked for half an hour's halt, when I found that we covered nearly two miles of ground, but before I could get all the men up, Colonel Gore had again moved on with the head of the column. We first coaxed the men, then joked them, then bullied them, and tried all means to keep up their pluck; but they were so completely fagged, that they fell on the road side, when we took their arms from them, destroyed their ammunition in the snow, and left them to their fate. Four or five of them were taken prisoners. After passing a bridge about four miles from St. Denis, we were met by an armed party, who had been sent to oppose us. Our march was impeded by the bridges being broken down, which caused much delay in crossing with the gun. We now found all the houses deserted, and on nearing St. Denis, we were attacked by the rebel skirmishers, occupying barns on the road and bushes on the banks of the river Richelieu. These were rapidly driven in by Captain Markham's company to the main entrance of the town, and I never saw anything so like rabbit-shooting in my life; all the men got so excited at the sport, that they had to be recalled by the bugle.

ST. DENIS

WE reached St. Denis at ten o'clock a.m., on the 23rd, after twelve hours' march, knee-deep in mud, over twenty-four miles of back road. St. Denis was found to be strongly occupied, and the entrance defended by a large fortified stone house, and a barricade of carts, trees, stones, etc., across the street, flanked by a building and many houses, from which a severe fire was kept up.

Our column was deployed, the two companies of the 24th on the left of the road, and two companies of the 66th on the right, extending to the river Richelieu. We then forced our way up to the barricade, keeping as well as possible under cover; nevertheless, many men bit the dust. The gun played upon the fortified house, but with little effect, for the balls either went clean through the windows, or only about three inches into the stone-work, without at all shaking it. It was calculated that in this one house, not less than one thousand men were armed, and they kept up a tremendous fire. Markham was wounded by two bullets through the neck, and was disabled, on the opposite side of the street to where my company was. The house he was in was only twenty-five yards from the full fire of Nelson's house; but hearing that he was down,[1] I rushed across the street to see him, and had to run about fifteen yards besides, up a garden to get in at the window. The showers of bullets that stuck all round me were just like a hail-storm.[2] Whilst I was talking to Markham, I stood with my back to a stove that was in the room where he lay. Here the riflemen caught sight of me, and let fly a volley that went "*whish*" over my shoulder, and I counted five of the bullet-holes

---

[1] I sent for Dr. —, of the —, to go and dress his wounds, but he funked, and said he should certainly be shot if he attempted it. I then asked the coward if he would cross with me, and take snacks in the luck. After much hesitation, he said he would.

[2] Dr. — still was afraid, and would not go; but remained where he was.

in the stove-pipe. I immediately shifted my quarters, and after promising Markham that I would look after him, in case of a move either to the front or rear, and that I would not leave him there, I joined my own company, meeting with the same reception from the rebels on my way back. The men were jaded, and so done up, that they cared little what became of them, and dozens I saw sitting quietly by the stoves in the houses we had taken, with the bullets going straight through the rooms they were sitting in.

It was now after two o'clock. We had fired sixty rounds a man, and the pouches had been replenished with thirty more. Only six rounds remained belonging to the gun, when Colonel Gore sent for me to where he was, near the gun. He said,

"Davenport, you have been in front all morning what chance of taking the place is there?"

"We'll take it in ten minutes, if you will only let us have a go at the barricades."

"But we shall lose an awful number of men, and I don't want to lose any lives."

"Why we certainly should lose ten or a dozen, but we shall have the place then, and be all right."

"Markham is wounded, I hear; what does he say of our success?"

"Markham's opinion is the same as mine."

"Well, if you can get to him without exposing yourself, go, and ask him his opinion."

"Very good, sir," I replied, and off I went; but some of the 32nd, seeing me about to cross the street again, caught hold of and stopped me, just in the fire of the rebels, and I had a narrow escape, as it gave them a sitting shot at me. However, I thanked them for their good intentions, and told them to let me go; but if I was knocked over in the crossing or garden, I should be obliged for their assistance in picking me up. I then ran the gauntlet to Markham and back again, and delivered his opinion to Colonel Gore, who thought it advisable to retreat, as the gun ammunition was expended. He therefore told me to pass the word to the front to retreat, and bring all the wounded we could. I accordingly did so, and made arrangements to carry Markham off. I tried first to have him carried on a bed, but it was so cumbersome, that it was found that plan would not do; so Sergeant Allcock and a private made a sort of seat between them, with their hands, and bore him off; but in so doing, we drew down upon us a brisk fire. Poor Markham got another bullet through the calf of his leg, and a second shot grazed his knee. The escort had a miraculous escape, having their shoulder-knots cut off with the bullets, and only a slight graze on the thumb of the sergeant. I, having run the gauntlet six times, came off without even my coat being touched!

Lord Cochrane, during the affair, took a sergeant's fusil, and blazed away. There was one Perault, a leader of the rebels, very conspicuous, waving his hat and encouraging his men. Cockrane had three shots at him at about fifty yards, but the fourth caused him to leap into the air and bite the dust.

During this action, the gun had been shifted to take up a fresh position; but the horses were so completely "used up" that it was a long time before they could move it, and not then until we had got many shoulders to the wheel. During these operations, hundreds were pouring into St. Denis, both from the skirting of the "bush" on the left, and crossing the Richelieu on the right, but no shot could be spared from the fortified house to obstruct their passage. It was now three o'clock, and it became necessary to fall back before the main bridges in our rear should be broken up, as the ground occupied could not be maintained during the night. After getting Markham away, I went to Jack Inglis,[3] Markham's subaltern, who was in the advance of the whole, and told him to retire

---

[3] Afterwards Brigadier Inglis.

with his subdivision. He replied, "Markham is down, and neither I nor my men leave here till he is safe." I told him I had made that all right, and we commenced the retreat, my company in the advance, and the 24th in the rear. The rebels followed our retreat, firing into us for three miles, but without much effect, till we got to a bridge where we were obliged to halt to try to get the gun over.

ST. OURS

THE roads to St. Ours were as deep and bad as those we had marched on the previous night, with the addition that it came on to freeze, which 'caused the bad roads to be jagged, and the men who had lost their boots in the mud the night before, suffered extremely. It froze so hard, that at nine o'clock that night, the ditches would bear a horse to stand on the ice in them. On crossing this bridge, the horses were completely done, and two of them fell. The Infantry immediately went to the gun, and every exertion was made to get it on, while sharp shooting was going on on each side. The horses of the officers and those of the ammunition were also put to it, but without effect. The wheels were now frozen and clogged with mud, and after *seven hours' toil*, during which Lieut.-Colonel Hughes got his toes frost-bitten, the medical officer reported, that if they remained there any longer, the men would be frozen. The gun was therefore spiked and abandoned, stuck fast in the mud. I proposed it should be taken off the carriage, and dropped through the ice into the river; but that was thought useless, as it was spiked. The march was then continued to St. Ours, which everyone knew was a "nest of hornets," but where Colonel Gore expected to meet the steamer Varennes, which had been ordered to meet us with provisions, etc. However, she had been attacked that day, obliged to cut her cable, and return to Sorel.[4]

All our clothes were frozen as stiff as boards upon our backs, and most of the officers (I believe I started the idea) borrowed a blanket from the men who did not want them, and used them as hoods, tying our sashes under the chin. I saw Colonel Gore get off his horse at a house to get some milk, and his cloak that he wore was frozen to the clothing of the horse, which it had on under the

---

[4] The captain was a rebel, and did all he could to deliver her and her stores over to the rebels; but the Commissariat officer on board (Leggate) produced his pistols, and swore he would shoot him if he did not return instanter.

saddle, and this was so stiff with ice, that it tore off all round, leaving him minus four inches of cloak. His feet were frozen in the stirrups, and I knocked them out with a piece of wood for him. I frequently had my feet frozen in the stirrups; but owing to having on two pairs of worsted stockings, to make a pair of seal-skin boots fit, I received no injury. We got to St. Ours at about two o'clock on the morning of the 24th, and as I was leading the Division, I discovered the churchyard as full of armed men as it would hold, and as we had to pass under the wall, of course, I thought we should get a good peppering; but, strange to say, they did not fire on us. After passing through St. Ours, we halted at some farmhouses, about a quarter of a mile out of the village, at about three o'clock. The men and officers all lay down in a heap for about a couple of hours. But before lying down, I went to see how my horse was put up, and, to my surprise, found the poor animal, which, like ourselves, had not tasted food for more than thirty hours, standing at the door, shivering in the cold, with another horse. I immediately took the two in one hand, and a pistol in the other, and went in search of a stable, which I eventually found, full of cows and pigs. There was a peasant rebel there, who had the impudence to attempt resistance to my approach; but I told him I would put a bullet into his carcase, if he did not clear the whole place, and put clean litter and forage for the horses, which he did in a little less than no time. I then returned to the house, and very luckily discovered that our Surgeon, Dr. Anglin was so ill that he could not eat the contents of his haversack. I, having lost my own at St. Denis, requested his, which contained some frozen ribs of mutton, and bread frozen as hard as a rock. These I ate, and never had such a delightful meal; but I doubt much if any beggar in England would have so much as tasted it. It had been in a night's rain and frost, a good deal knocked about; the bread was covered with the fat, and the meat with the frozen particles of bread. But it was the sweetest morsel I ever tasted.

St. Ours is only seven miles from St. Denis, and it took us from three o'clock in the afternoon till three o'clock next morning, to get over that ground. After feeding my horse, and eating the doctor's provisions, I lay down on the floor amongst the men, and had a long draw-well bucket for a pillow. But I had not enjoyed above an hour's sleep, when my pillow was kicked from under my head, and I was told to get up if I intended to get anything to eat before we marched.

SOREL

AT six o'clock, we were on the march for Sorel, twelve miles, where we arrived at two o'clock, looking something like chimney sweepers, being all begrimed with gunpowder and dirt. The loss in killed and wounded was six killed, and nine or ten wounded on our side; but the rebels suffered much more severely. We had been now from ten o'clock on the Wednesday night till two o'clock on the Friday afternoon on the march, (with the exception of four hours' halt at St. Ours,) and in the worst possible weather. Numbers of men went into hospital with colds, frost-bites, rheumatism, and other complaints, brought on by the severe work, and numbers of them died or were invalided in consequence. The officers fared but little better, though none died; for every one of that expedition, with the exception of myself, was laid up in the sick list for some time afterwards, and Crompton was obliged to leave the Service, from rheumatism which came on in consequence. The rebels now gained courage, and threatened to attack us in Sorel. We only had our two Companies, and one Company 32nd, with one six-pounder gun, which remained to strengthen us when Colonel Gore returned to Montreal with the force he brought down. Of course all the officers were much fagged after the march, therefore they determined to go to bed, which they all did as soon as the men were put into the barracks, intending to get up again in time for the mess dinner, at seven o'clock. I knew very well that if I went to bed, I should not so easily get up again at short notice; therefore, after getting a bath, I waited patiently for the hour to arrive, which I certainly should not have done, had we not expected reinforcements to come down from Montreal that evening, and the officers to dine with us. The dinner bugle at last sounded, and I was the only representative of the 66th Regiment forthcoming; but we sat down a party of about eight or ten. I sat president, and Bainbrigge, of the Royal

Engineers, sat on my right hand. I recollect helping the soup, and once or twice dozing during dinner. I also recollect the cloth being removed; but after that, I was not aware of anything that was passing or passed, till I awoke in my bed the following morning, at seven o'clock, when I was as perfectly refreshed as if I had not lost any of my usual rest during the week. I came down to breakfast, and inquired how I got to bed; when Bainbrigge said, "Why, you went to sleep after dinner, and knowing the fatigue you had gone through, we carried you upstairs, undressed you, and put you to bed, and you never awoke nor were conscious of our proceedings."

"I recollect going to sleep once or twice during dinner," I said.

"Yes, it was a most curious thing. You awoke to help people to your dish; you frequently dropped to sleep whilst in the middle of a sentence, and after a few minutes, you awoke, and took up the conversation that was going on, as if you had heard everything that passed."

I believe I was the only one of the expedition that appeared that morning at breakfast; and many of the others lay in their beds much longer than they had any inclination for. I attribute my standing the fatigue so well, first of all, of course, to an iron constitution; secondly, from having been the previous fortnight attacked with slight fever, *physicked*, and, in a way, put in order for hard work.

We now heard the report that Lieutenant Weir, of the 32nd, had fallen into the hands of the rebels, and had been murdered, which eventually turned out to be too true. He had been despatched from Montreal on the morning of the 22nd, by land, to order our Detachment at Sorel to be in readiness to join Colonel Gore's Brigade, on his landing that evening at Sorel from the steamer; but the roads were bad, and the troops named had arrived, and marched on St. Denis before he reached

Sorel. He took a calèche to follow us, as we had only marched an hour before his arrival; but unfortunately he drove along the front road, which goes through St. Ours to St. Denis, whilst we had marched by the back road. He therefore missed us, and fell into the hands of the rebels. He was treated well by them, and had breakfast with Wolfred Nelson, (their chief,) but it is supposed that when he heard our firing, which was so close to where he was a prisoner, he attempted to escape, when he was cut down by his guard, and murdered. On the 2nd of December, when we again entered St. Denis, the body of poor Weir was discovered in the river Richelieu, in about two feet of water, covered with large stones, which kept it down. The stones being removed, it rose to the surface. There was a sabre wound about four inches long, which penetrated deep into the bone on the forehead, and several small wounds, as if done by a sharp-pointed instrument. The back of the head was completely laid open. On the neck were several sabre wounds, and five other wounds in different parts of the body. The fingers were hacked and split to pieces.

The rebels having threatened to attack us in our barrack, we set to work to fortify it. The wooden market house near it was pulled down, and picketing and palisades (which were rendered ball-proof by inch boards being nailed against them) were erected. Patrols went out day and night, and we were kept on the *qui vive*.

COLONEL WETHERALL'S EXPEDITION

COLONEL WETTIERALL'S column, which moved from Chambly to attack St. Charles, was more fortunate than that of Colonel Gore. It consisted of five companies of the Royal Regiment, and one of the 66th Regiment, under Lieutenants Johnson and Carey, two guns, and a party of Volunteer Cavalry, amounting to about four hundred men. They, too, started on the same night as the St. Denis' expedition, and with similar orders; but the Colonel acted upon the spirit of his order, (whilst Colonel Gore acted upon the letter,) and did not arrive before St. Charles until the morning of the 25th of November, having left Chambly on the night of the 22nd. The distance from Chambly to St. Charles is the same as from Sorel to St. Denis, by the back road. Colonel Wetherall halted twice on the road, by which he brought *his* men fresh into action. He found Mr. Debartzch's house, and one or two other wooden houses, stockaded and defended by about one thousand four hundred or one thousand five hundred men, and two guns, under "*General*" Brown. He halted when within musket-range, and displayed his force, when a sharp fire was opened upon him. He then deployed, and after silencing the rebel guns, charged with the bayonet. Though four or five to one in number, the rebels, who at first stood fire well, broke, and ran in all directions; but not until the British troops were among them. About one hundred and fifty were left dead on the field, and twenty-seven taken prisoners. Colonel Wetherall had three killed, and eleven wounded. All the mounted officers' horses were wounded, and Colonel Wetherall's shot under him. That night he occupied St. Charles. On the going round at night to visit the sentries, he perceived that one of them, a man of the name of Sullivan, of the 66th Regiment, had his bayonet bent, upon which he said, "What have you been doing with your bayonet to bend it in that way?"

"I did it in the guts of a Canadian, yer honour, and its

grazy, (greasy,) now, would yer honour like to feel it."

Colonel Wetherall next day marched back to St. Denis, where he left his wounded under the charge of a doctor, a sergeant, and fifteen men, and proceeded to attack the rebels, who had collected at Point Olivier, to cut off his retreat to Chambly. These he sent flying with a few shots, and returned to Montreal with his prisoners, on the 30th November. On the same day, Colonel Gore left Montreal with one Company of the 24th, four of the 32nd, one of the 83rd, and a detachment of Artillery, and arrived at Sorel by steamer the same evening, with orders to attack the rebels again at St. Denis.

RICHELIEU

ACCORDINGLY, the next day, two Companies of the 66th Regiment at Sorel joined his force, and attempted to ascend the river Richelieu as far as St. Ours in the steamer; but the ice on the river was three inches thick, and after proceeding about a mile, it was found to be impracticable, so we had to return to Sorel, and march up the front road to St. Ours.

On entering the village, an unfortunate fellow was recognised by a man of the 66th Regiment, as having been one of a party of rebels who took him prisoner on the 23rd of November, and who, he alleged, had him out to be shot, with others in the same predicament. As soon as the fellow saw he was known, he ran away, when, without any orders, he was shot down by five or six bullets from the Light Company of the 32nd, and one or two from the 66th. Colonel Gore immediately inquired into the case, and finding no orders had been given to fire, nothing more was said on the subject; but it was no wonder the 32nd fired as soon as a rebel was recognised, after having one of their officers (Weir) murdered, and another (Markham) severely wounded, besides other casualties amongst their own comrades the previous week.

On the end December we entered St. Denis without opposition, the rebels having fled at our approach. They had made preparations for defending the place since we left it, by throwing up embankments and trenches; but they evidently thought discretion the better part of valour. Here we recovered our lost howitzer, which had had the spike beautifully drilled out, and the gun loaded up to the muzzle with all kinds of old iron. Search having been made, and no chiefs or a single rebel having been found, the work of destruction commenced. The distillery and other strong stone houses, from which the troops had been fired at on the 23rd November, were ordered to be burned; but as the distillery was full of whiskey, it was considered the explosion from it when ignited would cause great damage to all around, it was therefore burst open, and all the spirits in it, and all the wine in casks in other houses were let flow down the gardens into the river. No sooner was this place on fire than houses all down the road we had marched in from blazed away one after another, and houses in the town also were several times set on fire, but extinguished. Each time that a fresh house caught fire, the "turn out" for the troops sounded, as it was supposed it was they who were amusing themselves in this way. When we had been turned out about seven or eight times, on the bugle sounding, I was out in a minute, and after assembling my men, went back to see that no one was left in the house, when I found they had put all the wooden and rush-bottomed chairs on the fire, with the planks of the floor crammed into the fire also. I immediately set to work, and pitched the whole of the blazing chairs right into the midst of my men, (who were just under the window,) for their folly. If I had not done so, we should have had no shelter that night, for all the other houses not occupied by troops, had been destroyed. I believe the Volunteer Cavalry were the people who set the houses on the road on fire. I certainly did a little myself by burning down two houses, from which I had been fired at.

There was a strict order against plundering, and a picket paraded the streets to stop it. Nevertheless, I and my friend, Jack Inglis, put on our haversacks, and arming ourselves with short sticks, went in quest of fowls, and were caught in the act of bagging a couple by Colonel Gore, who shook his head at me, and said something about "bad example;" but I told him if I did not look out for my own dinner, nobody else would do it for me, upon which, he rode off with a smile.

The men we left behind us wounded, on the 23rd November, we found looking very well. They told us that Dr. Wolfred Nelson, the chief of the rebels there, had taken every care of them, treated them kindly, and visited them twice a day.

The 3rd December was occupied in searching for searching arms, but none worth anything were found, but a great lot of old rusty guns, which were immediately destroyed.

On the 4th, three Companies and one gun, under the charge of Major Reid, 32nd Regiment, were left in charge of St. Denis; the remainder of the expedition marched to St. Charles, where Colonel Gore was informed that the rebel chiefs and Papineau had gone to St. Hyacinths on the river Yamaska, where it was likely they had established themselves. My Company's knapsacks were at once taken off, and I was sent on with Colonel Gugy, as also another Company, to St. Hyacinths, to surround the house where the rebel chiefs were supposed to be. Gugy was a magistrate, and held the warrants for the apprehension of the rebel leaders. We accordingly surrounded the house, when Madame Solle assured us that no one was concealed there. Nevertheless, the place was searched by Gugy.

> "He searched, they searched, and rummaged everywhere,
> Closet and clothes-press, chest and window-seat,
> And found much linen, lace, and several pair
> Of stockings, slippers, brushes, combs complete,
> With other articles of ladies fair,
> To make them beautiful, or leave them neat.
> Arras they prick'd, and curtains with their swords,
> And wounded several shutters, and some boards:
> They open'd windows; gazing as if the ground
> Had signs of foot-marks; but the earth said nought."

And then we retired, and Colonel Gore came up in the evening, with the remainder of his force. The following day, he retraced his steps from St. Hyacinths, and returned to Sorel, thence to Montreal, leaving the 66th to occupy St. Charles.

On our march from St. Denis to St. Charles, we found that the wooden bridges had been half cut in two underneath, so that when any weight came upon them, they would break down. But our Engineers were not to be caught in *that* trap.

During the time all this was going on, Sir John Colborne collected troops from neighbouring provinces, concentrated them in Montreal, fortified that city, purchased horses for the Royal Artillery, built barracks, formed magazines of provisions and ammunition, organized several Corps of Volunteers, distributed arms to the loyal Militia, etc. One thousand five hundred men were now enrolled and organized in Montreal, and two thousand in Quebec. On the 5th December, Martial Law was proclaimed.

ST. HILLAIRE

I was now sent from St. Charles to St. Hillaire de Ronville, with about twenty men, to take charge of the wounded soldiers left there by Colonel Wetherall. I found Dr. Sewell, who had medical charge of them, a very good companion. We were both billeted on the "Seigneur," Colonel De Ronville, of the Militia, and were there for about three weeks, during which time many of the wounded died, and I and the doctor buried them. Only five or six lived to return to Montreal. This Colonel De Ronville was a rank old rebel at heart, though he tried to conceal it. I detected him making the "habitans" take the oath of allegiance to the Queen on an old Virgil, and we found out afterwards that he had sent sums of money and two small cannon to the rebels. It was a very stupid quarter, and nothing to be done but smoke over the stove in the Colonel's studio. However, the accommodation for the wounded, (a wash-house over a stream, which could be seen through the crevices of the floor,) and the intense coldness of the barn where my men were put up, having been reported to Head Quarters at Montreal, the remaining sick were removed, and I returned on 30th December, to join our detachment at St. Charles. The officers belonging to it were Captain Crompton, Lord Cochrane, and Dr. Auglin.

In the meantime, Sir John Colborne, in person, headed a Division to attack the rebels of the "Lake of the Two Mountains." He routed them in a short time at St. Eustace, and burned that place: also St. Benoit and St. Scholastigne. We were still kept alive by hearing that five thousand Yankees were coming to invade the country.

ST. CHARLES

OUR amusements at St. Charles consisted in sleighing, Crompton and myself having forage allowed us, as Commanding Officer and Adjutant and Quarter Master. Lord Cochrane and Auglin had each a horse; but the latter was one day driving himself down the ice to St. Denis, when the sleigh slewed against a knot in the ice, and sent him sprawling. He returned with his wrist a little hurt, swore he would never drive again, and handed his horse over to me, when I set up a tandem, and enjoyed myself. The dogs on the river were very annoying; flying at your horses' noses, or catching hold of the robes of the sleigh, so after a few of these attacks, I always took my large pistols with me, and generally killed two out of three that I shot at, going the rate of ten miles an hour; but then the dogs went the same pace. On one occasion, my servant boy, who was about fourteen years of age, was sitting behind me, and when I had just passed a house in the "bush," he cried out, and said that a dog had bitten him in the shoulder; upon which, I turned round, and saw a kind of large mastiff in the road, about forty yards off, looking at us. I knew he was the aggressor, therefore pulled up my horse, took a deliberate aim at him, and sent the bullet through his chest. He gave a howl, turned round three or four times, and dropped dead. Some of our officers passed the same place that evening, when the people of the house complained of the loss of their dog; but said it was the most capital shot they ever saw. I believe I must have put an end to nearly four dozen curs in this way on the river that winter, and when they got scarce, we took out a spaniel to run after the sleigh as a decoy; which afforded great sport, for if a cur got a glimpse of a strange dog, he was at him in a minute.

At other times, we took long walks on snow-shoes, and went into the bush to look for partridges, which are the only birds to shoot in the winter; but they are often. poisonous, and at all times without flavour.

About this time an order came for us to search for arms; but we found very few, and those rusty and double-loaded. The rebels here had now taken the oath of allegiance, and all appeared quiet.

CHAMBLY AND ST. JOHN'S

ON 17th February, we were sent from St. Charles to Chambly, a march of eighteen miles, and I recollect well what a piercing cold day it was. Many of the men got frost-bitten severely, and I got a bite under the nose like a white moustache, but was told of it in time to prevent any bad consequences.

Since we left Sorel on the 1st of December, we were not allowed any more baggage than a carpet-bag, or small portmanteau, all the rest of our kit, etc., being left behind. We, therefore, now began to have rather a curious and ragamuffin appearance; but nobody cared about dress. Some wore long mocassins up to the hips; some long worsted stockings which came up as high; some sealskin boots up to the calf; some black trousers, others blue, and so on; but our *faces* were all alike—as brown as a nut, and that kind of brown which nothing but exposure to hard weather can give. The weather was now becoming warm, and on the 15th of March, the snow had disappeared, and the ice on the River Richelieu began to break up.

SOREL

ON the 14th of April we left Chambly by steamer for our old quarters, (Sorel, forty-five miles,) and right glad were we to get back to our own mess and baggage.

I now laid my plans for shooting, and killed the first snipe of the year in Lower Canada. I had very good snipe-shooting for the time of year; but they begin to breed in May, when, of course, the guns are put up for a time.

We bought a very good four-oared boat, in which we spent a good deal of our time, and it was a source of great amusement to us. Our crew consisted of Captain Crompton, Lord Cochrane, Trench and myself.

May, June, and July having been allowed to the ducks and snipe to breed and bring up their young; in the beginning of August, I opened the campaign against them afresh. On the 6th of August, I went down to Isle au Moine, at the end of Lake St. Peter, with Lord Cochrane, and in three hours, we bagged sixteen and a half couple of snipe, when all our powder was expended, or we might easily have bagged twice that quantity. My general plan of shooting was, to get three days' leave of absence, and go down to Lake St. Peter with Edmund Peel, (a magistrate of Sorel,) and live in a "cabane," taking with us provisions for that time. Then, having engaged old Chaterau and his son-in-law with their canoe, we used to start immediately after breakfast, and taking luncheon with us in a despatcher, we shot snipe or ducks, sometimes both. We used generally to make very good bags, from sixteen to twenty couple a day. In the evening, we would get into a canoe, tether it under a bush, and fish for perch with a stick about a yard long, a piece of whipcord, with a lump of lead at the end, and a hook about three inches above it. In this way we had capital sport, and caught much more fish than we could use. We had to eat our snipe and ducks also, for they would not keep more than twelve hours, so that we could send them nowhere. The musquitoes were quite dreadful. I got bitten so horribly one night, that I had to return next day to Sorel, and put myself under the doctor's hands. The bull frogs there make a most tremendous noise at night, particularly before rain. They roar very similarly to the lowing of a cow, and may be heard at the distance of a mile. They are as large as a small-sized plate.

The Head Quarters of the Regiment were relieved in Quebec by the Grenadier Guards, who came out from England as soon as the river opened and was clear of ice. They proceeded to Three Rivers, thence to Sorel in August.

Rumours now got afloat that the rebels were again organizing themselves, and in September it was a well-known fact that they were drilling at night in Montreal. They engaged a Corporal of the Royals to teach them the different exercises, etc., thinking that he would join them on being promised a commission in their army; but they had not "calculated" sufficiently on this subject; for as soon as the proposal was made to him, he readily accepted it, and instantly reported what he had done to Colonel Wetherall. The Corporal was then ordered to go and drill them to their heart's content, by which of course all their proceedings were known to the proper authorities; but although the whole country was in an excited state, yet it was not thought there would be another appeal to arms.

NIAGARA

ON the 10th of September, I obtained two months' leave of absence, and started with John Parker on a trip to the United States. That night we went by steamer to Montreal; next day up the St. Lawrence to Dickinson's Landing; thence to Kingston, on the 22nd, and then crossed Lake Ontario, on the 24th, to Niagara. I wanted to go to Toronto first, but Parker, who had been there before, assured me there was nothing to see; therefore we passed it, and pushed on to the races at Fort Niagara. The races were pretty good; but there were one or two bad accidents. An officer of the Navy, who was riding in one of them, touched a post as he passed it, and broke his kneecap. I never saw so many drunken people any where. They were lying about the course in all directions, and put me much in mind of the dead and wounded lying about at St. Denis. On the 28th we proceeded to the falls, (twelve miles,) passing through Lewiston, and over the Queenstown Heights—very beautiful scenery. We arrived at the hotel at the falls at night, when we immediately rushed to see the sight, and as there was a splendid moon shining, we were lucky enough to witness a lunar rainbow. After all I had heard of the splendour and magnificence of this wonder of the world, I confess I was much—very much disappointed; for I expected to see the falls double the height they are; being only one hundred and sixty-four feet high, though three quarters of a mile in width.

The roar of the water as it falls, can be heard from five to twenty miles distant, according to the state of the atmosphere. It is sometimes distinctly heard across the lake at Toronto, a distance of fifty miles. The mist, arising like curling smoke, and forming into masses of clouds, is seen at distances of from three to fifty miles. This depends much upon the state of the atmosphere, the height of the sun, and the direction of the wind. We remained here two days, and the more I saw of the falls, the more I was pleased; but I had heard too much of them before seeing them. The —rd were encamped in an orchard close to the precipice of the river below the falls, and added much to the picturesque. But although we had paid every attention to them, both at Sorel and St. Charles, on their march up the country, they did not even ask us to dine with them.

Before leaving Niagara, we thought we ought to go behind the sheet of water which pours over the Canadian Fall. We accordingly procured the guides, (two negroes,) who supplied us with water-proof dresses for the purpose, and proceeded over some very slippery green rocks, for about one hundred and fifty-three feet, to "Termination Rock," holding well on by a rope which was attached to the rocks as a hand-rope, but which the guides warned us not to trust to, as it was certainly *rotten*. The day was dull, and the wind blowing against the fall, which caused a heavy spray to blow into the arch, and prevented us almost from opening our eyes. We, however, did as others had done before us; went underneath the falls, saw nothing, and got a right good sousing, for which we paid five shillings each to the guides. These two negroes had to undress, and change their clothes when we did, and I never in my life saw two such men. They would have made splendid bronze statues of Hercules.

STATE OF NEW YORK

WE left the Falls of Niagara with great regret, and went in a wagon to Buffalo in the Northern States, situated at the outlet of Lake Erie. It is one of the most rising towns in America. There is little to amuse the traveller in it; therefore we proceeded the following day to Batavia, thence by railroad to Rochester and coach to Canandagua. In this short journey through the State of New York, I met with more incivility and down-right impertinence than I ever did in my life before. The fact was, wherever we went we were immediately recognised as Britishers," and belonging to the Army, which was quite crime enough to insure our being insulted by the detestable vagabonds we met with in our travels. Canandagua is a pretty town, composed of very neat cottages, with a pretty garden round each. The country around is very beautiful; but as we were pressing on to New York, we only remained here one night, and merely saw it from the road.

SYRACUSE TO UTICA

NEXT day, we proceeded from Canandagua to Aubern, thence by a wooden rail, (on which the carriages were drawn by horses, at about seven miles an hour,) to Syracuse, where we had to go on board a canal-boat with seventy other passengers for conveyance to Utica; the said boat being capable of accommodating one third of that number. We did not get on board till four or five o'clock p.m., and the distance to go was about seventy miles. It was all very well as long as daylight lasted, and the weather was fine, for then we could remain on deck; but unfortunately it came on to rain heavily, when all pressed into the cabin, and packed like slaves. We now felt the disagreeableness of *equality*, and travelling with those filthy brutes (Yankees.) Each man chewed tobacco, and spit in all directions, and in a short time, the floor was covered with tobacco juice. About ten o'clock the steward came in to make up the berths for the night, and a most curious thing it was to witness. Each chair or seat of any description, tables, etc., etc., all fell to pieces, and by magic touch were converted into some part of the berths which were now erected, three deep, (one over the other,) on each side of the cabin, with about fourteen to eighteen inches between each. There was one unfortunate man amongst the rest, who was remarkably stout. He looked a long time at the apple-shelf (for it was much more like that than anything else) that he was to lay his carcase upon, and at last he attempted to get into it, which he eventually did with much difficulty. I could not help pitying him, although I was laughing in my sleeve, as often as I saw him, for he appeared to get a squeeze every time the occupant of the berth above him moved.

NEW YORK

HAVING arrived at Utica, not a little glad to be free of the canal prison, we took our tickets and places in the railway to Albany. As there appeared nothing particular to arrest our attention here, we got into a night-steamer, and ran down the Hudson River to New York, a distance of one hundred and forty-five miles. This was a great mistake, for the Hudson is one of the most beautiful rivers in America, and we lost the scenery by sleeping through it. We went to the Carlton Hotel at New York, and were surprised to receive so much attention and civility from everyone there, after the indignities we had been obliged to put up with on our way. Having met with several officers in New York, whom we knew, and who were, like ourselves, on leave of absence, we were induced to fritter away our time from the 4th to the 12th of October. New York is a fine city; but besides its principal street, Broadway, the Astor House, and one or two other places, there is very little worth seeing. The table-d'hôte at the Carlton is very good. We paid, I think, two dollars (8s. 4d.) a day for our board and lodging.

Of course wine was a separate item. The cheapest wine to drink there is Champagne, which costs about 7s. 6d. a bottle. Port wine is not drinkable under 10s. Sherry and Madeira from 8s. 4d. to 60s. a bottle. We attended the theatres every night, and had oyster suppers and porter afterwards. At this time, Abbott the actor was performing. We had seen a great deal of him when in Canada, and he was a great friend of Parker's. Parker, therefore, asked me and many of the other officers then in New York, if we would dine at Delmonico's to meet Abbott, to whom he wanted to give a dinner. Delmonico's is a celebrated house for dinners of the most recherché description. I believe we sat down, seven in number, at five o'clock, and left at half-past six, as Abbott had to go to the theatre. The bill called for and paid, *only* amounted to eight dollars forty cents. (or £1

15s.) each!

We intended to go on to Charlestown, staying a few days; but hearing that the "strangers' fever" (a kind of yellow fever which attacks all strangers, and is very fatal) was raging in both these cities, we changed our plans, and only went to Philadelphia.

PHILADELPHIA

WE had not been more than an hour at the hotel where we stopped, when General Pattison of the United States Army, came to call on us. We were out when he first called, but he left word he would call again in an hour's time. He did so, and was particularly kind and attentive to us. He made arrangements for our seeing all the sights in Philadelphia the following day. and sent us his carriage to drive to each of the Institutions, for which he procured tickets of admission. We visited the Penitentiary, Deaf and Dumb and Blind Asylums, the Mint and the Lunatic Asylum. In the latter place, the keys of some of the wards were kept by one of the patients. The General entertained us most hospitably, and got up a large dinner party to meet us, amongst whom was the celebrated Van Buren. The dinner was good; but what struck me most, was the custom of handing round Champagne in the drawing-room during the evening, after coffee. General Pattison pressed us very much to remain for a month with him to shoot, but we had no guns or shooting dresses with us, and were quite unprepared. However, he said he would supply our wants in every respect, give us clothes, guns, etc., and he would either go into the "bush" with us, to shoot bears, deer, and other animals, or he would give us the best partridge (quail) shooting in America. I could not remain, for all my money was spent, and I had to borrow £10 from my friend Parker to carry me back to Canada. He remained in Philadelphia with Miles, of the 1st Dragoon Guards.

MONTREAL

I LEFT on the 18th of October, and went direct through New York, up the Hudson, that splendid river, to Albany and Whitehall, thence down Lake Champlain to St. John's, and through Chambly to Montreal, where I arrived on the 23rd October. The next day I took my passage from Montreal to Sorel, intending to finish my leave (which did not expire till the 10th November) there amongst the islands of Lake St-Peter, shooting snipe and ducks. However, Major Johnston, who was at Sorel with the Head Quarters of the regiment, hearing that I was down there shooting, sent me a message to say that if I continued shooting about Sorel, I must rejoin, and do my duty. This I thought a hard case, as I had come so far for the express purpose of shooting over the only good snipe ground I knew of in that part of Canada. I therefore kept very quiet, and was seldom seen by anyone, except Lord Cochrane, with whom I stayed.

On 7th of November, I was in Montreal, and found the rumours of war, which had been spreading for some time, were quite true. The whole country was in arms. The rebels had attacked Beauharnois, and shot some English farmers in cold blood. At Napierville, four thousand rebels had assembled under the command of French officers, and a Pole named Hinderlang. Sir John Colborne resolved to attack them in person on the 8th. I was told that my Regiment would have to move against the rebels at St. Ours, twelve miles from Sorel. I therefore gave up my leave, and rejoined that night. I went down in the same steamer with the orders for us to attack St. Ours the following day.

RICHELIEU

WE marched accordingly with two guns, and arrived there the same night; the insurgents dispersing on our approach. We halted there for the night, and marched on the 9th through St. Denis to St. Charles, the roads dreadfully bad, and up to our knees in mud. At night it froze hard, and rendered them almost impassable. It was therefore decided the following day, that we should proceed by the steamer to St. Hillaire, where the rebels had collected in force, but as the horses could not be got on board, those of the Artillery, and the officers who had horses, were obliged to travel on the banks of the river, each man armed with a musket; but I, having a large brace of pistols, dispensed with the heavier tool of war. We arrived there, however, without having been attacked, and found that the enemy had again *"moved on."* The next day, Sir John Colborne attacked the rebels and Yankee sympathizers at Napierville, and as we were aware of this, we got permission (a party of the officers) to ascend the St. Hilaire de Ronville mountain, but with strong injunctions to go armed, in case of an attack. From thence we had a magnificent view of the country for many miles, and saw Sir John's work, in three towns blazing away at the same time.

BOUCHERVILLE

WE were now informed that an insurgent camp had been formed on Boucherville Mountain, only twelve miles from us. Major Johnston, upon this news, went with a party of mounted Artillerymen and one or two officers to reconnoitre, and nearly dropped upon the rebel outpost at Vingt Quatre; but their spies discovered the party, and they all retreated to their camp in the mountain. Two Companies with Captains Gordon[5] and Michel,[6] Lieutenant Daniell, myself, and Trench were sent forward that night to the rebel outpost just named, which we found vacated. Here we took up our abode for the night, the two Captains occupying the bed, and the subalterns the floor; after a very good dinner of Irish stew, which Daniell manufactured. Here we were at the foot of Boucherville Mountain, and only three miles from the rebel camp. The following morning, the Major joined us with the two other Companies, and two guns. We then advanced on the mountain and the rebels, and after taking every precaution against surprise in the "Bush," with which the mountain is covered, we marched straight up to a mill in a very strong position, and well loopholed. The rebels had again fled on our approach, but left behind them three guns, (one a nine-pounder,) forty muskets, some dozen pikes, and a great deal of powder and ammunition. This was all taken possession of, and we marched to return to our billets in Belœil and St. Hilaire but the men were fagged, the roads being knee-deep in mud; the rain came down heavily, and it was freezing very hard at the same time; the men began to lag, and many remained on the road-side. It became pitch-dark before we got half-way back.

---

[5] Sir William Gordon.

[6] Major-General Michel.

BELTIL

THE Major was obliged to billet many of the "done ones" on the road, and it was nine at night before we got to our old quarters at Beloeil. Two of the Companies had then to be ferried across to their quarters on the opposite side of the river, and it must have been eleven o'clock before the men could have got their accoutrements off, which was a hard day's work for them, having paraded that morning at five o'clock. Many was the hearty laugh we had that night, after getting under the shelter of the house, and before the roaring wood-fire, which I shall ever remember, at the grotesque appearances some of us made; having changed our clothes for those of the "habitans" in whose house we were. I had a coat, the sleeves of which came but little below my elbows, and trousers that reached somewhat below my knees. Another man (Biscoe) was dressed up in women's apparel, not being able to find any other. The night previously to this, I was orderly officer, and visited the sentries, whose orders were, that on anyone's approaching their posts, they were to challenge three times, and if they got no answer they were to fire; which I told them was quite correct. About six o'clock the following morning, when quite dark, the sentry in the square opposite the chapel, saw a light moving across, about one hundred and sixty yards from him. He immediately challenged the person with the light three times, but receiving no answer, he took a deliberate aim, fired, and down dropped the lantern. The guard turned out, and discovered a poor old *deaf* sexton on the ground, having his three fingers of the left hand cut off by the sentry's ball. The poor old man was going to ring the bell for early mass, and could not hear the challenge. A subscription was got up for him, and he received about twenty-eight dollars, which quite compensated him for the loss of his fingers.

From Beloeil we marched to St. Mary de Monoir, and thence to St. Corsair, where we were ordered to live in I free quarters,' that is, upon the stock belonging to the rebellious party. The people at first raised the prices of everything to double their market value, but that was not to be stood, so we sent out foraging parties every day under an officer, and took whatever was wanted for the Regiment, paying the regular prices established before the outbreak. After remaining there a week or so, I was sent with Gordon, Parker, and the Grenadier Company, to St. Pic, and thence to St. Hyacinths, where we were joined by the Head Quarters of the Regiment.

After remaining about a month at St. Hyacinths, we left it for Chambly. Thence we proceeded to St. Athanase and St. John's, where we were quartered for a few days, when a report was spread that the Yankee sympathizers were coming in at Henryville on the boundary line. We were immediately ordered to march there with the Artillery, three hundred and fifty of the Guards, and half of the 15th Regiment. We remained there a few days, all being quiet, then returned to St. John's. It was now January 1839.

ST. JOHN'S

We found St. John's rather a nice quarter; and the frozen River Richelieu gave us good roads for driving. We had three days' rapid thaw, which melted all the snow, with the help of rain. The thermometer then suddenly dropped, and remained from ten to below zero, therefore we had the glare ice to drive on. I once drove down from Isle au Noix (fourteen miles) in one hour's fair trotting. The 15th Regiment were quartered at Isle au Noix, 1st Dragoon Guards at Chambly, (twelve miles,) and the 71st at Lacadie, (seven miles from St. John's.) We therefore had always some place to drive to, after our long and tiresome parades. At the end of January, we left St. John's, and marched to Chambly, where we were "doubled up" in barracks, two and three in a room, and without bedding, except what we got from the stores. We were attached to the 1st Dragoons, and lived at their mess—a very good one.

Our amusements were chiefly in walking into the "Bush" with our axes, and trying who was the most expert at cutting down trees and building wigwarns, or huts. I found that after a little practice, I could build a hut weather-proof, with the boughs of the fir-tree, in about an hour. Some of those we built were afterwards inhabited by some wandering people for six months.

LA PRAIRIE

IN the end of February, we got our orders to march to La Prairie, where were also a Squadron of the 7th Hussars. Being hard-up for amusement, the officers
Being
of the 7th Hussars and 66th, who were quartered in the barracks at St. John's, bought a spade each, and we set to work to drain the space of ground between our quarters and the town, for the purpose of forming a race-course, and in about six weeks, we had made a very good one. The best horses of the Canadas, and of the Northern United States attended the meeting, and the owners all admitted it was the best course in Canada, if not in America. The races came off in the middle of July, and were very good; but "Britishers" carried away the greatest portion of the prizes, to the great disgust of the Yankees.

We invited two tribes of Indians to come down to these races, which they did, the one from "The Lake of the Two Mountains," and the other from Cauguawaugha. They ran matches between the races for purses allotted for them, and afterwards the one tribe played against the other at a game similar to "hockey," with long rackets, for a prize. They were remarkably strong-made men, and very fast runners. They all appeared in their war costume, and with only the girdle on.

On the 24th of May we had a grand Brigade Field-day, in Montreal, and all the troops within eighteen miles of the town were called in, the 66th amongst the number. We were Brigaded with the Grenadier Guards, under Colonel Ellison. There were also the Royals, 15th, 24th, 71st, the 7th Hussars, 1st or King's Dragoon Guards, and all the Field Artillery; the whole under Sir John Colborne. We were under arms at six o'clock a.m., at La Prairie, crossed the St. Lawrence in the steamer, and marched on to the ground at ten a.m., when the fight began. It continued till near five o'clock in the afternoon, when a feu-de-joie was fired, three cheers, and one cheer more were given for the Queen; marched past, saluted Sir John, and returned to our respective quarters. The field-day passed off very well, Sir John expressing his satisfaction. The ground was very wet, and full of blind ditches. The 24th Regiment had at one time their pouches under-water, and the whole were knee-deep at one part of the field, in black bog-mud. Lady Colborne gave a grand ball in the evening, to which we were all invited.

On the 10th of June, I got ten days leave, and went down to Sorel, crossed the St. Lawrence to Berthier, and drove "aback" to Rawdon to fish. I got amongst some beautiful lakes and rivers, but the musquitoes and "brulo," or sand-fly, were so thick and hungry, that I was driven away in two days, having caught (between two rods) sixteen dozen trout.

SOREL

August 25th, I obtained leave of absence till the end of October, and went straight down to Sorel with my horse, dogs; gun, and servant. Here I put up at O'Neil's hotel, (he formerly was a sergeant in the 66th Regiment,) and I drove down nearly every day to the islands in Lake St. Peter to shoot, which I found a much better plan than I had adopted the previous year, in living on the ground for three or four days together, and without a bed. I went out with my gun thirty-six times, but sometimes only for an hour's potter about Sorel. Other days I used to drive the nine miles, and canoe it two more before getting to the ground. The total of game bagged was three hundred and twenty-eight head, in thirty-six days; two water hens, six woodcocks, seventeen ducks, two partridges, two hundred and thirty-three snipes, eleven bitterns, three pigeons, and two herons, (one stood five and a half feet high.)

LA PRAIRIE

MY leave having expired, I rejoined the Regiment at La Prairie.

* * * * * * * * *

Daniell and I having made up our minds to go into the "bush" for a time to hunt deer, used to take long walks every day, in order to put ourselves in training to walk with the Indians. Generally after luncheon we would take a "stretch" of twelve or fourteen miles. On one of these occasions we met our doctor, (Auglin,) who was a very lazy fellow, smoking his cigar just outside his lodgings in the town; we requested him to take a walk with us, but he refused, however, he said he would not mind going as far as the railway bridge with us, (about two miles,) so away we went. On arriving there, we persuaded him that if he went beyond the next "cutting" he would get the nicest milk possible: by this persuasion we got him on two miles further. After a rest, we told him that a little beyond was a capital view of the country, and he could see Lacadie, where the 71st were quartered. This got him nearly two miles farther from home, and then, as he was longing for some beer, we proposed to go to Blairfindy to the public-house, which he agreed to, and then we had taken him over nine miles of ground. Just as we were drinking our beer, we discovered it was five o'clock; we dined at half-past six o'clock, and had nine miles between us and the table. We started off at our best pace; the road was bad, as there was a quantity of rotten ice and snow on it. Daniell and I did the nine miles into La Prairie in one hour and thirty-four minutes: poor Auglin came in about ten minutes afterwards, but only to go to bed, where he stayed for three days, at least he did not make his appearance for that time.

Captain Biscoe and myself having got leave, started on the 3rd of February to Beauharnois, on a deer-shooting excursion. This place is about thirty miles above La

Prairie, on the right bank of the Saint Lawrence. Having stayed here three days, and finding only one deer, and seeing no tracks of any others, we left that part of the country; the one we did find was run down fairly by a hunter named Maturin, and killed with a stick. He ran the deer for about five hours. The snow was so light and fresh that it let us (who had small snow shoes on) in to a considerable depth. Maturin's shoes were immensely large, and bore him over the top very fairly.

THE BUSH

ON the 6th of February, having procured an Indian named St. John as our hunter and guide, we struck into "the bush," about twenty miles to the south, up the English river. Having come to the edge of "the bush," our provisions, blankets, guns, &c., were divided into three bundles, the guide taking the largest, and ourselves the other two. The snow-shoes being put on, each one slung his burden on his back, and away we went, about five miles into the original bush, straight-on-end, when we came to a little bark hut, which was deserted, filled and covered with snow. Here we made up our minds to live, and accordingly set to work and cleared out the place, felled small trees for firewood, and made our beds of the branches of the fir-trees on each side of the hut, in the centre of which we always kept a roaring fire. Here we remained for a week, five miles in the forest, with no habitation near, except a wigwam belonging to an Indian hunter, a little way off. We had no dogs; indeed, if we had, they would have been of no use to us, for we had to run the deer down by following his track in the snow, and often we followed one for six or seven hours, without ever seeing him. We were very unfortunate in the state of the snow, for at first it was like feathers, and let the snow-shoes sink deep, and, of course, in raising the foot again, about three pounds of snow had to be dragged up on the top of the shoe. The weather then changed, and the snow turned to "slush," after which it froze on the surface, just sufficiently hard to let the shoe through, and catch the toe on coming up, with the crust, which caused innumerable tumbles. The following day it was frozen as hard as a turnpike road, which let the deer, and us too, go as fast as we liked, but not being so swift on foot as deer, we gave the thing up in disgust. Our Indian hunter went out on the Sunday during the "slush," and killed a fine doe, which was the only thing we got on this excursion, except some spruce partridges that we shot.

The proper state for the snow to be in for deer-hunting is this. It ought to have a sufficient crust on the top to bear the weight of a man on the broad snow shoe, but not so strong as to resist the sharp foot and weight of a deer. It ought just to let the animal's legs through as he trots along, which not only causes great impediment in his speed, but if long run, will at last cut the legs against the crust, when he will give in almost immediately, and the sportsman gets up to him, and gets his shot. We returned to La Prairie on the 13th, bearing with us as a trophy, the doe which the hunter had killed. It turned out to be "*a very good one and a fat*," as a friend of mine in the 7th Hussars expressed it.

MONTREAL

MAY the 1st we crossed over from La Prairie to Montreal, and relieved the Grenadier Guards, who went down to Quebec. The change for us was much for the better, and a great comfort in many respects.

* * * * * * * * *

One day a servant boy I kept to groom my horse, and look after my sleigh, informed me that my soldier servant who acted as valet, decorated himself in my clothes every evening after he had seen me go to mess, and paraded himself about the town. At first I doubted that it could be the case, but the boy persisted in his story, so I had Mr. Rowland, a grenadier, searched, when I found he was totally rigged (in the day-time) with my shirt, drawers, socks, etc., underneath his own clothes. So much for your trustworthy "gentleman's gentleman" from the ranks.

Montreal was the first place worthy of being called a town that we had been in since we left Quebec in 1837. There was society to be had at some times of the year, but I did not consider it so refined as might have been expected, and from several occurrences that took place there, it took very little "summing up" to come to the conclusion that the morals of both sexes in society were as loose as they need be.

About the middle of May, Captain Biscoe and I had made up our minds to visit the townships with our fishing-rods, but our Colonel was quite of another way of thinking, for he told us that it was near the time for the general to inspect the regiment, and that he could not let us go until that was over. General Clitherow heard of our fishing propensities and longings to be off, through his "son John," who was his A. D. C., so he sent a message to Colonel Johnston that the two officers who wanted to go fishing might go at once, and that he would put off his Inspection till their return. Accordingly, on the 3rd of June, we crossed to La Prairie, took rail to St. John's, and next day steamer up Lake Champlain to "Rouse's Point," where we disembarked, got a wagon to Moortown, at which place we roughed it for the night, and proceeded next day in another wagon to Chateauguy.

As we drove along the road from Moortown towards the Lake, clouds of pigeons kept constantly crossing us, and after we left our wagon to walk through the bush the last mile, we came upon these birds in thousands, sitting in the trees, and so tame were they, that we threw several stones at them without disturbing them. I was much struck by the circumstance of all the cock pigeons (known by the reddish brown breast) flying in one direction in the morning, and returning in the afternoon, when the hen birds took their flight, and returned afterwards. It appears that these flights are taken to a distance for their food, and whilst the one sex is away, the other sits upon the nest.

CHATEAUGUY

HAVING arrived at Chateauguy, we immediately made ourselves acquainted with Mr. Weeds, the proprietor of a saw-mill at the outlet, and requested permission to put up at his house during a stay of two or three days, which he most civilly consented to. Having made these arrangements, we put together our fishing-rods, (which were "Bowness's" light trout rods,) much to the amusement of the workmen about us, who laughed at the idea of pulling a fish out of the water with such flimsy "*fish poles*" as those. Again were they astonished at our small flies, and "*guessed*" we should catch nothing with them, for the trout were two or three pounds' weight in the lake, and would smash to all eternity all our fish-gear. However, their astonishment did not reach its climax till they saw us catch fish, and land them almost as fast as we threw in the line. We fished only for about two hours in the evenings, and the same in the mornings of Saturday and Monday, and our sport was as follows— Friday evening, six dozen and six trout; Saturday morning and evening, thirteen dozen and two; Monday morning, eight dozen; making a total of twenty-seven dozen and eight trout. The men now admired our tackle and "fish poles" as much as they had at first despised them, and were quite annoying from their incessant begging for some of our flies, which of course we were not very willing to part with, not only because we had just started on our fishing excursion, but because we could not get another supply nearer than England. They requested us to bring a stock of flies with us when we went again, and said they would pay any price we liked to ask for them. However, we said good-bye, and never saw the place again.

We left the Lake on the 9th of June, and returned to St. John's, from whence we started afresh on the 10th in a wagon, and arrived at a very comfortable little inn, called Richford, the same evening. It has been said that no cream, like the Devonshire, can be made out of that county, but at Richford we had as thick, clotted, and beautiful cream as any I ever saw about Plymouth.

Here we had the Misisquoi River to fish, which I found far preferable to lake fishing. We fished in the mornings and evenings only, and killed on Thursday, Friday, and Saturday, eleven dozen and five trout. These fish average three-quarters of a pound. The water in the river was very low and almost hot. I found the best fish lying where the cold springs from the hills ran into the river.

We now determined to "move on," and upon inquiring from the innkeeper how we were to get to Sherbrooke, he informed us that the next day being Sunday, "*the Colonel*" would have nothing to do, and would most likely be very glad to drive us to Darby-line. But we, not having been introduced to "the Colonel," did not know how that was to be managed. We came to the conclusion at last that we would go and call on him, and having found out that he lived at Priddy's Burn, about two miles off, away we started. On arriving at the said "Burn," we discovered that "*the Colonel*" was a blacksmith, and that he was hard at work on his anvil. We soon introduced ourselves, and made known our business, which "*the Colonel*" immediately took on hand, engaging to drive us to Darbyline the next morning, for a consideration. "*The Colonel*" was as good as his word, and drove up to the inn door for us at ten o'clock. The conveyance was a wagon and "span" of horses, (i.e., a pair.) He proposed driving to Troy, halting there to bait and dine, and doing the remainder in the cool of the evening, which we acquiesced in.

On arriving at the inn at Troy, we found some dozen lazy fellows (the sort who are always found at a public-house on a Sunday) assembled there. We alighted, and ordered some eggs and bacon for dinner, but, unfortunately, we were put into the same room with these snobs, who immediately found out that we were "*Britishers*," and not only that but *officers*, upon which they began to insult us in every possible way. However, we kept very quiet, and took no notice of them. At last Biscoe left the room, and one of these "*sympathizers*" with the Canadian rebels, addressed me. "I say, Mister, so it appears Miss Bull (meaning the Queen) has made a fix of it. These papers say the man she's married had a woman living with him before at Saxe Coburg, and that she has come to England and claimed him. How does that go down with you Britishers?" I replied, "If that was the first their papers had of it there, they must be three months behind the rest of the world, for it was quite an old story, so old indeed, that it had now been forgotten." They went on in this strain talking at me for some time. I felt my blood boil. I saw some billiard cues in the corner of the room, and was just in the act of getting up to break one across my knee for the purpose of clearing the room, (which I certainly should have done, and have broken most of the eight or nine heads there into the bargain,) when my arm was arrested by "*the Colonel*," who dragged me out of the room, saying, "It won't do, don't answer them, keep quiet, and you annoy them more than if you thrashed them all round." He then blew up the master of the inn, and blackguarded him well for allowing those brutes to annoy passengers, and he swore he would never bring any there again if he permitted it. Now "*the Colonel*" was a Yankee himself, and held the colonelcy of some U. S. militia regiment. After getting our eggs and bacon, and coffee for dinner at two o'clock, we proceeded on our journey, and reached Darbyline, where we remained for the night. Next day, after wishing "*the Colonel*" good-bye and success, we went on to Sherbrooke. On the 16th of June we drove over to Lenoxville, and on the 17th, Biscoe went to fish in Lake Memphramagog, where he had most excellent sport. From some cause or other, I did not accompany him, but stayed at Sherbrooke, amusing myself by sketching, and playing quoits with the landlord of the hotel, who was a regular Pickwick.

June 18th. Paid our bill, and returned to Montreal.

On Saturday afternoon, the 20th of June, Colonel Johnston sent for me to ask if I would carry despatches to Quebec for Government, as some important ones were to be sent there immediately, and the steamer had left. I replied I would be ready in twenty minutes. Accordingly I packed up my carpet bag, took a calèche out of the street, and was at the Government House within that time, and received my letters, with instructions to lose no time. I applied to a livery stable keeper to send me down, but he recommended me to pick up changes of horses as I went along the road, as much the quickest way of going, so I took the calèche to the bottom of the Island of Montreal, there crossed the Ottawa River, got a wagon and "span" to Berthier, another from there to Three Rivers, a calèche to Champlain, which I exchanged for another to St. Anne's, got a cart from thence to Deschambault, a calèche to L'Eaurent, another to Lorette, and a third to Quebec, where I arrived on the night of the 21st, (Sunday,) at eleven o'clock, having left Montreal at three o'clock the previous afternoon, and having performed the journey of two hundred miles in thirty-two hours. The roads the whole way were in a most horrible state with ruts in them; without exaggeration, they let in the wheels up to the axle. I had to get almost every change of horses out of the fields, which caused me much delay, and when I arrived at the St. John's Gate, at Quebec, I was detained there for some time, as no one was allowed into the city after ten o'clock: however, upon saying who and what I was, armed with despatches from the Government, I was admitted. The only delays I made on the journey were, to sup at Berthier, breakfast at Three Rivers, and dine at Desehamvault. I went to Payne's Hotel, and never was I more glad to get into bed. I had had such a shaking, that I could scarcely swallow anything. My inside was regularly churned, and an attack of diarrhoea came on in consequence, which stuck to me for several days afterwards.

Before leaving Montreal, I had obtained the Colonel's

sanction to remain absent till the end of the month, after delivering the despatches. I therefore stayed at Quebec for more than a week, during which time I took a trip down to St. Anne's to see the waterfalls once again. The Coldstream and Grenadier Guards were then quartered in Quebec. I returned to Montreal by steamer at the end of the month, but here I was not suffered to remain long, for on the 8th of July I got my orders to escort ammunition from thence to Kingston, in Upper Canada.

On the 9th of July I paraded my escort of a sergeant and fifteen men, took over from the Ordnance three "bateaux" laden with ammunition, and escorted them by canal to Lachine, where I discovered that one of the bateaux was unserviceable, and had to send back to Montreal the following day for another in its place. During this delay, the crew, who were Canadians, got drunk, and one, who was not drunk, told me he would not go with me, so I gave him in charge of the sentry. He then said he would not work if I kept him; however, I quietly told him that go he should, and that if he would not work, I would tie him at the bottom of the boat, and he should neither eat nor drink till he changed his mind. When the time came to exert himself, he turned out the best of the lot. We were obliged to remain at Lachine all Friday, the 10th, but left it on the 11th, and arrived at St. Anne's Rapids, which took us three hours to get over. We remained here all night.

July 12th. Left St. Anne's Rapids, killed a few pigeons on the way up, and pitched the tents about six miles below Carillon, on an island, where the musquitoes were in millions. However, before I went into my tent, I lighted a fire in it, and filled it with smoke, which I allowed about ten minutes to rise a foot above the ground, when I crawled in on my hands and knees, and lay down, having shut up the entrance to confine the smoke. From adopting this plan, I did not get a single bite.

July 13th. Left the island at half-past five, a.m., and

got up to Carillon, where I breakfasted with Ensign Trick, of our Regiment, who was there on detachment, and went on to Grey's Point.

4th. Got up to the head of "Longue Soult" Rapid to breakfast, and pitched our tents in the evening at the mouth of Red River.

15th and 16th. In consequence of head winds against us, could only proceed very slowly.

17th. Tremendous thunder-storm, and rain all night. It rained through the tents and put out all the fires.

18th. Tremendously hot sun, which affected my head so much that I could not rise from a sitting position. Got up near Bytown.

Sunday, 19th. Bought a bark canoe from some Indians at the mouth of the Calinot river, and arrived with my charge at Bytown. Here I got rationed for nine days, and passed through the locks of the Canal, twenty-four in number, which are a most magnificent work. The scenery about Bytown is very beautiful. I was more pleased with it than with anything I had before seen. There were nineteen boats waiting at the bottom of the locks to pass through, but were not allowed, as it was Sunday.

10th. Were detained here till ten o'clock by the baker, who supplied us with nine days' bread. He told us at the same time that it would keep good for three days! We got up to the Black Rapids, where we pitched the tents. I killed a brace of partridges and a pigeon. I found the bass take the "kill devil" very well in the rapids.

21st. Proceeded about seventeen miles. I killed a pike, (three pounds,) and ran several others with the bowl of a tin spoon: killed several bass and white fish.

22nd. Reached within three miles of Merricksville; killed a couple of black ducks, (young ones.)

23rd. Went in my canoe in advance of the bateaux, and killed a couple of ducks. It rained heavily all day. Pitched the tents at Kilmarnock locks; rained in torrents all night; found the tents of little use.

24th. Took one hundred and fifty buckets of rain water out of ONE bateau. Saw a good many ducks; caught some bass; entered Green Lake, and a fair wind springing up, enabled us to sail fifteen miles through it, when we halted after dark on an island that was so rocky, we could not pitch the tents.

25th. Caught lots of fish; got through two more lakes.

Sunday, 26th. Proceeded on our journey, and put up for the night about eighteen miles from Kingston.

27th. Started at four a.m.; saw several eagles, a fox and a deer, and arrived at Kingston about half-past six, p.m., having been twenty days in getting up seventy miles of the Ottawa River, and one hundred and ten miles of the Rideau Canal. During the whole journey, the sun was intensely hot, and we had no means of putting up an awning over the boats, as it would have been in the way of the oars. The dew rose so heavily every night, that when I awoke in the morning, the whole of my clothes were completely saturated, and in that way I put them on to dry on my back in the sun. The Rideau Canal was begun in the year 1826, was opened for navigation in 1830, and has cost upwards of a million; the object of it being to provide a communication by water from Montreal to Lake Ontario, without encountering the rapids of the St. Lawrence, some of which are insurmountable. It commences at Bytown, where are the most splendid locks in America, joining the canal with the Ottawa River. From these locks it proceeds by artificial cuts and natural sheets of water, which are again backed up by other locks, to Kingston Mills Locks.

I was detained three days at Kingston, where I lived I was detained by my old friends the 24th Regiment. I then went to the Acting Quarter-Master General, and after some difficulty, got him to order me to return to Montreal by the Saint Lawrence, there being an order that troops should always be sent *viâ* the Rideau Canal, in consequence of some detachment who were descending the river, having forced the boat's crew to take them to the American side, when they all deserted.

I represented that if we were to wait till an opportunity occurred of sending us in tow of the steamboat per canal, we could not get back to Montreal for a week, whereas by going down the Rapids of the St. Lawrence, we should get down in two days, or three at the most. Having at last got MY orders, I distributed my men equally among the three bateaux, and left Kingston about six o'clock a.m. The weather was beautiful, and we were soon sailing down with a light breeze amongst the Thousand Islands. Some of these are eight or ten miles long, but dozens do not cover more than an acre of space. They are for the most part rocky, rising in abrupt cliffs from the water; but others are low. The whole are well-wooded, and form very beautiful groups. That day we got down to Prescott, a distance of seventy miles. Here we remained for the night, started by daylight the next morning, and reached Dickenson's Landing about two o'clock.

This place is just above the Longue Sault Rapid, the most dangerous of all. I could not get the crew on board at this place for a long time, nor would they come, till they had had "one other glass" to give them *strength* to go down the rapid; (i.e., give them pluck.) However, at last we started, and as soon as we got into the turbulent water, each man lay upon his oar, with his eye on the steersman, ready to either pull or "back-water" as they might be directed. There was a man also at the bow of the boats with a long pole, on the look-out for rocks, and ready to fend off any we might come near. Down we went, amongst these foaming waves and breakers at the rate of twenty miles an hour, sometimes actually jumping from the top of one wave down into the hollow of the next, half the keel of the boat being often out of the water at a time. On we went, rushing at an awful pace, sometimes straight for a huge rock, and just when almost about to strike it, a word from the steersman, "*pull larboard,*" and a dip of the oars would send us clear:

onward we went, now into a tremendous whirlpool, in which it would take the whole strength of the crew to keep the boat at all straight and prevent her being whirled round and round: out of this, then into the breakers again, down between immense rocks, (which it is wonderful how we cleared,) till we reached the comparatively smooth water below. In going down this rapid, my bateau was the last of the three, so we had an opportunity of seeing how the other boats behaved. At one time, we missed one boat for several seconds, and the Captain said it must have struck and gone down. However, it soon turned up again, for it had only got into a whirlpool, and had been wheeled about in a helpless state until it got under the cover of a large rock. To avoid this rapid, travellers are obliged to go by coach down the banks of the river for twelve miles, to Cornwall. Having passed the Longue Sault, we rowed away down Lake St. Francis, and landed for the night on a point of land about halfway down, having got over about seventy miles. It being quite dark when we were crossing this lake, I was much struck by a number of lights, which appeared to me to be those of a large town; but the crew informed me there was not even land where the lights were, but that they were the torches used by the Canadians for the purpose of spearing fish, and placed at the head of their canoes.

The following morning, we were on the 'move at four o'clock, and got down to Couteau du Lac. Here, again, are other rapids, which cause the traveller a land journey of sixteen miles. Down these we went at the same speed, and in the same manner as down the Longue Sault, to the Cascades at tie junction of the Ottawa and the St. Lawrence. Leaving the Cascades, we descended the St. Lawrence, shooting the Lachine rapids to Montreal. Thus ended my escort duty to Upper Canada.

MONTREAL

JUST outside of Montreal was the kennel of the Garrison hounds. The pack was kept up not only by members of the Garrison, but civilians also put down their names. The hour of meeting was six o'clock in the morning, before the sun got too hot, and we were generally back before nine o'clock. As for sport, there was none. The hounds were thrown into cover, or rather the low bush, generally found a fox, or perhaps half a dozen immediately, and ran them up and down the bushwood for an hour, but not one bit of the run could anybody see. The horsemen cantered and trotted, following the pack by their ears on the outside of the bush, and found always plenty to do in the leaping way, for there were generally post and rails from four to five feet high every fifty yards. I have heard people there talk of a run of eight or nine miles over what they call the "Barn" country, which is clear of bush; but they do not get into that country twice in the autumn. I used to -o out regularly with Captain Michel and Hon. Edward Lambert; but it was more for the sake of hearing the note of the hounds, than with any hope of having a run. On one occasion, Stackley, V.S., (who kept the hounds,) had a bagged fox, which he had kept at the kennel for a week before he turned him out. He was "shaken" one morning in about two acres of low bush-wood, and having had about ten minutes to think where he was, the pack were thrown in. I got on to the end of this cover to view him away, and after sitting quietly there for some time, he trotted into a path quite near me, but was not inclined to leave. A young hound came up on the scent of the fox till he found him. The fox very deliberately squatted. The puppy, thinking he was for a game at play, began his pranks, and played round him until some of the old stagers came up, and put an end to my fun, and the fox's existence. I one morning saw five foxes break cover together, but they only ran out one field, when they doubled back.

There is some good snipe-shooting, and woodcock too, to be had about nine miles below Montreal, nearly at the extremity of the island.

The Garrison consisted of ourselves and the 85th, and at St. Helen's the 15th Regiment Infantry, the Royal Artillery, and the 7th Hussars. In the beginning of October, one Company of the 66th Regiment left Montreal, and embarked in the Sapphire steamship for England, under Captain Dames. On the 24th October, our Head Quarters embarked on board a steamer at Montreal, which carried us down to Quebec, and the following day, we were trans-shipped to the Athole troop-ship, which had been sent out to bring us home. We were relieved at Montreal by the 23rd Royal Welsh Fusiliers, and right glad we were to see them. The ship was tremendously crowded: we had over three hundred men on board, besides women and children.

VOYAGE TO ENGLAND.

WE left Quebec in a heavy snow-storm on the 28th October, beat down the river about fifteen miles, and next day ran aground opposite Grosse Isle, about two miles from land. However, the return tide floated us off, and we got good anchorage for the night, which came on to blow terrifically. On the 31st, we passed the "Traverse," and anchored off the "Pilgrims." November 1st, we discharged the pilot, passed the Brandy Pots, with studding sails set. Off Cape Chat. On the 2nd, we passed Cape Gaspe and the Percy Mountains on the starboard, and Anticosti just visible on the larboard. On the following day, passed the Magdalene and Bird Islands. Cape North and St. Paul's on the right, and Cape Ray and Newfoundland on the left. On the 5th, it came on to blow from E.S.E., took in a lot of sails, and got up a stay-sail; the sea getting up and much swollen. This weather continued till the 9th, when it increased to a heavy gale. The Colonel had two horses on board, which he had been advised to leave behind, as they could not cross the Atlantic safely at that time of year. On the 8th, the little mare became perfectly mad, foaming at the mouth, and making efforts to leap out of her box. I recommended that she should be bled; but the Colonel said, *No!* I knew that if she was not bled she would die, and at five o'clock a.m. she did die. At two o'clock p.m. the ship was "put about," when it affected the other mare so much that she became furious, and managed to get half out of her box in a state of madness. She was immediately stunned by a couple of blows from a large hammer by a sailor, and then had her throat cut, and was thrown overboard, apparently dead. However, the cold water revived her to a certain extent, and she was seen swimming about for several minutes afterwards. It was a sad butchery, but could not be helped. On the 9th, it blew a heavy gale, top-gallant masts were lowered, and top-gallant yards brought in. At night blew a perfect hurricane: we shipped several seas, one of which carried away the bulwarks of the larboard bow. The storm staysail got loose, gave a flap, split the block on the fore yard-arm, and buried the hook in the deck of the ship, hooking in the beam underneath. The next flap sent the sail to smithereens. The noise it made was very like the discharge of a cannon; everyone turned out, thinking the masts had gone overboard. That hurricane was the most awfully grand sight I ever witnessed. It happened that I was on watch that night from eight to twelve, during its height. The sea was in mountains, and each sea crested. These came rolling down upon us, towering twice the height of the masts, as if each one would roll right over their tops, but as if by magic disappearing astern of us. It was a rather dark night; but occasionally the moon shone out from the heavy black masses of clouds, and showed the state of the ocean. The wind roared and whistled through the rigging to such a degree, that the Captain (Bellamy) could not make himself heard through the speaking-trumpet half the length of the ship. In this magnificently awful din, the sailors were attempting to do what they could. The ship was pitching and rolling so tremendously, that everyone was lashed; the sailors had ropes run fore and aft, by which to hold on as they moved along the deck. I lashed myself to the bulwarks on the poop, and was frequently swung off my legs. The hatches were battened down, and no one but the watch allowed on deck. However, after calling another officer to relieve me at twelve o'clock, I remained on the poop till nearly one o'clock, watching the storm. I then went down, and went as fast asleep as if I had been in my - downy bed at home. It was a curious thing to see how those stiff lower masts of the Athole swished to and fro during that hurricane. The ship was uncommonly leaky, the lower decks swimming with water, and all the berths were wet. The tiller was kept rigged below, and all the axes were up on deck, ready to cut away the masts if they went overboard, which there seemed every chance of their doing. Captain Bellamy said he had been forty years at sea, and never experienced such weather before.

During the gale, which lasted nine days, we drifted bodily to leeward, fifty miles a day, (to the south.) We got down to lat. 38°, nearly halfway between the St. Lawrence and Bermuda. Here the wind was as warm as in summer, the thermometer standing at 66°, the water at 67°.

On 17th November we were put upon a short allowance of water: viz., one pint a day; and on the 27th we were further reduced to half a pint a day. On the 28th we were only allowed one cup of tea or coffee for breakfast, and those who had tea in the evening, could get no water for their brandy. It was therefore always asked who was for tea, and who for brandy and water. The sails were spread upon the deck to catch the rain; but after filling one or two tanks, it was found to be so salt, from running off the canvass that had been covered with spray, that it was found to be quite useless.

When we arrived at Spithead, I found from the purser that there were only three days' provisions in the ship. There were nine deaths on board, seven of which were children, owing, it was supposed, to the crowded and wet state of the ship. Three births also occurred during the passage.

Tuesday, December 1st, we made land for the first time, St. Alban's Head. We passed through the Needles, and dropped anchor opposite Newton at seven o'clock p.m. On the 2nd we got up to Spithead, when a steamer came out and towed us into the harbour about four o'clock, p.m.

PORTSMOUTH

WE disembarked the next day, and marched up to Forton Barracks, Gosport.

It was generally supposed that the run home from the St. Lawrence at that time of year, would not occupy more than twenty-five days, in consequence of the prevalence of north-westerly winds; but during our whole voyage, we never got one puff from that point; and the people at Portsmouth began to be very doubtful of the safety of the Athole. The Serpent man-of-war of sixteen guns was in the same gale of wind, but arrived several days before us at Portsmouth. She also gave doubtful stories about our ship, as she had not seen us since the hurricane. She had to throw several guns overboard, and, unfortunately, had three men washed away.

Never shall I forget the pleasure I experienced on once more seeing English ground, English fences to the fields, and those fields of immense size. I fell into a reverie. I was hunting, skimming over the country, hallooing in my mind—in fact, I was in a state of madness in my dreaming thoughts. After three years and six months, I had returned to England. Merry old England!

Our depot, which had been quartered at Sheerness, joined us soon after our disembarkation at Gosport.

We had very good barracks at Forton, but found both that place and Portsmouth very stupid in general. Southampton, which was only sixteen miles from us, was quite a different place. Balls were very frequent there, and the Committee never forgot to send free to the officers of the Garrison at Portsmouth. We found it very good fun in going there. We had our old friends the 15th Regiment on the Gosport side of the harbour at Haslar.

On the 26th May, 1841, I got leave from my Captain till the end of the month, packed up a few things in a valise, which I attached to my saddle, and went over to the Isle of Wight with poor Scott, (who was after• wards killed in the Phenix Park, Dublin, by his horse running away, and dashing his rider's head against the branch of a tree.) We rode the first day from Ryde through Brading to the Culver Cliffs, which are four hundred feet in perpendicular height above the sea. After seeing these, we proceeded on our ponies to Shanklin, where we put up for the night, and the next day continued our journey through Bonchurch and Ventnor, admiring the beautiful cottages at these places, which were otherwise rendered peculiarly interesting by the great numbers of invalids whom we saw reclining at the windows, on sofas or in armchairs. We went on along the coast road to Freshwater, where we halted for the night. All that part of the coast was bare and uninteresting.

On the 28th, we hired a boat, and rowed to "The Needles," having a look into the caves as we went along. The cliffs between Freshwater and the Needles are about six hundred feet high, and as perpendicular as a person can conceive; yet smuggling is carried on there on stormy nights, the men carrying casks of brandy or bales of tobacco up the almost inaccessible cliffs. The birds of different descriptions, such as the cormorant, razor-bill, and the puffin, which build in these rocks, are innumerable. After visiting the Needles, we returned to Freshwater, got on our ponies, and cantered off to Carisbrooke Castle, the place of imprisonment of Charles I. In this Castle is a remarkably deep well, which furnishes very excellent crystal water. Its depth is about two hundred and ten feet. The water is drawn by an immense wheel, worked by a donkey, which quietly walks into it as soon as required, and walks away inside till he sees the knot on the rope just above the bucket appear at the top of the well, when he immediately stops. One of these animals died a few years ago, having done this service during forty years.

Having baited our horses at Newport, we went on to West Cowes, where we staid for the night, and next day, after looking over Norris Castle and Osborne, we returned through Wootton to Ryde, and crossed over to Portsmouth, very well pleased with our trip.

Being here in July, I took the opportunity of attending the Goodwood Races. I had a capital hack which I bought out of the mail, and put in condition. This I rode (Daniell accompanying me) to Chichester, 'sixteen miles and back, in the afternoon: from thence we went in a coach to the course. We did the distance to Chichester in two hours, and the same back again, without my horse "turning a hair." This little mare, though not more than 14h. 2in., could carry me (thirteen stone six) over all the stiles round Portsmouth, and often I have "set" Lambert, when he has been riding a seventy guinea horse, having decoyed him into some narrow lane, ending in a stile.

There was a curious fellow in the 34th, then quartered at Gosport, named Duff, (a brother of the celebrated Duff: celebrated for being concerned in rows in London, and every other place he went into.) He would dress himself up as different characters, and walk about the streets. Sometimes he would put on a black wig, which he would occasionally change for a red one, a white neckcloth, and a suit of black: then he was the parson. At other times, he has dressed in women's clothes, and at a fancy ball he went as a convict, having obtained the dress and ring for the leg from the convicts' stores. He always carried his coffin about with him, and had it kept under his bed. On the march he used it as a packing case. He was a most singular fellow. One night he had some friends dining at mess with him, one of whom was staying with him. This one he pitched upon as a victim, and before he left the table, Mr. Duff had picked his pockets of everything, and robbed him even of his breast-pin, which Duff wore the next day in his own scarf, much to the astonishment of its rightful owner. Of course the thing was only a joke, and the articles were returned in due course of time. He was a great favourite with the lower orders, from his being always up to some fun or other. One night he took a suit of his own clothes, stuffed them well, put boots into the legs of the trousers, and a smoking-cap on the top of the pillow which served for the body. He then put a rope round its neck, and hung it out of his window, which faced the road. The following morning he and everyone else were awoke by loud cries and lamentations from a large crowd that had collected outside his house, and who were deploring poor Duff's fate. "Ah! poor Duff! poor Duff!! well he was a good gentleman; and who'd a thought it would have come to this! Poor fellow!" and so on; when up jumped the living man, and hauled his effigy hand over hand into his room, much to the surprise of the assembled multitude, who had been so well taken in, but who gave him a cheer and a hearty laugh.

WINCHESTER

IN September, our old friends, the 32nd Regiment, arrived from Canada, and were quartered in Portsmouth; but we were not long with them, for our regiment was ordered to Winchester. The Head Quarters to which I belonged marched on the 22nd of September. The barracks at Winchester are splendid, having been originally built for a palace. The town is very agreeable, and well situated, with a number of nice people in the neighbourhood. There are beautiful rides about the country, and a gallop on the Downs which surround Winchester is quite delightful. There is a beautiful trout stream here, preserved from time immemorial by a club; but I have no doubt any gentleman could get a few days' leave to fish in it in the season.

On the 1st of October, I got a fortnight's leave, and went home to Davenport, where I had some capital shooting. My father made me a present of a fine bay colt by Emancipation, five years old, which I took down to Winchester, and amused myself by breaking. My Portsmouth hack I sold, as I did not want two.

A man with horses might have had very good hunting from here, as there were several packs of hounds within reach; Mr. John Long's, the Hambledon and Ashton Smith's, not a great way off; but we were not contented with this, so got up a subscription, and purchased six couple of harriers, with which we never had any sport.

The North Hampshire Yeomanry Cavalry were called out for a fortnight's drill: Mr. Lefevre, the Speaker of the House of Commons, was their Colonel. Their Head Quarters were in Winchester, and we found them a very nice gentlemanly set of men. They were a great loss when they were dismissed.

During our stay at Winchester, there were several public balls at the hotel, which we enjoyed much, though they certainly were rather mixed, the "belle of the ball," on one occasion, being the butcher's daughter.

Although we had left Portsmouth, the good people of Southampton had not forgotten us, for they never had a ball at the Assembly Rooms without sending us *free* tickets.

ROUTE TO MANCHESTER

On the 17th November, 1841, we left Winchester by railroad for Manchester; arrived in London at Vauxhall, and marched through the Park to Paddington.

Head Quarters were fixed for the night at the "King and Queen". My Company was billeted from thence all the way to Kensall Green, about three miles, and we were ordered to go round each billet to see that the men had their dinners! It was dark before I had got half my men into their billets, and when I had done so, I returned to the "King and Queen," got leave, and dined with my bonnie sister Lizzie.

On the 18th, we were to be at the Euston Station at seven o'clock; but not being able to collect the men, it was nine o'clock before we got into the train. It cost me 3s. 6d. in cab-hire to get round my billet that morning, but I might have saved myself the trouble, for none of the men remained in the houses that I had placed them in the previous night, having been "paid out," (i.e., had money given to them to find other lodgings,) which is allowed, but ought not to be sanctioned by Government, as it entails an immensity of trouble on the Officers, and puts their men quite beyond their control, as they can never find out where the men have gone to after being "paid out."

We arrived at Birmingham that afternoon, and marched up to Dee's Royal Hotel, in the Old Church Yard. This was the Head Quarters and billet for the officers. By the time we had reached this place, it was perfectly dark, snowing and sleeting fast.

The whole of the billet tickets were jumbled up together in a confused heap, nevertheless our chief ordered us to keep our Companies separate in the different parts of the town, and to go round the billets and see the men's dinners! I asked for seventy-nine tickets, and went off with my men to the first tavern I came to, which was the "Black Boy;" here I gave each man his ticket for a billet, and his shilling, telling him to find out where the ticket directed him, and ordering him to parade there the next morning at seven o'clock. I then returned to the Royal Hotel, changed my wet clothes, and sat down to dinner at nine o'clock, but some of the officers did not come in until long after that. Instead of parading at eight o'clock at the station on the 19th, we did not get down there till near nine o'clock, as the men could not be got together in consequence of the way in which they were dispersed in their billets. I had ten men absent of the Grenadiers, who came in about eight o'clock. These men had been lodged three miles away from the Head Quarters. We arrived at Manchester on the 19th November, relieving the 78th Highlanders in Salford Barracks, two Companies being sent to Tibb Street, which is a desperate low and beastly part of Manchester.

Manchester I considered a very bad quarter. I *never* saw a *gentleman* in the streets. Luckily I was only there for three weeks; but during that time we had scarcely a fine day. I recollect a fog that came on about three o'clock one afternoon, and was so dense that you could not see the people in the street until you nearly ran against them.

We had the *remains* of our scratch pack of harriers, some of them having been stolen on our march through London. We used to go out and draw the country (including gentlemen's coverts) without leave or licence, but of the many days the "pack" were out, they only found one hare, which they lost in three fields. This splendid kennel was eventually sold to some man in Lancashire, who never paid for them.

The roads about Manchester were anything but pleasant to ride on, being paved for some six or seven miles out of the town; nor was the country at all interesting: nothing but manufactories, tall chimneys, smoke, and clay! Society, we had none.

DAVENPORT

On the 8th December, I got leave to go into Shropshire till the 14th. With joy I left Manchester, and arrived at Davenport, where I found that my father had been keeping all the best shooting for me, and had bought a weight-carrying mare for me to hunt. Here I enjoyed myself considerably, going out shooting with my brothers, and also hunting with them. Many were the happy evenings we passed, relating to my father the events of the day. On looking at my game-list, I find, that the game that fell to my own was as follows, during the months of December, 1841, and January, 1842 –

26 brace of pheasants
33½ brace partridges
8 brace hares
12½ couple rabbits, etc.
Total – 184 head.

On the 28th December, I went coursing with my brothers and Johnson. We made it a fine of a shilling for any one that rode through a gateway to shirk a fence, except when the dogs were in a course. We at last came to a "*whopper*," which was a ditch, a hedge about four to five feet high on a bank, with a regular "Yawner" on the other side. William and I both went at it, and cleared it well into the turnips in the brick-kiln field at Catstree. He, on the roan mare, cleared twenty-one feet; I, on the Stableford mare, eighteen feet, which was not bad for a young'un, with fourteen stone on her back. On the 17th February, I was riding the same mare with Jasper's harriers, and in a run near Chesterton, I *set* the field twice. She cleared double post and rails with quick hedge between, and covered nineteen and a half feet (measured.)

December 16th, 1841. The Albrighton hounds met at Coton, where we found three foxes, and ran one to Dudmaston, where we rattled him about for some time in the woods, till he took to the house, finding the hall door open, and was bagged in one of the bedrooms. He was turned out about half an hour afterwards, and had three fields law, but being stiff, could not go, and was run into in about six fields. I must record the following good day with the Albrighton hounds.

January 1st, 1842- Met at the "Hem," found a brace of foxes in Hem Coppice, ran round by Sturchley and back to Hem Coppice in thirty-five minutes; country tremendously deep. Drew Hatton Gorse, found, and ran by the "Manor House," through the Hem country by Wyke, etc., to the Lizard, where we lost him in a turnip-field, after one hour and twenty-five minutes good going through a country uncommonly heavy. My mare carried me right well, and was all right on arriving at her own stable; but many horses in the field were dead beaten, F—, —Lancers, amongst the number. I passed him under a hedge, quite done, leaving him my brandy-flask to administer to his horse. He "too larky was by half," for all the morning he had been bragging how he would show the field the tail of his horse if we got a run. We afterwards heard that our fox had been caught by some colliers, and carried off, being dead beaten. I got an awful roll.

"Cigars are thrown down in a hurry,
And bridle-reins gathered up tight;
See, each is prepared for a scurry,
And all are resolved to be right.

"Tally ho! cries a clod from a tree,
Now I'll give you all leave to come on;
And a terrible burst it will be,
For right o'er a fine country he's gone.

"Now, the fences made skirters look blue,
There was no time to crane or to creep;
O'er the pastures like pigeons they flew,
And the ground rode infernally deep.

"Oh, my eyes! what a fall.[7] Are you hurt

---

[7] E.M.D.

No, no, sir, I thank you; are you?
But who, to enjoy such a spirit,
Would be grudging an odd rib or two!

"Now the stragglers come in one by one:
Holloa! where, my dear fellow; [8] were you?
Bad luck! in the midst of the run,
My poor little mare lost her shoe.

"But where was that Gemman[9] in pink,
Who swore at his tail we should look;
Not in the next parish, I think,
For he never got over the brook."

On the 4th of February, the Albrighton drew Barton gorse, which contains only two acres, found and rattled him about up and down the cover for *two hours and ten minutes*, when he at last broke over two fields to another acre of gorse, where, after another half-hour's rattling, he was killed. Never was such a determined dunghill fox before known. However, we had a burst of thirty-five minutes hard going afterwards from Walton Wood. My mare went beautifully, and fenced magnificently.

On 21st February, I rode with a patent saddle-cloth, which during the run shifted forward on to the mare's withers, and pinched her so much, that she was afraid to rise at her fences. She went clean through one or two, giving both herself and me tremendous rolls, and came home that night quite crippled, not being able to walk down-hill without great pain, which I thought at the time was in her feet, but the next morning, the sore showed itself. This caused fistula in the withers, and I never rode her again, but sold her for £13. If it had not been for that, and my hurry to get rid of her, she ought to have sold for £70 or £80.

---

[8] E.S.D.

[9] F —, Lancers

ON the 27th of February, (Sunday,) my poor father died very suddenly in his bed, from a spasm of the heart, at about three o'clock p.m., which caused a great change in all our minds from the happiness we had been experiencing. On that day, and the two days previous, he had been much better than usual, and was just going to get up. He was reading the newspaper when the spasm struck him; the paper fell from his hands when asleep, and he was gone without a struggle: Dr. Thursfield said, without pain. Oh! what a loss was there! What a blank that cannot, and never will be filled up! Never was there a more kind and indulgent parent. He always anticipated the wishes and pleasures of us all, and seemed only to live to gratify them.

On the 8th of March, the funeral took place, and my poor father was buried in the Family Vault, under the altar at Worfield. Mr. Bates, of Willy, read the service, but had great difficulty in doing so, from the effects of the loss of one of his last and oldest friends.

* * * * * * * * *

On the 9th of March, an express arrived from India with the intelligence of the destruction of Caubool, five thousand troops killed, and sixteen ladies taken prisoners by the Affghans. This was afterwards confirmed on the 6th April by further accounts of between five and six thousand troops being cut to pieces near Caubool, and only one European and three Sepoys having escaped.

March 14th, Colonel Goldie, Captains Michel, Turner, and Lambert left Manchester with two Companies, to be quartered at Carlisle.

During the month of March, I had some very good trout and grayling fishing, commencing on the 17th, at Worfield, killing sixty-eight trout and grayling in seven mornings.

GLASGOW

My leave of absence, which had been extended to the 15th April, coming to a close, I left Davenport to go to Bolton, to inquire about some property which had been left me by my father. After leaving directions with my tenant as to the rent, I proceeded by rail to Lancaster, which I found a very nice clean-looking town, the houses being built of white stone; very different from Bolton, where there were no lights in the streets at night, except what may escape through the chinks of some shop-window shutter. I went into the Market Place at about eight o'clock in the evening, when I found the Boltonians selling their crockery-ware, etc., by the light of torches and coal fires, which appeared to me what I might have expected some hundred years previous. 13th of April, I left Lancaster, arrived at Carlisle, and went up to the barracks, where I found Colonel Goldie and the Detachment, with whom I dined at their mess. On the following day, I got on the Rapid (the best two-horse coach I ever saw) at half-past three p.m., passed through Gretna, and a beautiful country, arriving in Glasgow at twelve o'clock.

The inn at Crawford is one of the places where the Rapid changed horses, and during the time they were doing so, I went in and had supper, which consisted of a large plate of cold beef and bread, and a glass of whiskey, for which "entertainment" the landlady demanded *sixpence.*

Glasgow is a very fine large town, with about 300,000 inhabitants. Argyll Street is magnificent, when properly seen. The time to see it is, when it is empty at about day-dawn, for it is so crowded all day, but particularly about four o'clock, that it is difficult to get along it on foot. On Saturdays, the crush is awful; any stranger would fancy that the whole population had moved into that one street. We gave a detachment under Daniell to Dumbarton Castle, from the top of which is a most splendid view of Ben Lomond and up and down the Clyde. This we found a lounge, as it was a nice trip by the steamer and back.

We had but little amusement at Glasgow. We played quoits a good deal in the mornings. The band used to play at Woodside Crescent every Thursday, which was a lounge. The fishing about Glasgow was bad. I had permission to fish at Mr. Mc Call's, at Daldowie, on the Clyde, but I never succeeded in catching anything worth having. The "otter," with some dozen flies, is used so very much about Glasgow, that a fisherman with his three flies has not a chance.

The barrack-master used to fish a good deal with the minnow on Loch Lomond, and, according to his own account, used to catch an immense quantity of fish. His tackle, certainly, was very good. I have adopted myself, and find that if a trout runs at all at the minnow, it is certain of being hooked either inside or out. It is made thus-

Mr. G told me that he had been fishing in Loch Lomond one day with his son: that they had put up their fishing tackle, and gone to the shore, and were watching a cow that was up to her belly in the water, swishing the flies about with her tail. He saw a pike, about ten pounds weight, snatch at the end of her tail, as it touched the water, and the next swish she gave, she threw the fish right on the land

On the 4th of July I got my orders to hold myself in readiness to proceed on detachment to Fort William, in the Highlands. Wishing to see Edinburgh whilst in the neighbourhood, I went there by rail with Taylor. We went all over the Castle, down the Canongate, and were shewn over Holyrood House, where is a gallery covered with the portraits of the old kings. It struck me that there was a great family likeness in them all, and that, if possible, they had been *daubed* (I cannot call it *painted*) by the same man at the same time. After seeing all the curiosities of the Palace, we ascended Calton Hill, where we had a magnificent view of the city and the surrounding country.

July 9th we embarked on board a steamer at Gran-ton Pier for Stirling, stopping to land passengers at Queen's Ferry, Kincardine, Alloa, and Cambuskeneth Abbey; at the latter place we landed also, walked up to Stirling, and visited the Castle, from whence we had a most splendid view, which included Ben Lomond, Ben Ledi, and Ben More in the distance; the Grampian Hills, Abbey Craig, St. Ninian's, Bannockburn, and Achill hills, all rendered so interesting by Walter Scott. After gloating over this scenery, we drove to Castlecary, where we met the five o'clock train, which took us back to horrid Glasgow at seven, p.m.

July 12th, I embarked in the steamer at Glasgow at half-past three o'clock, a.m., for Fort William. We had a beautiful passage, and saw the Hills on the Clyde to great advantage. The scenery as we passed Donoon and Rothsay was very splendid, and all the way from thence, through the Kyles of Bute to Fort William, was magnificent, particularly about Corran Ferry, between Loch Linnhe and Loch Leven, where the view up Loch Leven and the entrance to Glencoe opens itself. We landed at Fort William at a quarter to eight, p.m.

FORT WILLIAM

I made acquaintance with a fellow-passenger, who turned out to be a most excellent friend to me, Mr. Platt, of Denny Park, near Horsham, Sussex, and who was then going to Fort William on a fishing and shooting excursion. He was one of Mr. Scarlett's (now Lord Abinger's) party, and had preceded his friends by a month. As we were going to the same unknown place, we agreed to dine together at the hotel. This dinner made us more acquainted, and the end of it was, that we lived there together for a fortnight, at the expiration of which time I moved into my rooms in the dilapidated old Fort.

On calling for my bill at the hotel, I was told Mr. Platt had got it, so I requested to know the amount of my share, when he replied, "This is my bill, you have nothing to do with it, it is all paid and settled but I insisted upon having my share, and he insisted as positively that I should not, saying, I had sent wine to the table which was quite equivalent to anything that might be charged against me, and so it ended. I believe the bill was about £14 or £15.

About a week after our arrival at Fort William, Mr. Platt asked me to take a ride with him, as he was going to call on Mrs. McDonald, of Killichonate, a tenant of Mr. Scarlett's, where he would introduce me. I went accordingly, and met some other ladies. Mrs. McDonald said they were getting up a picnic for the following Friday, to go to the top of Ben Nevis, and asked me to join the party, which I said I would, with great pleasure. The party met at John McDonald's, of Milburn, at the foot of Ben Nevis. We left the house at half-past nine, to ascend the hill, and arrived at the top at three o'clock, p.m., having lunched and dined on our way up at different springs. There was still a great quantity of snow on the top, so we "set to" at a snowballing match. The view from the summit is beyond description; you can see such an immense distance. It can only be comprehended by being seen. The stillness and grandeur are almost awful. Here you overtop the whole of the surrounding hills, which look like a rough sea that had suddenly been turned into grey rocks; then between the near ones you see the green valleys, with the rivers and streams running through them: the little specks of houses, and, with a telescope, may be seen the sheep browsing hundreds of feet below you. The height of Ben Nevis is 4750 feet.

After remaining on the top for about an hour, we left to descend, and got back at seven o'clock to Mil burn, where there were refreshments provided, but where little was eaten, though a great deal was drunk.

Mrs. Batten was an elderly lady, was the mother of twelve, and grandmother of thirteen children. She rode, as also her daughter and the other ladies, nearly half way up, and walked, assisted by the gentlemen, the remaining part. This party gave me introductions to an immense circle of people, who, in the kindest possible way, gave me invitations to visit them at their places. They were not the unmeaning invitations which are commonly given, but real warmhearted, good-natured ones, sincerely meant, and this was afterwards proved by the unparalleled hospitality and kindness I received from all, during my stay of more than twelve months in the Highlands, when I formed friendships which will never be forgotten.

The commencement of the shooting season now being near, I wrote to Donald Cameron, (the Chief of the Clan Cameron,) to allow me to shoot over his unlet grounds, or any part he might think proper to point out, as I was likely to be quartered at Fort William for the next twelve months, to which I received a reply that I might shoot over his estate from Fort William to Ballachulish. I also wrote to Sir Duncan Cameron, of Callart, to the same effect, and from him also I got a courteous answer, that I might shoot over his grounds near Fort William, and upon his farm of Blarmachfulach; so that I now had moors extending seven miles in length, by from three to

111

five in width, and although it was much poached, I expected to find amusement on it. Having obtained leave to fish in the rivers Lochy and Spean, I amused myself most of the summer in that sport, and although I did not catch many salmon, I occasionally had some capital trout fishing in the Lochy, near the Ferry at Milburn. I have there caught "finnock," a kind of sea trout, weighing about half to three-quarters of a pound each, very fast indeed, and soon filled my basket. A large black fly, with a little silver tinsel at the tail, was the most killing of all. I have also caught salmon in the Nevis when there has been a "fresh" in the river, but the Spean was the best river for salmon, *out-and-out*.

On the 3rd of August I went on board the Rob Roy steamer, at Bannavie, at half-past five, a.m., and proceeded to Inverness.. Here I was met by Rainsford, who drove me to Fort George, where he was quartered with Caulfield. The scenery up Loch Lochy, Loch Oich, to Fort Augustus, also on the lower part of Loch Ness, is very fine and bold, but after we passed Medfourvoine Mountain, it gradually became tamer, and beyond Inverness, all the way to Fort George, it is actually flat. I remained at Fort George, which looked like a deserted town, (the barracks being built in streets, and capable of holding two Regiments, but now only occupied by *part* of one Company,) till the 7th, when I went in to Inverness, and the next day returned to Fort William by the Caledonian Canal, right glad to be amongst the hills again.

August 12th. First day of grousing. I was up at five, and off by six o'clock, seven miles to Lundirra, where I commenced shooting, having John Cameron, an old poacher, with me, to guide me as to the whereabouts of the game. We went over the hills to the top of Ouich. I found three or four covies of grouse, and killed nine grouse, two blackcock by mistake in the dense fog, three snipe, and one hare. I began to shoot at nine o'clock, but had to leave off at half-past twelve, on account of the mist, which came on so thick, that we could not see more than thirty yards. My two dogs being very fat, knocked up in about two hours, and I, having a flask of port wine in my pocket, gave each of them a glass, which completely revived them in a quarter of an hour, and I believe they would have worked on for two, or even three hours, if I had required them. John Cameron knew every inch of the ground, and when the mist came on, we agreed to meet the steamer at Corran Ferry to return to Fort William, but the mist puzzled my guide, and we descended at Ouich, four miles from the place we intended. However, we were in time to catch the steamer. On board I found my old dog "King," a Russian setter, which I shot over all the time I was in Canada, and a famous dog, and cunning was he. He had been sent up to me from Shropshire, where I had left him. Also on board I met a lot of Liverpool sportsmen on their way to their moors. Some of them were wise (?) enough to enquire if the heather was yet in blossom.

Having obtained leave to shoot over a large extent of hill and dale, I was anxious to explore the ground, therefore, on the 15th of August, I started from Fort William at about nine o'clock, beat the hill side down to Corran, from thence turning on the left, to Lundirra and Blarmafulach, where I left off, having beaten an extent of moor of 21 miles as the crow flies. I got back well beaten myself at six o'clock, being soaked with rain and mist the whole day, and having only bagged one grouse and a couple of snipe. I saw a lot of grouse and black game, but in consequence of the rain, I could not get within a mile of them.

Mr. Scarlett (now Lord Abinger) having arrived in the country, gave me leave to shoot on Ben Nevis, and in the Corrie.

August 27th. Scarlett's keeper came by appointment to show me the ground at nine o'clock. I had not been in bed above three hours, having been dancing all night at Inch. I awoke with a tremendous headache, and could scarcely see; however, I was not long in getting ready, and we ascended to the Corrie. My dogs Ben and King worked well, but I had such a headache that I could not see them, and whenever they pointed, the keeper called my attention to the fact. Strange to say, I killed my birds right and left, and once front and rear, without missing a shot, until the sixteenth. The total of my bag was eight brace of grouse and one snipe, and this on nearly the same ground that Sheriff Fraser had bagged twenty brace the day previous.

October 3rd. I had a day's shooting on the Marquis of Douro's hills at the back of the Corpach.

The grouse were all in large packs of from fifty to one and one hundred and fifty. However, wild as they were, I picked up a few stragglers. My bag at the end of the day turned out six and a half brace of grouse, four and a half brace of ptarmigan, one snipe, one brace of hares and one plover, total, twenty-six head; which was not so bad for the 3rd of October.

My total head for the season was two hundred and sixty-one. Number of days out, forty-two.

September 9th. I took a trip with Doctor Crichton to Inverary. Having sent his horse on the night previous to Ballachulish, we drove my pony down there, and then changed at half-past eight, a.m. We then drove through the most splendid scenery up Loch Leven, and entered that magnificent gloomy pass of Glencoe, which looked even more imposing from the clouds of mist which rolled in heavy masses along the high, rugged tops of the hills on each side of the glen. For six or seven miles we ascended through this mighty and. awfully grand pass, till we found the level of the Black Mount, Lord Breadalbane's deer forest, and then we proceeded to King's House Inn, where we got eggs and oat-cake for breakfast, and fed the horse, after which we pushed on to Inverouran for the next stage, expecting to see Prince Albert's deer-hunt, as he was then with the Marquis of Breadalbane, but in this we were disappointed.

Inverouran is the shooting box of the Marquis on Black Mount. We then went on, leaving the dreary mountain, over the Bridge of Urchy, and down Glenurchy to Dalmally, where we dined; then leaving this place early, we went on our journey by Cladich, and arrived at Inverary at nine o'clock, having had a splendid view of Loch Awe and Ben Cruachan, (on leaving Dalmally,) and passing through some fine wooded scenery of the Duke of Argyle's into the town. Inverary is a neat little town on Loch Fine, which is so celebrated for its herrings. It was a curious sight to witness the fishermen hauling in their nets at night, the thousands of herrings which they caught, looking like so many bits of glittering silver in the nets. The country and scenery around there is very beautiful. Inverary Castle is a fine building, and has an imposing appearance, with the Hill of Dunquoich at its back, rising seven hundred feet in nearly perpendicular height. The fir-trees here, particularly the silver firs, are said to be the largest in Great Britain. On the following day we left Inverary at half-past four, p.m., passed Cladich to Port Sonachan, where we crossed Loch Awe, having a magnificent view of the lake, Ben Cruachan, and the island with the old Abbey of Kilchrenan. We then proceeded through a wooded glen to Bernau and Taynuilt, where we put up for the night. The next day we rose with the lark, and journeyed on down the left side of Loch Etive to Connel Ferry, which we crossed, having a fine sight of Dunstaffnage Castle, one of the oldest edifices in the Highlands. It is a Royal Castle still, the Duke of Argyle its keeper. Next we crossed Loch Creran at Skian Ferry, where we made out a sort of breakfast, and arrived along the beautiful shore of Loch Linnhe at Ballachulish. Here we crossed Loch Leven, and returned to Fort William at five o'clock, having travelled over most part of Argyleshire in three days, and with one good old horse.

On the 16th of September, Daniell, my old friend, came to spend a fortnight with me, and have some shooting. I shall not forget his astonishment one morning when I put him at the "Cow Hill" after breakfast to begin his day's work with, (the Cow Hill close to the Fort is nearly perpendicular, and about five or six hundred feet high,) nor was his surprise lessened, when I informed him that that hill was *nothing*, that after getting to the top, and beating it, we must descend to the level of the sea, again to ascend Auchintour, which I pointed out to him in the distance.

On the 24th of September, I drove Daniell, in a borrowed cart and harness with my mare, to Corran, to shoot on the Ballachulish Hills. I remarked on going to the ground, that I never saw the mare go so freely and well. After shooting there, Daniell put the mare in harness, and told me something was the matter, as she reared up on coming out of the stable. However, we put her into the cart, and away she went, very freely. The mare wanted to gallop, but I thought that not prudent, so she stepped out in style at the trot for about a mile, when, on going down a hill, she let fly her heels, the belly-band broke, the shafts went in the air, the swing-seat upset backwards. Daniell was pitched out at the back, with both guns in his hands. I was dragged ten or fifteen yards on my head, before I could disengage my legs from the cart, still holding on by the reins till they broke, trying to guide the mare, when she kicked away, and jumped off the road over the ditch into a bog, having divested herself of all the harness excepting the collar! I went and picked up Daniell, who was almost stunned, and then we looked to the wreck. The mare was standing on three legs, not being able to put the other to the ground; however; we got her back to the road, when we found she could walk pretty well, and not very lame, so having tied up and put the rotten harness on again, we put her in the shafts, and made her draw the cart with the dogs up to Fort William, which she did with ease, and apparently without being in pain. That night, I had a doctor to examine the fetlock, which he said was sprained, so I had it fomented for a couple of hours, and afterwards a bran poultice put on it for the night. The following morning, my groom came to inform me that the mare's leg was broken. As he was a great fool, I told him it was impossible, and to put another poultice on. He went away, and did so; but as I was going to church, I looked into the stable, and found the fetlock joint was out, (the off hind fetlock.) I called in Dr. Kennedy, who said it was impossible to set the joint; therefore, I instantly went for my gun, shot her to put her out of pain, and had her buried immediately, giving a boy a shilling to dig her grave. This turned out a grave offence to the Presbyterians, for the elders and clergy made a great fuss about my "breaking the Sabbath." They sent for the policeman to go and arrest *"the Officer,"* as he had broken the Sabbath by shooting a horse on a Sunday. The policeman told them he would do no such thing, unless they gave him a written order; but this thin,, they declined. They then sent to the Procurator Fiscal, and ordered him to have me arrested, but he laughed at them; when they ordered him to go to the Sheriff to get an order to have me taken up, but he also laughed at them. One of the fools declared he would write to the Queen to report me, and, as he said, to have me dismissed the Service. One of the others was for arresting me himself, upon hearing which, I sent him an invitation, promising to show him a shorter way out of the house than down the stairs; but he did not come. They had meetings in their church twice a week, to talk over this awful crime, and preached sermons on the subject for a month. As for the poor unfortunate fellow who dug du the hole to put the mare in, he was excommunicated at once. They persecuted the Fiscal so much about arresting me that he wrote to the Queen's Counsel in Edinburgh, to know what he was to do, when he got an answer to mind his own business, and let the clergy do likewise. After this had been going on for a month, the clergyman of Kilmanaveg, who had attended all these meetings, wrote to Sheriff Fraser, stating that it had *"just* come to his knowledge that a breach of the Sabbath had been committed by *"the officer"* in Fort William, and begged to point out several Acts of Parliament for the punishment of such offenders," requesting him to take notice of the offence. He referred to an act of Queen Anne, which stated that any person breaking the Sabbath shall be fined one pound *scot*, (i.e., one shilling,) and in default of payment, he shall be tied to the tail of a cart, drawn through the town, and publicly flogged, and that in the event of the Sheriff not seeing this punishment carried out, he is liable to the same punishment himself. The Sheriff wrote him a *"stinger"* in reply, and the thing dropped.

On the 30th September, I went with "Long John McDonald and Sheriff Fraser to join in a deer-hunt in Glen Lye, near Achnacarry, the Marquis of Douro's shooting box, on Loch Loehy. About nine of us were armed with rifles, and posted by the forester under the direction of Captain Corkran, in the most likely spots for a deer to run out of the wood. All being settled, the beaters were put in with a lot of cur dogs, and soon disturbed a stag; but he could not be induced to break, so he was given up. Captain Corkran was just lamenting that we were all deprived of the expected sport, when one of the foresters discovered a stag and five hinds near the top of the opposite hill. The question then arose who should stalk them. I was asked to go, but saw so little prospect of getting near them in such an open place, that I declined, and preferred awaiting the result of Sheriff Fraser and Donald McDonald's stalking skill. The deer were so high up, that they could not be distinguished by the naked eye from where we stood at the bottom of the glen.

Fraser and D. McDonald started with the two foresters, one of whom led two magnificent Scotch greyhounds (belonging to Colonel Ross, of Tindrish,) up a burn to leeward of the deer, and after about forty minutes' climbing, they got nearly to the level of the game. (The scene was most exciting, and can only be known by experiencing it.) However, now the wind began to veer, and several times had they to stop to consult how to get round the deer without being scented by them. During one of these halts, one of the foresters lighted his pipe, (a most unheard of and outrageous proceeding,) and on being remonstrated with by Sheriff Fraser, said there would be no harm in it, as the wind was in their favour. They were now getting near the game, and were within eighty yards of them, when Fraser took an aim, but the forester arrested his arm, and prevented him from firing, thinking to get nearer by going down a little burn. Just then the wind changed, and carried the scent of the tobacco (which stuck to their clothes) down to the deer. Up jumped the stag and five hinds, and away they came down the hill at an awful pace, the hinds leading, and the stag coming up in their track. In an instant they were out of sight of the stalkers, and seemed to be coming straight for where we were standing. We gave the foresters signs of the direction they had taken, and the two dogs were let loose. The oldest of the two singled out the stag, and coursed him *through* the herd of hinds, taking no notice of *them*. The other dog, a young one, took two hinds over the hill, and we saw no more of him or them; but not so with "Oscar:" he took his game along the side of the hill, and kept rather above it to prevent its turning upwards, and such a splendid course never was witnessed. It lasted half an hour in full view of us all. Oscar succeeded in getting the stag to the low ground, and drove him so hard that he jumped into a high sheep-fank[10] and out again, when the poor dog was beaten, but the stag was then chased by collie dogs into Poltheron Wood, (the one we had beaten,) and hunted up and down, round and round for half an hour, when he broke cover, and made for the hill we had first discovered him on. In doing so, he had to cross our party, and run the gauntlet of many rifles, one of which (the forester's) took effect in the hock, which it

---

[10] Sheep-yard.

broke, and the noble stag, which weighed twenty-one stone, was pulled down by the greyhounds.

On the 15th of October, I went, by invitation, with Fraser to meet Colonel Maclean of Ardgour, and Lord Dalhousie at Stronreatghan, to drive the glen for a stag. After getting our orders that we were to shoot anything we could, *except a hind with a calf at her side*, we started to our several positions. Colonel Maclean remained at the bottom of the glen. Fraser was posted on one of the lower passes, Lord Dalhousie on the centre and best. I went up to the top of the glen, and secreted myself in what I considered a good spot. After we had time to get settled, the beaters were heard at the bottom of the glen; gradually ascending, at last there was a shout, "Look out," and smack, smack went two rifle barrels; then the shouts were redoubled and came nearer. I waited to hear Lord Dalhousie fire (as I knew the shots I had heard were Sheriff Eraser's;) but no rifle did he fire. In about a minute, a fine hind with a calf at her side cantered up to within thirty yards of me, and stopped. I took a deliberate aim, and then lowered my rifle again, remembering the orders. Fearing that should again stag (which I supposed had been fired at) come up, and see the hind standing aghast at me, he would turn off, I waved my arm at her, and she trotted quietly round one, describing a half-circle to get on to the track she wanted.

Presently up came Lord Dalhousie, the Sheriff, and the keeper—the two last in a dreadful state at my not firing at the deer. I merely said it was against the orders I got to do so. Lord Dalhousie made the same excuse. Upon inquiring what Fraser shot at, he could scarcely tell at the time he fired, but thought it was a stag. However, there was no stag in the glen. We then tried the wood on Loch Eil side, where there were no red deer, but two or three does, at which no one could get a shot. We then got into Colonel Maclean's carriage, and drove to Ardgour, where I remained for a few days shooting and fishing.

On the 12th of December, Mr. McGregor, of the Bank, drove me to Stroutean, a neat village at the head of Lock Sunart, in Ardnamurchan, the property of Sir James Riddell. This place is noted for its lead-mines, one of which I entered with an old miner, who conducted me through a horizontal shaft or "level," and we went to the end of it, about three hundred fathoms. I was much gratified by what I saw, and returned with a good specimen of the ore, which some friend afterwards relieved me of.

The drive from Fort William down to Corran Ferry, and from thence through Glen Tarbert is very beautiful.

On the 17th of December, we experienced some very heavy thunder and lightning, more vivid than I ever saw it anywhere before. One flash was so bright and vivid that I was blinded for several seconds afterwards.

Having received an invitation to spend the Christmas in Badenoch, I left Fort William on my horse Emancipation, and arrived at the house of my host, Mac Nabs, of Dalwhilly. Here we met the Christmas party, Mac Nabs, of Sherabeg, Mr. and Mrs. McPherson, of Chapel Park, and a lot of others. After dinner, we set to, to dance, and kept it up till five in the morning. The following day, the whole country (gentlemen) assembled to play shinty, alias hockey, for our special amusement. On the 28th, we amused the ladies, and took some walks with our guns, but had no sport. Dined at Mac Nab's, of Sherabeg, and danced reels to the music of a couple of Jew's harps, played by Ranald Mac Nab, a good part of the evening, which was concluded by romping and blind man's buff. On the 29th, we all made a start for McPherson's, of Chapel Park, about fifteen miles off, (calling on our way at Cluny McPherson's, a very nice and well-kept place.) Here we dined and danced all night, and got up late in the morning.

Chapel Park being fifty - three miles from Fort William, and I being obliged to muster my men there the following day, made up my mind to return as early as possible. However, I could not stir my friends before twelve o'clock, when we started, and, calling at Dalhwilly on my way, to take leave of the Mac Nabs and McDonalds, I proceeded on my journey alone.

Having remarked on going up the country, that if any rain fell, that part of the road which crossed a corner of Loch Laggan would be flooded, I pushed on as fast as I could, for a great quantity of snow had fallen and thawed during the last few days. I got down about twenty-four miles to Laggan Inn before dark, where I met a carter who told me the road was flooded, and that I could not cross, except by daylight. I got on my horse immediately, and rode down the eight miles to the Loch; but it was pitch dark before I arrived there, and I could not see the road. The rain, which had been coming down in torrents the whole day, increased, and a gale of wind was blowing and howling in my face. I saw a light just off the road in a shepherd's house at Moy, and called to the inmates, and asked for a guide, but none would venture out "sic a nicht." However, after a good deal of persuasion, I got one of the shepherds to say he would guide me through the water on condition I would pay him well. I told him I would give anything he demanded, as I was *obliged* to go on that night. We went down to the water that covered the road, when he said he would not attempt it for £5, but would take me over the mountain. Now, it was so dark, I could not see my guide or my own hand. I attempted to ride my horse; but on going off the road, he tumbled into the ditch. I then got off and led him, being led myself by the guide, he holding one end of my pocket-hankerchief and I the other. At first I tried to follow him by putting my white handkerchief on his back, but it so soon got the same colour, that it became invisible, when I took to the leading plan. The track he led me was only a footway over immense rocks and stones, and along the top of precipices. It was with much difficulty I climbed over some of these and got down again. How my horse managed it, I cannot say, but he came as quietly, nimbly, and gently as a dog would, after he was once frightened at the start, by getting his hind legs over a precipice, from which he recovered himself. After some time, we got to the top of the hill, and into a quantity of bog, which we crossed with the horse with much difficulty. Here I could track my guide well by the phosphoric matter which stuck to his feet as he proceeded. In order to get out of this bog, he went to his left out of the proper track, and kept telling me to keep *still more* to the left, but I found I was on hard rocks, and could see water immediately below my feet, which turned out to be "the Loch," some two or three hundred feet beneath! I therefore altered my course to the right, till we came to a mountain stream, which was foaming and rushing down with immense force, swollen by the deluge of rain. Now how to get the horse over this was the question. I knew that if I attempted to lead him, and he refused it, I should have the greatest difficulty in riding him over afterwards if it came to that. It was so dark that I could not see the ground we were standing on, or where we were likely to land on the opposite side. I instantly resolved, got on his back, and rode him at it. He took a tremendous leap and cleared it, nor did he stir a foot, after landing on the other side. I again dismounted, and was led by the shepherd about half-a-mile further, over rocks, and through some beech-wood, down the hill, until we gained the level of the lake, which we skirted for a while, till we came to a small island between us and the road. Here we scrambled through the water up to our middles, the horse plunging through it on to the road, where he arrived on his knees. Having thus gained the road again, I asked my guide what was his demand? He replied, "Oh Sir, a shilling will recompense me very well." I was quite surprised, thinking a guinea was the least he could expect, and it was only by great persuasion I got him to accept of five shillings.

Being now about twenty-six miles from Fort William, I determined upon stopping for the night at my friend Greig's of Tulloch, but was afraid of missing the turn off the road; however, my horse had been there before, and I trusted to him. I once *saw a light in the distance, and fancied that must be it; but on trying to turn my horse in that direction, he seemed unwilling, so I let him have his way, and he took me all right to Tulloch, where I got a hearty welcome and a change of clothes, a good dinner and a comfortable bed. The next morning, I examined my horse's knees, and found he had not even a scratch anywhere. It was given out the next day all over Badenoch, that I had been drowned in trying to cross Loch Laggan. I was afterwards told by a gentleman who has Moy Farm, and by other people who knew the ground, that I could not cross in the day-time with my horse the places I went over that night, and that it was only my not knowing my own danger that enabled me to do it. After breakfasting with Greig, I returned to Fort William, mustered my men, and then went with Mac Gregor to spend New Year's Day with the Stuarts of Ballachulish.

Having been out somewhere or other dining and dancing almost every night, it came into our heads that we might get up a Subscription Ball at Fort William to keep up the excitement. Duncan Cameron, Donald Mc Donald, and I, were nominated stewards to make the arrangements, which we accordingly did for the 15th of February; sent out invitations to all the gentry of the country; and got the music, which consisted of three violins and a violoncello, from Greenock. There were forty-eight gentlemen subscribers. The evening arrived, and so did the beauty and fashion of fifty miles around. The ball commenced at half-past eight o'clock, and was kept up till daylight, about half-past six the following morning. They danced in the Mason's Hall, the supper was laid out in the George Inn just opposite, and refreshments in the Master Mason's room next the Hall. Sixty-two ladies and gentlemen sat down to supper, after which the health of the stewards was drunk.

As I had received so much kindness and unparalleled

hospitality from all about Fort William, I wished to show that I appreciated their goodness towards me, therefore before the Subscription Ball took place, I made up my mind to give one myself to all my friends, both in Lochaber and Badenoch. I accordingly fixed the 17th of February, and issued sixty-five cards of invitation, (Mrs. Fraser, the Sheriff s wife, kindly undertaking to matronize the party for me,) but only forty-three were able to attend. The music was the same as that at the subscription ball, which I detained for the purpose. We danced in the large room at the George Hotel, refreshments were in the small room off it, and supper in the dining-room. The company began to assemble about nine o'clock, and to dance immediately. We kept it up till twelve o'clock when we went to supper, after which my health was proposed by Mr. McIntyre, of Blarour, in a long speech, praising me to the skies in every possible way, which was drunk with three times three and one cheer more with Highland honours. Commenced dancing again, and kept it up till about half-past five with a spirit I never saw before. I never saw people enjoy themselves so much as they did. At last my matron got so tired that she was obliged to leave, when all my friends took their departure, highly delighted with the party; all thanking me as we separated, and leaving me their good wishes and invitations to their respective homes.

March 3rd. I was staying with the MacDonells, at Inch, and being a beautiful day, it was settled that I should drive Mrs. MacD— and Mrs. F— in the dog cart up to Glen Roy, to see the "Parallel Roads." The road which winds up the glen on the verge of a deep ravine is extremely narrow, and with many very sharp turnings in it. On driving round one of these, the brute of a horse would not answer the rein, but pulled his head round and gave his body to the inside curve of the road, trying to *hug the turn*. The consequences were very near being fatal. I looked down at the wheel and saw it going right over the precipice; I flogged, and almost lifted the horse away from it with the whip. I felt no alarm myself, as I never do when in real danger, but I saw the soil and gravel of the road rolling down into the ravine, two hundred feet beneath, from under the wheel. It was only with the aid of the whip in making the horse *spring* that prevented us, cart and all, from going over into the chasm below. The danger being over, I turned to look how it had affected the ladies, and found they had both fainted!

These "Parallel Roads" of Glen Roy are about seventeen miles above Fort William. On the face of the hills on either side of the glen are three roads (or rather the appearance of them) rising one above the other at regular intervals as if by stages, and running in parallel lines for nine miles. They are said to be sixty feet broad and two hundred feet distant from each other. Some people imagine that they were formed by the ancient inhabitants to assist their kings and hunters in the chase, and this is the tradition respecting them. The hunters stationed themselves at particular places whilst the animals were driven towards them through the only outlets left. Other people imagine that this glen was once a lake, and that these ridges are the effects of the deposit of mud, etc., at successive heights. They are well worth examining.

April 7th. Angus McDonell drove me into Arisaig, to Borrodale, the residence of McDonald of Glenaladale. We stopped at Glenfinnan, at the head of Lochshiel, a lake of about twenty miles in length, which is only separated from Loch Eil by a few hundred yards of land.

Near the Inn at Glenfinnan, and at the head of Lochshiel, is an obelisk to commemorate the spot where Prince Charles Edward Stuart first unfurled his standard on the 19th of August, 1745.

The glen beyond the Inn is exceedingly wild, and the view from it, looking over Loch Ailt and the Atlantic, is very beautiful. After baiting our horse and ourselves we drove on, fifteen miles to Borrodale; remained there the night, and next morning drove through the village of Arisaig, and from thence to Morrar to pay a visit to Mrs.

McDonald and Eneas of that name. Here I was introduced to Miss McDonald, one of the most beautiful girls in Scotland. I fished in the Morrar river, caught a 9th salmon, and was pronounced to be the best "Sassenach fisherman" that ever came there by an old adept in the art.

This is a most wild and desolate part of Scotland, the house is situated on the sea-shore, without any protection from the weather; almost without a road up to it, and amongst the most bare and inhospitable rocks, opposite to Skye, Rum, and Eig; but the *inside* of the house had quite a different appearance, and hospitality there reigned to the highest degree.

On the Sunday, while my friends (who are all Roman Catholics) were in chapel, I walked about Lord Cranston's grounds, visited the burial place of the McDonalds, and saw an immense heap of skulls of departed McD—'s. It is a custom of the Clan always to throw out the old skulls, whenever the vault is opened and place them in a heap in a corner. The following day we returned to Borrodale, stayed the night, and found them all very nice people. Here I tasted whiskey and gin both forty years old. I returned to Fort William much pleased with my trip.

May 11th. I was staying at Inch, and after dinner we all went in a cart to a Highland wedding, by invitation from the bride and bridegroom. He was a shepherd and she a housemaid. On arriving at the cottage on the side of a hill near Tulloch, we were ushered into a small room where there was supper laid out (for the bride and the lairds who attended) in the shape of cold fowls, tea, (?) and whiskey. After going through the form of partaking of the repast, we adjourned to the dancing-room, which was a long, low, narrow, mud floored barn, and which being on the side of a hill, the ground not having been levelled to a nicety, was on a considerable slope. Down the centre were four boards placed to dance upon, and right merrily were they used in turn by the gathering, which numbered about one hundred and eighty people. The music was a fiddle in the room, and the pipes for a lot of dancers outside. We all retired for the night to Greig's of Tulloch, after dancing no end of reels with the shepherds' daughters. All my time for the last four or five months was spent in visiting from one house to another; the only difficulty was to get away from a house when once they got you under its roof. Every house was a home.

On the 20th of July I suddenly got the route for Edinburgh, on being relieved by the 24th Regiment. I had now only to make my calls and bid adieu to my friends; the kindest and most hospitable I ever met with, and it was with deep regret that I did so.

July 25th. I embarked on board the Rob Roy Steamer, at Fort William, with my Detachment at five o'clock, a.m., and proceeded on our voyage; all well till we got about three miles south of Eastdale, where we ran upon a sunken rock with immense force. However by shifting the cargo, (salmon,) rocking the vessel, reversing the paddles, and with the assistance of the rising title we got off without damage, and landed in Glasgow next day at ten o'clock, a.m. I left it again with my Detachment at one o'clock by train, arrived in Edinburgh at a quarter past three, p.m., and marched up to the Castle. This afternoon we received orders to hold ourselves in readiness for Ireland.

EDINBURGH

WHILST quartered in Edinburgh, which is a beautiful town and a capital quarter, I received a good deal of kindness from many friends whose acquaintance I had made in the Highlands, amongst whom were Sir David and Lady Wedderburn, of Rosebank, close to Roslyn Castle; also Lord Robertson and his family, at whose house I used to spend a great deal of my time, and join all their picnics and riding, parties almost every day. I got leave with Langton till the end of the month, and we started off on our way to Loch Lomond and Loch Katrine, by Glasgow and Dumbarton Castle and Rock are amongst the most prominent and interesting objects in the west of Scotland. The rock is five hundred and sixty feet high, the sides nearly perpendicular, and the base washed by the Clyde and Leven. The form of the rock is very picturesque, the view from the top very grand. To the north is seen the Vale of Leven, with the windings of the river like the twisting of a serpent, beyond which is Loch Lomond, with Ben Lomond rising from its margin in awful majesty, and surrounded by other hills of less magnitude. Looking up the Clyde the prospect is also beautiful.

From Dumbarton we went to Balloch, about four miles, where we went on board the steamer on Loch Lomond, and *I* enjoyed tile magnificent scenery beyond anything, but Langton put a cigar in his mouth, lay down on the baggage, and looked at nothing, his excuse being that he had been there before! On the right the immense Bell rises from the smooth surface of the lake to the height of three thousand two hundred and sixty two feet. The islands of the lake, of which there are more than thirty, give a pleasing variety to the immense sheet of water which is thirty miles in length and eight in width. We went to the head of the lake, then returned to Inversnaid, where we left the steamer and crossed the mountain paths, walking five miles to Loch Katrine. Here the passengers assembled in so large a number that two large boats had to be procured to convey them and us across the lake. After a delay of an hour we were all seated. Ours was a four-oared, the other a six-oared boat.

Langton, having been there before, knew that if we did not reach the Trossachs before the larger boat we should not be able to get a bed that night. We there- fore stimulated our crew with promises of whiskey to do their best. They did so, and there was a race of six miles all down the lake. Both boats bumped the shore at the same moment. Langton, knowing the hotel, left me in charge of the baggage, and raced up to the house with a stranger who had a large party with him. However, the length of Langton's legs proved an advantage, for he was enabled to secure two rooms, one of which we afterwards gave up to some ladies. The other we kept, although the "gent" who ran the race wanted us to give up both. Here we got an execrable dinner and worse port wine, after which we retired to our double-bedded room, where we found the beds made in a large box, similar to a wild beast's cage with the bars out. The whole of the bedding was wet, we therefore had to get up, dress, and sleep in our clothes. The room was evidently a stable which had been converted into a sleeping apartment *pro tem*. The scenery on Lock Katrine is not nearly so fine as that on Loch Lomond. That in the Trossachs is beautiful and pretty, being wooded with silver birch and other small trees. Ben Venue on the left is a magnificent mountain. We had a boat and visited all the lakes and lions in the Trossachs, and having made some sketches, proceeded along Lochs Archray and Venacher, to Callender. Here we visited the bridge and falls of Brocklyn on the river Keltie, took a sketch of that, and afterwards of Callender with Ben Ledi on the right and Ben Venue on the left—a splendid view. That night we indulged ourselves with a good bed and dinner in Callender, and a bathe in the river Teith the following morning, when we took coach to Stirling. Here we breakfasted, left again per coach, and met the train at twelve o'clock, at Falkirk, which took us back to Edinburgh by one O'clock, on the 31st of August.

September 3rd. We received the route to proceed to Glasgow on our way to Ireland. Next day we marched at half-past one, and having got over seventeen miles of ground, arrived at Linlithgow at eight o'clock, and dined at nine. I wished to see the old Royal Palace, but had not time, as we paraded at six o'clock next morning and marched to breakfast at Falkirk. The men were very much done up, going so far with empty stomachs. We marched again and reached Cumbernauld very considerably beaten. Left Cumbernauld on the 6th of September and marched to Glasgow, where we went immediately on board the Aurora, and sailed at ten p.m. for Belfast. We had a beautiful night, and a capital passage, arriving at Belfast at ten o'clock on the 7th of September, and disembarked in ould Ireland, relieving the 53rd Regiment, who were on Detachments all over the country.

BELFAST

ON landing at Belfast, and marching up to our quarters, we found the barracks in a state of defence, the walls loop-holed, platforms erected round the inside, the gates barricaded and loop-holed, and double sentries posted at night; three days' fresh provisions were always kept in the store in addition to the salt; in fact, the place seemed quite in a state of siege. The populace, who had been rendered disaffected by Dan O'Connell, had threatened to attack the barrack, and burn it down, seize the arms, and set fire to the town. The consequence to us was that we had a great deal of duty to perform. We gave a detachment of one Company to Carrickfergus Castle.

Belfast is a very good town, about number three of those in Ireland. Of the society I cannot say any- thing favourable; it was seldom there was a party of any kind given. The 66th gave a grand ball, with the idea that it would induce the gentry to return the civility by asking the officers to their houses, but although numbers attended, only one house returned the compliment; the others laughed at the Regiment for being such fools as to throw away their money for nothing- During my sojourn there, I only became acquainted with one family, the Goddards.

On one occasion I was riding out with Daniell through White Abbey, when we saw on a door the notice,

"White Abbey National School,
M. Sinclair, Master.

Daniell was struck with an idea, which made him burst out laughing. He said, "Let us send Jacob (i.e., Captain J—), who was on Detachment at Carrickfergus) an invitation to dinner from Sinclair." "Agreed, and a good joke." We returned to barracks, when Daniell wrote the note as follows;-

"Mr. Sinclair presents his compliments to Captain J—, and hopes he will excuse this short notice, having called personally, and that he will give him the pleasure of his company at dinner this evening at half-past six o'clock.

White Abbey, October 1st, 1843."

This was duly forwarded with Mr. Sinclair's card enclosed, just in time to prevent J—,s inquiring who Mr. Sinclair was. He therefore ordered a car at six, bantered his two subalterns at having to dine at home, when he was going to revel in the choicest claret at his "friend Sinclair's," as he termed him, and away he went, five miles to White Abbey, but on arriving there, no Mr. Sinclair's house was to be found. In vain did the driver protest there was no such person living at White Abbey for the last twenty years, but he said there were two old ladies of that name living in the square house.

Well, "drive up there," was the order. He knocked at the door, walked into the drawing-room, where he bowed to an elderly lady, and sat down to converse. However, in a few minutes, the other lady came downstairs, much surprised to see a stranger in the room. She said, -I beg your pardon, Sir, but I think you have made some mistake."

Oh really! I beg your pardon, is not this Mr. Sinclair's?"

"There is no one of that name near here, with the exception of my sister there and myself."

"Why, I received an invitation from a Mr. Sinclair, of White Abbey, to dine with him, and here is the note," pulling it out of his pocket. The ladies laughed, and said they thought somebody had played him a trick, but that if he would remain and partake of their dinner, they would be very glad. This he declined doing, and returned to his Detachment in no very good humour, just as his two subs, had finished dinner. He tried very hard to find out the author of the trick, however, we knew too well how to keep a secret to say a word until the danger was over.

The Barrack Square at Belfast was as good as any

military bully could have wished; many were the pairs of soles ground away on it, marking time.

* * * * * * * * *

Sir George Barkley on one occasion inspected us, and had a grand parade and sham fight. Colonel Napier was the Assistant Adjutant-General. The Barracks were supposed to be attacked, the alarm was sounded, the Companies rushed to their different posts and loopholes, when Napier's voice was heard, "Sergeant Major, bring up the gun," and up came the *double-barrelled roller*, drawn by eight men at the "double," there being no real gun to bring up. The country was supposed to be in such a disturbed state, that all Officers were ordered to rejoin their Regiments, and no leave was to be granted, but one day we were kept an unusually long time on parade, and I instantly resolved to go to England. I had received one or two letters stating that my brother had been very poorly. I therefore sent in my application, making out a dreadful case as far as truth would admit of, and received an answer in the affirmative.

Accordingly I left Belfast, went over to Liverpool, and into Shropshire, where I surprised all my friends by my sudden appearance amongst them, and had some capital shooting, killing sixty-nine head in eight days.

* * * * * * * * *

I returned to Belfast on the morning of the 30th, thinking how much more pleasantly I had spent my last three weeks than I should have done, had I remained at Belfast.

On the 23rd of December I went to shoot with Maxwell at Templepatrick. We had not very good sport, but in returning, we met with an accident, which reminds me of the day. On getting on our car, which was a hired one, we soon perceived that the driver was drunk; however, as long as he drove us quick, we little cared.

After going some four or five miles, we went to sleep, and came in contact with some heavily laden dray cars, the wheel of one of which completely cut off the footboard of my seat, my legs only escaping by cocking them over the well. Maxwell, who was sitting on the other side, was thrown some distance by the violence of the concussion, and landed flat in the mud. The horse shot completely out of the harness, the driver was pulled to the ground by the reins, and the car smashed in pieces. It was so broken that we took our guns on our shoulders and walked in, about eight miles. Christmas Day, or rather the afternoon and night of it, I spent in the House of Correction, being on piquet.

Our Detachment at Carrickfergus consisted now of Captain Biscoe, Lieutenants Downman and Astley. On the 18th of January, 1844, I went down there to have a day's shooting with Downman. After breakfast we started off for the Common, about five miles away. The first hill out of the town is a regular blower, and I found myself very weak, and not up to my work, however, I went on, thinking I should get better. We walked a good deal, had but little sport, and on turning our faces homewards, I was quite done, and eight miles from home, without any chance of getting a lift, "Pluck has it," thought I, and put my bristles up, but it was no go. I had to lie down three times on the road to rest, and when walking, was reeling about the road, and as blind as a drunken man. When I did get back to the barracks, I took a hot strong glass of brandy and water, lay down for an hour, and at the end of that time I was quite recovered, and ready for dinner.

Daniell and I used generally to shoot together, he having bought a hack car and horse from off the stand in the town for the purpose. The shooting grounds around Belfast are so separated and distant from one another, that it is quite necessary to have a car to meet you at different spots during the day's shooting.

February 3rd I went with him to Straid. It was a

miserably cold evening, freezing hard, and as we were wet to the middles, we had occasionally to jump off the car, and run for half-a-mile to get our blood into circulation, The following morning I arose with a tremendous headache and cold, but thought my cold bath would put me all right, but in this I was mistaken. Pains came all over me; my head got worse; the doctor saw me, and ordered me instantly to my bed; I had fever. That evening I suffered most acutely, and requested the doctors to bleed me, but *no*—they said there was no necessity. About mess-time, I sent for Maxwell to ask him to send for Doctor Purdon, a civil practitioner, as neither Doctors G— nor M— would relieve me by bleeding, which I knew, from being in a similar predicament at Sorel, would give me ease immediately. Maxwell recommended me to wait till after mess, when he would bring both doctors to me. He did so, when old M— looked very wise, and said in his Scotch accent, "Well G—, I think you may as well take a little blood from him, it will do him no harm." G— whipped out the lancet, and instead of cutting *up* the vein, cut right across it, and took about thirty ounces of blood from me, which immediately relieved me of all pain but left me in a faint. He seemed not to have the least idea of tying up the arm, as he made a hard wedge out of an old shirt, and tied up tight with a bandage; the consequence was, that in ten minutes my hand was blue, all circulation having stopped. I then sent for him again to rebind it, which he did, just in the same way as before. I tried to go to sleep, and at last dropped into a slumber, out of which I soon awoke, and found myself lying in a mass of jelly, the bandage on my arm having come off, and the vein having opened again in my sleep. The fever left me, and I was allowed to get up on the 6th, but I was on the sick list, with my arm in a sling, and poultices on, until the 22nd, from the ignorance of *Doctor G—!*

On the 29th of February, the barrack was in a state of excitement, as Private Corderoy (who had been for some time my servant, but at this time was servant to his victim) shot Sergeant Dodd in the Barrack-room. It appeared in evidence that Corderoy had been absent from tattoo the night previous for half-an-hour, when Sergeant Dodd threatened to put him in the guard-room if it occurred again, and said he should report him to the Captain of the Company for the present time. Corderoy used always to have tea with Dodd and his wife, and they were very good friends up to this time. However, on the morning of the next day, Corderoy loaded his musket quietly, took a deliberate aim, and shot Sergeant Dodd dead. He was given over to the civil power, tried at Carrickfergus before Judge Perrin, convicted, and sentenced to be hung, but was, before sentence by the Judge, recommended to mercy by a most enlightened jury, on the ground of his having been *always on such good terms with his victim*. Of course this recommendation could not be listened to, and he was hung at Carrickfergus on the 15th of May; Colonel Dames, Captain Biscoe, and Lieutenant Astley, with eighty rank and file, being ordered down to *view* for the moral effect on the Regiment. When the sentence on Corderoy was made known, Colonel Johnston got one or two letters, saying that if he did not use his utmost efforts in getting the man off, he would be shot. Of course, these letters being anonymous, like all such, turned out mere puff.

March 4th. I obtained leave for four days, and paid a visit to Goddard's, of Tully, for the purpose of shooting. I found the best in Mazzarene Park, where the snipe lay beautifully in the grass.

Immediately after this, my dear old dog Ben was stolen out of my stable yard. I informed the police, got hold of all the dog stealers I could find out, offered rewards, and at last, in about nine days, discovered the whereabouts. I then sent a policeman to arrest (log and man, had them up next day at the Court, and had the pleasure of hearing the villain sentenced to a fine of £5, or one month's imprisonment with hard labour, which latter he paid.

As soon as poor "Ben" was brought into court, he looked round the bystanders, and at last saw me, when he set up such a whine of recognition, and made such attempts to reach me, that it was exclaimed through the court, -There is no doubt who that dog belongs to."

Ben was a great favourite. I bought him from Mr. Scarlett's keeper, above Fort William, in Scotland, as an unbroken dog, for, I think, £5. I broke him myself, and if any one had offered £25 for him, I would not have accepted it. Poor Ben! he was the most splendid dog I ever saw on a mountain for six hours a day, three days a week. He got quite foundered latterly when I was at Philipstown, in 1845; it was painful to see him walk along the road. I then gave him to Mr. Magan's keeper, an old man of sixty-five, who said he was just the dog he wanted to potter about with but I heard he would not stay with him, and that he attached himself to an officer in the 47th Regiment at Tyrrel's Pass. Another dog, poor old King—I often think of the happy days when we were young, and lived so merrily together. How those old dogs used to jump, bark, and skip whenever they saw me or heard me with my shooting boots on, but when I was in uniform, they lay as quiet as lambs. Poor old King! often have I seen him crawling on his belly behind me, when he has seen me doing the same in Canada to get a shot at ducks. He, poor old dog, *would never work for anyone but me*, and that was the reason Lord Cochrane made me a present of him. One day at Carrickfergus "King" pointed; I went up and saw nothing, but he was very sure, so I looked minutely into the grass, when I discovered a jack snipe, which allowed me to pick it up in my hand; I thought it extraordinary at the time, but have often done the same thing since. "Bonnie," my retriever, which I bought at Dundonald, I had great difficulty in breaking. I could not correct him by beating, therefore took the last chance, that of shooting him in the rump, which had the desired effect. One day I sent him for a snipe I had knocked down at a long distance; he went and brought it, but in doing so, he turned it several times in his mouth. This I saw, and thought he was eating it, I therefore scolded him, and told him to drop it; he looked me very wisely in the face, as much as to say, "You are a great fool, but I can't help it," opened his mouth wide, and away flew the bird, at which I fired two more shots, and missed, and never saw any more of it.

Captain King's troop of the 5th Dragoon Guards were quartered with us at Belfast. On the 3rd of April I went with him to Dundalk, on a visit to the Head Quarters of his Regiment.

* * * * * * * * *

Getting again tired of the drill and marking time, I trumped up a story, not without foundation, that my presence was required in England, to remove some money, of which I had a share on mortgage. I therefore made an application for leave till the end of the month, which with some difficulty succeeded, and I went home.

* * * * * * * * *

My leave being nearly expired, I left Worfield with my brother Shell, in his dog-cart, to attend the Shrewsbury Races on my return to join. Soon after we got into the cart, I fancied the mare looked like kicking, so kept a sharp eye on her; however, we went very well for sixteen miles till we got near Atcham, when going down a slight hill, we met some cattle, which the drover was trying to drive out of our way. The mare saw his stick up, got frightened, and set to work to kick, sending her heels right into the cart. If the kicking strap had not broken, we should have been all right, but she lashed away till she fell down, when I was shot into the hedge, and lit on my feet. My brother was not so fortunate, for he got kicked between his knees, though not much hurt, and afterwards somehow got in between the mare's hind legs and the cart. Luckily she was now so hampered, that she could do no more harm; some people came to our assistance, and shortly we got the mare out, found her knees smashed, and the shaft broken. In struggling with the mare to keep her down, I strained a muscle in my arm, which gave me a good deal of pain for a long time afterwards. We had to walk to Atcham. The Races were not good, and the attendance of gentry worse. I was rather glad when the day was over.

I went on to Belfast *viâ* Holyhead and Dublin. My object in returning through Dublin was to see Scott, of the 5th Fusiliers, who had been in the 66th Regiment, but on arriving, I found my time was so short, that I was obliged to leave without even calling on him. I heard afterwards that he had been killed in the Phoenix Park by his horse running away with him, and dashing his head against the bough of a tree. He, poor fellow, was buried in Dublin on the 6th of May.

May 28th. I went to Dundalk on a visit to my friend King, 5th Dragoon Guards. That day a party of us went over to Claremont to shoot rooks, where we slew about five dozen of them.

* * * * * * * * *

King and I walked to the top of Fahey Hill, which overlooks Carlingford Bay and Rosstrevor; from this height is a very fine view of the surrounding hills and scenery. I returned to Belfast on the 30th, to the old system of worry.

Dan O'Connell's trial for High Treason was now concluded, and he was sentenced on the 30th of this month to one year's imprisonment, and a fine of £2000, and to find sureties for his good behaviour at the expiration of the term of his incarceration, but from some flaw in the proceedings, he was released after a time.

July 8th. I got four days' leave, and went with Hawkins, of the Engineers, by coach to Coleraine.

We went to the salmon-leap, and tried the fishing, but caught nothing. We witnessed the curious sight of the eels' spawn, or small eels, about two inches long, swarming up the side of the river from the sea, and crawling up the straw ropes which are let down the rapid to enable them to reach the water above, which they do in myriads. Besides the assistance they get by the ropes, people are employed to lade them up in buckets. These then go on to Lough Neagh, grow large, and descend the river again to return to the sea; it is at this time that such immense numbers are taken at the weirs. The weirs at Toome Bridge, close to Lough Neagh, let for £000 per annum. The people here have a great aversion to the lamprey, of which they catch numbers, and boil them for their pigs! We dined at the Hotel, which was comfortable enough for an Irish one, and slept there. The following morning we took some coffee early, and proceeded per car to the Giant's Causeway, stopping on our way at Dunluce Castle, which is built on the brink of a precipice rising about one hundred and fifty feet from the sea, and insulated from the mainland by a chasm twenty feet broad, and about one hundred feet deep, across which is a very narrow path. The numerous turrets and pointed gables of this ruin give a good idea of what it has been in former times. It is said that in 1639 the Duchess of Buckingham and Marchioness of Antrim resided there, and one stormy day, whilst dinner was preparing, the kitchen and rock on which it stood, with the cook and eight other people, were precipitated into the sea, which so alarmed the Duchess, that the Castle was never inhabited again. After seeing Dunluce, we proceeded through Bushmills, (a place celebrated for its whiskey,) and arrived at the Causeway Hotel to breakfast, about eleven o'clock, after which we procured guides and boats to visit the Grand Cave and the Causeway. The Grand Cave, only visitable by water, is a fine chasm, but nothing very wonderful. The Causeway is curious, it projects from the base of a cliff nearly four hundred feet high into the sea. The basaltic columns of which the

Causeway is composed have been computed at thirty thousand, are perpendicular, closely compacted, and the sides and angles so closely fitted that it is impossible to get the blade of a knife between them. We slept at the Causeway Hotel, and went on next morning in a car to Carrick-a-ride, which is a basaltic rock about three hundred feet h separated from the mainland by a high chasm of sixty feet wide, and eighty in depth, over which is thrown a bridge of ropes, for the purpose of assisting the fishermen to reach this island, where there is a good salmon fishery.

At the Inn we got a very bad dinner of bad eggs and bacon, but made it up with some capital toddy, and tumbled into a comfortable bed, but in consequence of the bad fare, we resolved to go on to Larne next morning to breakfast, but fared no better on our arrival there. We then went on to Carrickfergus, lunched with our Detachment there, Captains Daniell and Holmes, and afterwards returned to Belfast.

DUBLIN

AUGUST 10th. Maxwell and Light Company sailed for Dublin. On the 14th, Colonel Dames, Captain Johnson, Lieutenants Birch, Kebble, Monckton, and Ross, embarked for Dublin. I accompanied them, and we marched up to the Royal Barracks the next morning, where we found the 16th and 24th Regiments, also the 1st Dragoons and 3rd Dragoon Guards, with the 11th Hussars, in garrison, under Lord Cardigan. We met also in Ship Street our old friends the 32nd, and in a few days, the 73rd arrived in the Rhadamanthus. On the 18th, Captains Michel, Blount, Mainwaring, Benson, and Langton, arrived in Dublin, and on the 23rd, the Head Quarters of the Regiment.

We were now in the Royal Barracks under the eye of General Wyndham, which was a great comfort to us, as we could only do as other Regiments; no extra parades or worrying drills, no marking time, right about turn, etc., etc., which we had morning, noon, and night at Belfast.

On the 28th, 29th, and 30th of August were the Garrison Races in the Phoenix Park, which caused great excitement throughout the Barracks. Our messes constantly full with officers from all parts of Ireland and England.

August 31st- I obtained six weeks' leave.

SCOTLAND

HAVING obtained leave, expressly for the purpose of grouse shooting, so went in the application, (and which was granted on that head only; another application merely for leave "*without mentioning for what*" was refused,) I embarked with Maxwell from Dublin on the 3rd of September, at eleven, a.m., and landed at Greenock at half-past seven next morning. After breakfasting at the Tontine Hotel, Maxwell moved off towards Glasgow. As there was no steamer direct to Fort William that day, and only the "heavy goods boat" the next, I determined on posting across the Black Mount, and leaving my dogs, Ned and Ben, at the Tontine, in Mr. Mc Donald's charge, to be forwarded by the first boat. I left Greenock at ten, a.m., in the steamer which plied up Loch Long to Arroquhar, from whence I crossed to Tarbes, and posted from there up Glen Fallach, by Tyndrum and Inverouran, to King's House on the Black Mount, where it grew so dark that I determined to pass the night. On crossing the Black Mount, which is Lord Breadalbane's deer forest, I saw a great number of deer.

September 5th. Left King's House at six, a.m., rattled down that splendid pass of Glencoe in a dogcart, the road running all the way on the verge of a precipice with innumerable sharp turnings, but these my driver was quite accustomed to, and rattled full tilt all the way to Ballachulish, where I called and breakfasted at Charles Stuart's, then rowed across the lake to Ardgower. Here my dogs were to meet me, but by some mistake they did not arrive. Nevertheless, I went out shooting next morning with an old dog of Colonel Maclean's. The Colonel said, "You had better put a bullet in your gun, as there are deer on the hills, and you may get a crack at them." Knowing pretty well where the deer usually were, I and Duncan the keeper crept stealthily up the hills, keeping a good look-out for about an hour and a half, but not seeing the expected game, and arriving at a place where Duncan said were two or three coveys of grouse, I thought it no use wasting time. I discharged my bullets to load with shot. At the report of the gun four fine stags and three hinds sprang from behind some rocks not more than two hundred yards off, and went trotting down the hill and across the valley into the Loch-wood. Great was the disappointment! but never having found the advantage of fretting over mishaps, I made the best work I could out of the grouse. These were few and far between, however, bagged four brace and a half, which they considered good sport.

On the 7th September I left Ardgower and went on a visit to the McDonells of Inch. Here I remained till the 26th, shooting, visiting my old friends, receiving their hospitality which was unbounded, and enjoying myself very much. I shot on Mr. Walker's grounds behind Inch. Lord Abinger also gave me leave to shoot on Corry-na-owen, but there were but few grouse here, and the walking was bad. The second steamer from Greenock after my arrival brought me up a brace of pointers, but not my own. They had been left at the Tontine Hotel to be forwarded to Liverpool to somebody who had returned from his shooting. The landlord made a mistake, sent mine to Liverpool and this man's to me. They were not good dogs, and half starved, however, I kept and used them until my own arrived, which was not till the 15th, when I returned the strangers. I shot with North on Glenfintaig, Mr. Drury at Urrachan, (one day I bagged eight brace of grouse with him and he did not kill a shot,) with Greig of Tulloch, and bagged sixty-five head in seven days. After spending a very pleasant visit, Angus drove me to Fort William to meet the steamer. I went on board at half-past five, a.m., on the 27th, and made acquaintance with Captain Bonham, Lord George Beauclerk, Lord Garvah, all loth Hussars, and Mr. Leigh of Liverpool, returning from their shooting. We had a miserable wet day which did not tend to keep up our spirits. Captain Bonham had eight or ten beautiful trained hawks with him. We dined together at the Tontine in Greenock. I and Mr. Leigh had to wait in that horrid place all the 28th, till five o'clock in the evening when we went on board, and arrived in Liverpool at twelve o'clock next day. I went on home. Here we went out with gun and dogs daily. We had one day at Gatacre, when we bagged twenty-one partridges, thirteen hares, four rabbits, and one pheasant, between two guns. This on the 10th of October.

LONDON

October 11th. I went up to London, and on the following Sunday I was walking in the Regent's Park when I heard terrific screams; on looking round, I saw a gig being run away with. It contained a Mr. and Mrs. Norbury and a child. It went at a most tremendous pace, (how it escaped other carriages I know not,) till they came opposite the gate leading to Avenue Road, when the horse chested the stile posts at the corner of the footpath, smashed the gig to atoms; Mr. and Mrs. N— both pitched out; the former lighted on his head and never stirred, being killed on the spot. Mrs. N— was picked up insensible, and the child went flying over the horse's head, but was not hurt or even frightened. Mr. N— was carried into the gate lodge after a great deal of *resistance* from the lodge-keeper!

On the 28th I was present at the opening of the New Royal Exchange by the Queen. On her arrival the bells of the Campanile Tower struck up for the first time "God save the Queen." The reading room was fitted up as a throne room, the walls were hung with crimson velvet, and the floor covered with crimson cloth. At one end, on a dais was a throne of crimson velvet, backed by a curtain of the same bordered with gold lace. The Queen having taken her place, and all the public functionaries being arranged, the Recorder read a loyal and congratulatory address from the Lord Mayor and Corporation to Her Majesty, hailing in suitable terms the presence of Her Majesty in the heart of the metropolis, and recalling the occasion of the visit of her great predecessor, Queen Elizabeth, for a like purpose, and requesting Her Majesty's favourable regard and sanction to the work which her loyal citizens of London had just completed. Having returned a gracious reply, she gave the Lord Mayor her hand to kiss, and announced her intention of creating him a baronet in commemoration of the day. Her Majesty then with numerous distinguished guests partook of a sumptuous déjeûner; such a déjeûner, such capital wines and dishes, I never saw before or since. At the conclusion of the repast the Queen ordered the Lord Mayor to give a toast, "Prosperity to the city of London," which she drank herself, after which she and Prince Albert proceeded to the Quadrangle in the centre of which Her Majesty stopped. The members of the Corporation and the Ministers formed a circle round the Queen, and the heralds having made proclamation, and silence having been commanded, she said in a loud tone, "*It is my Royal will and pleasure that this building be hereaftercalled the "Royal Exchange.*" This closed the ceremonies of the day, and the royal cortege returned to the palace. But just as the Queen was going out of the Quadrangle a man, in his anxiety to see her, overbalanced himself, and fell from the top of a tower over the entrance door, through a skylight, on the pavement close to her feet. He never stirred, being killed on the spot. As it was certain there would be a crush when the Queen left, I went according to appointment for my sister to the throne room, at the door of which I found a great crowd assembled trying to force their way in against the halberts of the "Beef Eaters" who guarded the entrance. The crowd increased every instant, at last a move was made and I was carried off my legs into the centre of the room. Then came a pretty scene of confusion and dismay. The ladies who were in the room jumped up from their seats, ran over the tables in all directions, upsetting tarts, and putting their white satined feet into others. In the melee some ladies got much crushed, and Lady Sale was knocked down and nearly very much hurt.

On the 29th October I called on my doctor, got a sick certificate from him, and went to the Medical Board in St. James' Street, who gave me six weeks' sick leave. I then returned to Worfield for some hunting with the Albrighton hounds, and remained at Worfield and Davenport till the 11th of December, when I went up again to London, and sent in Captain Rainsford's papers to sell for me. On the following day, I again visited Dr.

Sampson and obtained another sick certificate; when I went with it to the Horse Guards to obtain an order from General Brown, Quarter-Master General, to appear before a Medical Board. On my applying to him he laughed in my face—my red face—and asked if I was joking; but upon my assuring him I was not, he replied, "Well, I'll give you an order at all events, but I don't think they will give you any leave." The next morning I walked down from Haverstock Hill, the cold, frosty morning adding more colour to my already red face, and attended at the Medical Board, producing my certificates; I was examined by Dr. Gordon who refused to recommend a further extension of leave. I therefore rejoined the Regiment in Dublin, with my horse Emancipation. Bates offered to get me £180 for him, but this I refused as I should not be able to get re-mounted.

DUBLIN

DECEMBER 23rd. Went with Astley to meet the Garrison hounds at the Black Bull and lost my purse containing £8 on my road thither. Uncarted the deer at two o'clock, and had a middling run of an hour over the largest and deepest ditches I ever saw. They funked my horse, and I found I could not ride half of it.

27th. Met the Garrison hounds at Kilrue, and being determined my horse should not shy his fences, the first we came to I crammed him into it, and got up to the saddle in chick-weed and water. On getting off to allow the horse to come out, he made a jump; my one foot on the ground slipped, and down I went under his belly and came up like a drowned rat. However, I was soon in the saddle again, and got into my place, but which I could not keep, as I and my horse got into three ditches in two miles, the third being so deep that I had to lead him half round the field before I could find a place that he could get out of. This completely threw me out; however, I thought that perhaps the deer might be headed, or take a ring, so I continued in the line and arrived in time to see the Ward Union pack uncart their deer. I took the lead for about ten minutes, when a bank twelve feet high presented itself. This my English horse could high not get over, and in the attempt he slipped back into the ditch, so as soon as I could get him out, I rode home with the certain knowledge that a horse fresh from England cannot go in the Dublin county.

This year was finished by my being gazetted Captain to Rainsford's Company on the 31st of December, having paid him six hundred pounds over Regulation.

There was plenty of hunting about Dublin. Be. sides the Garrison and Ward Union stag-hounds, there were the Kildare fox-hounds, but they met at long distances from Dublin, and had indifferent sport, therefore few went to their Meets. A very good pack of harriers were kept in the neighbourhood. With them were generally to be seen three ladies, whose names I forget, but they were "divils" to ride, and beat many of the men.

The shooting round Dublin was very indifferent. I used sometimes to go by rail to Drogheda, where Captain Michel and Ensign Benson were quartered; it was considered a good country for snipe, but I never had much sport.

* * * * * * * * *

Colonel White, of Killakee, on the mountain, had very good rabbit shooting. I went there one day, and bagged ten rabbits, two woodcocks and one hare, in about two hours' shooting. This was on the mountain, where the rabbits cannot burrow on account of the rocky soil; they live and breed in the gorse bushes, which are thick, and afford capital shelter. Colonel White's keeper had three dogs, a breed of his own, the best rabbit dogs I ever saw; they are between a terrier and a spaniel, and are not so large as a good-sized rabbit.

My game list for the season of 1844 and 1845 shews total of two hundred and forty-seven head. Number of days out, thirty-one.

We had but little society in Dublin, except a Dance occasionally. I used to attend all the Lord Lieutenant's Levees and Drawing-rooms, which were always crowded to excess, and the Ball on Saint Patrick's Day was so full, that it was almost impossible to move from one end of the room to the other. The Roman punch given at the refreshment table was so good, that I believe numbers attended solely on its account. Here we met people of the highest rank, down to your tradesmen's wives and daughters, some of whom became very lively, particularly after a glass of the inimitable punch.

March 29th. My eyes were attacked by some epidemic. They felt as if there was a quantity of sand in them, and were very painful. I immediately consulted Wilde, the oculist, who said it was lucky I attended to it so soon, as otherwise I might have lost my sight. I was in the sick list with this for some days, and remained in Dublin, where I lived with the 32nd Regiment. Meantime the 66th Regiment marched out to different places; Langton marched with my Company for Philipstown, and the Head Quarters left for Birr.

PHILIPSTOWN

Soon afterwards I said good-bye to Dublin as a quarter, and proceeded to join my Company at Philipstown. I was surprised to find it so clean a place as it appeared to be, and the people so clean, in the middle of the "Bog of Allan." It scarcely deserves the name of town, only consisting of one street, about a third of a mile long, and claiming not one good house. When a gig or car drives through the street, all the doors and windows shake and rattle. There was a rule some years ago that no car should go faster than a walk through the town, or incur a penalty, as the jolting was liable to break the windows. It is built entirely on the boggy land of the "Bog of Allan." How it got the name of "town" I know not, unless I may draw an inference from a conversation I had with a Patlander one day I was out shooting at Maynooth. I enquired of him if there were any partridges about there, and if he knew where to find them? Faix, yer honer, there's plenty of them; there's not a night I don't hear them *roaring through the town.*" As there was no town about there, I was at a loss to know his meaning, but upon inquiry, I found he meant the *fields* adjacent, and what he called "*roaring* through the town," meant that he heard them calling. Nevertheless, I did not find these roarers.

I made inquiries as to the fishing near there, but all the answers I got were to the effect that there was *none*. "Is there no stream or river anywhere?" "None!" was the answer. "What becomes of all the water?" "Absorbed in the bog," was the reply. However, I one day took a walk towards Esker, on the Clonbullock road, and in about three miles crossed a little stream. A boy was near at the time, and I asked him if there were any fish in it. He said there were *pikes and eels.* I fancied I saw a fish rise at the time in a deep hole. The river was very deep, from five to six or eight feet deep, but so narrow that I could jump over it; it ran through the land that had been reclaimed from the bog. The following day I went down with my rod, and some preserved minnows. The very first spin I had, I caught a trout as black as my hat, about three-quarters of a pound. I fished on, and caught a few more good fish, and returned to the barracks with a secret nobody knew, that there was fishing at Philipstown.

These black fish, when cooked, cut up as pink as salmon, and were, without exception, the best river trout I ever saw; they take the minnow and May-fly voraciously. I always got a good basket full whenever I went there, and fish from half-a-pound to one pound and three-quarters in weight. With a strong breeze and rain the sport was capital all the way to the Police Station at Esker. One man found out the place by seeing and hearing of my fishing, but I don't think he ever caught much.

There ought to be good snipe shooting all round Philipstown, particularly during the time of the light nights, as the place is surrounded by red bog, which the snipe always frequent when there is a moon at night. At the time of dark nights they will be found in the rushy fields, and scarcely any in the red bog.

One day I was crossing part of the bog, trying a young dog, when suddenly I came upon a cabin. The owner asked me in, and sheaved me a brace of grouse in a cage, formed by cutting a hole in the wall about two feet square, with bars in front. The birds were quite tame, but he never let them out without a string to their legs. The one he said he had had for two years, and bred the other from it just a year ago. When the breeding season came on, he used to tether the bird on the bog at night, where she always found a mate, and he took her in during the day. She laid seven or eight eggs, but the "chiller" ate most of them, and he only reared two young birds.

We had no society at Philipstown, and but little amusement except fishing, (which the state of the weather often prevented,) and driving over to the

Detachment at Tullamore. Langton and I at last used to walk through the town at four o'clock, when the National School closed. We collected some dozen and a half of boys, and took them outside the town to the meadows, and then gave stakes of twopence or threepence to run for, over two or three fields through which a deep brook ran, and which they had to jump twice in the course; frequently one or two of them went plump into it on the run home, but they cared little for that. Our own exercise and amusement were in fixing a certain point, and going over hedge and bank there and back; or taking a walk of eight or nine miles.

One day we were rather surprised to see the Police bringing in two prisoners, to whom we had seen the sentry at the Barrack-Gate carry arms. These proved to be Holmes and Astley, who made a bet the previous night to run against each other from Birr to Philipstown, twenty-eight Irish, or thirty-five English miles. They started, and kept together the whole way, stopping only for a moment in Tullamore to get a drink, and reserving their strength for the run into the Barracks, but just on entering the town, a policeman met them, and taking them for deserters, (they having only flannels and wide-awake hats on,) had them arrested as they passed the Police Station. It was all in vain trying to persuade them that they were officers of the 66th Regiment running a match, so they marched them up prisoners, to give them over to us, and were not a little surprised at the sentry saluting them. They ran the distance in six hours and a half. Poor Holmes was very tired, but "little Jack," who was a light weight, was fresh enough, and after some luncheon, accompanied Langton and myself in a run across the country. On the 10th of June I rejoined Head Quarters at Birr.

BIRR

Is not a bad town for Ireland. It has three or four streets, and a few miserable shops, but at which you can buy stationery, and that sort of thing, also powder and shot. It possesses a very tolerable Hotel, to which is attached a billiard room.

Lord Rosse's domain is in the town; the grounds are very pretty, with the River Bresna running through them, where are to be seen the trout, almost tame, from never being disturbed, rising to the flies on the water. Lord Rosse allows all the respectable people of Birr, and elsewhere, to make a promenade of his domain, and it is the only place about there where ladies could find a nice walk for half-an-hour. There is little or no society at Birr, most of the respectable people being badly off, with the exception of His Lordship, who *never asked* one of the Regiment into his house.

The only places I visited at were the Walshe's, of Walshe Park, Mr. Stoney's, of Portland, Lord Avonmore's, and Captain Pigott's, of Eagle Hill. I found Lord and Lady Avonmore's a very nice house to visit, and often went there. Mr. Walshe was also very kind to me.

The fishing about Birr was bad, decidedly bad. There was the Upper and Lower Bresna River, the upper being above the town, the latter below; and it is the same stream which flows into the Shannon below Banagher. I have fished this stream often, but never had sport, though I sometimes got a good trout or two of one pound weight. There is a diminutive little stream, or rather drain, behind the Barracks, which comes out of a peat bog; in this and the great holes which have filled from the stream are good trout, and scarcely any one knows the fact. It is not more than a mile from the gate, if so much. I frequently went to fish for salmon in the Shannon at Meelick, two miles below Banagher. I have fished there half-a-dozen times, from four in the morning till nine or ten o'clock, and again in the evening, from four till dark, but never had much sport. I caught a ten pound salmon on the *14th of June* at Meelick Ford, and another on the Whiteford on the *15th of July*, (with an eel's tail,) weighing seven pounds and three quarters. These two were the only ones I caught in seven journeys to Meelick, eleven miles from Birr.

On the day I was fishing at Whiteford, an old man who rowed my boat, manufactured my bait to troll with, (an eel's tail,) and after I commenced fishing with it, he kept continually saying, "God bless it, it's saying illigant bait. A *tousand* pounds but you'll have him wid it, God bless it. Who knows what He is doing? We may have a fish yet. Try again, God bless you. By my faith, but you have him! God bless him! I *tould* yer honer you would. God bless you! Who knows? we may have another yet," etc.

In June we got orders to form the Head Quarter Division for foreign Service; accordingly they were named and separated from the Depot Companies.

On the 26th of June the Head Quarters marched out of Birr for Cork, to embark for Gibraltar, consisting of Lieutenant-Colonel Johnston, Brevet Lieutenant-Colonel Dames, Lieutenants Birch, Langton, Saunderson, and Dr. Miller.

June 27th. The second Division of the Regiment marched out to follow Head Quarters, consisting of Captain Maxwell, Lieutenants Downman, Astley, Cooper, Benson, and Melsop. They were joined by Captains Michel and Coates at Roscrea.

ATHLONE

JULY 23rd. Lieut.-Colonel Goldie and I had made up our minds to travel through Galway; accordingly we left Birr for Athlone, there to obtain Sir Guy Campbell's leave for a few days, but he would not give Goldie his, as the Command of the Depot during his absence would devolve upon a very junior officer. We dined with our old friends, the 32nd, in the Barracks. Athlone is a horrid, dirty, stinking hole, with only one redeeming quality, i.e., that the Shannon runs through it, and there is good boating on the lake above.

I was up at half-past three in the morning, to get on the Galway mail, but when it arrived, I found it was full, therefore ordered a car to Ballinasloe. However, just as the mail was starting, and my car at the door, a Mrs. Gilligan recollected that she was to alight there, which she did amidst the laughter of the passengers, and the curses of the coachman. I then got her place and arrived in Galway at eleven o'clock.

Next day, after breakfast, I got on the Galway mail, and arrived at Clifden at six, p.m., passing through Oughteherard, near which place I saw two women walking at a good pace round a well, the bushes overhanging the place being covered with little strips of coloured cotton and other rags. Upon inquiry I found that these unfortunates were there doing penance, having to walk round the well so many times, and each time to say a Pater Noster. The dress of the peasant women in this part of Ireland is very picturesque, being made of red flannel; but they are the most ugly set of mortals I have ever seen. They have a peculiar way of riding, sitting upon the horses' rumps behind the panniers, which is astonishing to a stranger, for he cannot imagine how they stick on; but I suppose it is all practice.

The scenery from Oughteherard to Clifden is wild enough; nothing but barren moors. On the left, about Ballinahinch, are the twelve Pins, which are bold and rise to a good height.

July 26th. Got up at half-past five, a.m., having had a comfortable bed at the Hotel, which is not bad. My guide McDonald, whom I engaged the previous night, took me to Ballinahinch, Mr. Martin's, (the famous Cruelty Act man,) about seven miles from Clifden. Here I sent in my card and asked permission to fish in the river, which was granted immediately by Miss Martin, her father not being at home. We then proceeded to the river, which is only half a mile in length, and not more than two hundred or three hundred yards of it fishable by rod and line; however, I caught one salmon, hooked another which broke my tackle, and rose two others, all before ten o'clock. It being Saturday, Mr. Robertson, who rents the fishing, then brought up his nets to draw the weir where I was fishing, and to take the accumulated masses of fish which had collected there since the previous Sunday evening. This spoilt my fishing for salmon, so I then tried the river above the weir for sea trout and caught eighteen. I saw Mr. Robertson take at one haul of the net, out of one hole, ninety odd salmon, and at the second haul about half that number. On returning to Clifden to dinner, I met hundreds of people riding, walking, driving, sometimes riding three upon one horse, going on their way to the rendezvous for to-morrow, about eight miles from Clifden, it being Garlic Sunday, or Pattern (Patron) Day. At this place, on the side of one of the Pins, is a holy Well, and a cave where they all assemble to do honour to the Saint, and encamp or lie on the open moor for a couple of nights. I hear that a great deal of whiskey is expended on these occasions, and other villanies committed.

After seeing Clifden Castle, (nothing particular in itself, although the sea-view from above it is good,) and viewing Clifden from D'Arcy's Monument, which looks well, backed by the twelve Pins, I left Clifden and travelled through a very fine country, having the said twelve Pins on my right, and occasional peeps at the sea bays on the left, till I reached Kylemore, which is a splendid hill with a lake at its foot. Having driven through this Pass, I proceeded to Killery Harbour and went up the Bay to Lenane, a small Inn where I stopped to luncheon and had a capital chop; I then took a boat across the Bay to Delphi, (the Bishop of Tuam's fishing lodge,) where I caught the Bishop's brother fishing the lake for salmon, and with him I had a chat. The hills here are magnificent, and well worth one's being imposed upon by the boatmen charging 2s. 6d. for boat hire instead of 6d.

I left Lenane at eight, p.m., driving through Joyce's country; so called from there being a race of immense men named Joyce living in that part, but now only one or two remain. I went on to Maam, a beautiful drive *when it does not rain*. Here I arrived at half-past nine, p.m., (having gone at the rate of four and a half miles an hour,) and found a very comfortable Hotel. The waiter, who had been in the same situation at Cork, understood his business, which is a comfort to travellers.

Maam is only an Hotel, not a village, and is situated at the North West corner of Lough Corrib. Hearing that there was good trout fishing in the Maam River, I was up at seven, a.m., to try my luck, but found it was *all talk*. I only caught three trout and a perch. A man there, a boaster, went with me to the river, and whilst doing so, sounded his own praises very loftily, which I encouraged him in. He told me he was the fox hunter of the country, that he was well known, as the best walker and runner in the counties of Galway, etc., etc.: that there was not a man between there and Dublin that could go over a mountain with him! Here I interrupted him by asking how long it would take to ascend the mountain behind the Hotel. He said it could not be done under an hour up, and the same time down. I told him I would go up if he would *show me the way*. I then partook of luncheon with some porter, (not good things to walk upon,) and we started. He took the lead at five miles an hour along the flat, but I cried out and said I was not going at that pace directly after eating and drinking, so he pulled in. We then began the ascent, and in about ten minutes I passed him, leaving him behind crying out for me to stop or I would "*kill*" myself. However, I climbed away and arrived at the summit in thirty-nine minutes from the Hotel door. My guide came up in about ten minutes afterwards, quite blown. I bullied him, and said he was the *worst walker I ever saw*. I then commenced the descent; running down almost all the way on my heels, and arriving at the Hotel in fifteen minutes. My guide was so ashamed of himself that he would not come to be paid for his trouble, and I had to send him a shilling

I left Maam at five o'clock and drove twelve miles to Cong, the N.N.E. corner of Lough Corrib, through a most uninteresting country, composed of masses of rock and stones; the latter piled up like haycocks. At Cong I found a very diminutive Inn, or rather no Inn at all, but a house where I got a bed and a grilled fowl for dinner, and where I saw the prettiest girl I ever saw in Ireland.

July 29th. Rose at six and went to see the caves through which the river runs underground for four miles, emptying Lough Mask into Lough Corrib. The "Pigeon Hole" and "Horse Discovery" are the best worth seeing, as they penetrate a long way into the bowels of the earth, and look very fine when lighted up with torches or bundles of straw. In caves are eel weirs, and I saw several small trout there also in the stream. Having returned to breakfast, I hired a capital four-oared boat, and had a beautiful breeze all down the lake, arriving in Galway about half-past two o'clock. It being the assize time in Galway, beds could not be procured at any price scarcely, but I had no sooner stepped out of the boat than I was accosted by somebody's "tea-boy." "Want a bed, Sir? Get one at Mrs. Lynch's, Sir. Only one left. Seven counsellors in the house. Now Sir, one left this morning. Only a guinea, Sir." Not wishing to pay a guinea to be in the same house with seven counsellors, I went up to Tongue's, where I dined. In the evening we went to the Assize Ball.

Here I was introduced to a host of Blakes, Burkes, and Lynchs, whom I found a very nice set of people, and with much of the manner and hospitable ways of the Highlanders of Scotland. It was a capital Ball, and was kept up till half-past four, a.m.

Next day I inspected the town, and found it to answer the description of most Spanish towns, which I believe it originally was. It is very filthy in the back streets, and particularly about the market. There is a race of people in Galway called the "Claddagh," whose sole mode of living is by fishing. They are an extraordinary race of people, keeping entirely to themselves, having their own laws, and all their disputes being settled by their own king. The men are a fine, stout, hardy set, and the women, with their peculiar dress, red stockings, and very robust appearance, are extraordinary to look upon. Galway in the summer is resorted to by all the fashionables from long distances round, being a great place for bathing, and I think more carriages are seen driving along its narrow streets than even Cork can boast of.

The people here, ladies included, as at Portobello, near Edinburgh, bathe along the rocks, close under the public promenade and drive. At Portobello the bathing sand was the principal promenade and ride, and I believe made so on purpose that they might witness the antics, splashing, etc., of the bathers.

After seeing the town, I fished for an hour in the river above and under the bridge in the town, where I saw the salmon lying as thick as they could, waiting to get up, but I could not stir one of them, and returned with only one sea trout. It is very seldom that the salmon will rise there. A shrimp to troll with is the best and surest bait, but it is not allowed. *Why?* I can't tell

I heard a man speaking of some woman and telling an anecdote of her. I inquired if she was good-looking?

"Indeed, then, she wasn't, she wore a bonnet!" was the reply. Now, I could not find out if her being ill-looking obliged her to wear a bonnet, or whether good looking women did not require them to set them off. These Patlanders are queer fellows. I heard two men arguing a point, when at last one of them said as a clencher, "*Bad luck* to your *lice!*" and walked off.

The following day I left Galway for Portumna, where I dined with the 32nd and got back to Birr at night.

August the 14th was Portumna Regatta, when I had an invitation from Lady Avonmore to join their party, which I accepted. The day was calm and no breeze for the contending boats. Our shore party in the morning had nothing to do but to walk about with the ladies, however, in the afternoon I proposed we should get up foot races among the natives who were assembled. Barry Yelverton collected the subscriptions and laid out the course in the meadow below the house. We gave shilling stakes to be run for. The last leap on the course was the dock cut in the meadow for Lord Avonmore's yacht. This was sixteen feet wide and as many deep, a good jump for the natives when blown, and much too wide for many; some three or four out of eight or ten would clear it, but most of the others went splash into the middle. We had a Ball in the evening which went off very well, the people not going away till three o'clock in the morning.

August 19th. I joined Lady Avonmore's party at a luncheon, where were about fifty ladies and gentlemen who assembled in Birr for the purpose of seeing Lord Rosse's telescope. I had seen it before by night, when I had a look through it at the moon, or rather at a section, for the telescope magnified it so much that only a portion could be seen at a time. The moon through this had the appearance of newly molten silver which had dropped on the ground, with all the irregular pinnacles on it consequent upon its fall. It was as bright, and had the same appearance as silver, the outside edges being rough. We could also see dark spots like valleys or craters in several places. This was not the very largest telescope but the next to it, the speculum of the large one not being complete. It is suspended between two very high walls in the domain. The tube is so large that a man can walk down it without stooping. All the most beautiful workmanship of this telescope was executed by Lord Rosse himself.

August 18th. It being now the grouse-shooting season, I received a note from Mr. Walshe, of Walshe Park, saying he expected a friend down from Dublin to shoot on the 20th, and hoped I would come once to dine and sleep, to be ready to join him in the sport. I gladly accepted the kind offer, which was quite unexpected by me.

August 20th. Saw me up at three o'clock. a.m., and on the bog at half-past four. I shot till breakfast, and killed two and a half brace. I had to return to Birr for a Court-Martial, but went back in the afternoon and met Willington. We shot together with the keeper, Jemmy Mara. The total bag of the day, which was considered good, was nine brace. We remained at Walshe Park to dine and sleep, and were up at six the next morning, killing seven and a half brace of grouse. We picked up a brace of grouse *alive*! They must have been too frightened, or fascinated by the dog's eye to move.

Jemmy Mara, the keeper, was a queer fellow. Mr. Walshe always had him into the smoking room after dinner to give him his glass of grog, and hear him talk. He used to attend Mr. Walshe when out shooting, always carrying a gun himself for his own protection; even when he went to chapel, he never was without his gun. However, on two occasions, Mr. Walshe had narrow escapes. Once, on going through a hedge, Jemmy was following, when his gun went off, and the charge went between Mr. Walshe's arm and his side, luckily without injuring him. Another time they were together, Master Jemmy's gun went off, the charge closely passing Walshe's head. These were accidental circumstances, and

Mr. Walshe said *he did not think* Jemmy *intended to shoot him*; nevertheless, he did not like going with him again, and gave up shooting in consequence. Jemmy was not a good-tempered man, and would not brook an insult. One day a carman, with three horses, met him; he began to laugh, and call Jemmy names, when Jemmy a deliberate aim at his nether end, and let fly. The man and horses got awfully peppered; the consequence was, that a warrant to apprehend my friend was issued, but he told his story to his master, who very considerately kept him in close confinement in his cellar till the affair had blown over. One of the days he accompanied Willington and myself out on the bog with his gun, he missed one or two shots. In the morning we went to the house for lunch, all the guns being placed for security in the smoking-room. During the time Jemmy was eating his luncheon, we drew the shot out of both his barrels, and on going out again, we bet him five shillings that he missed the two first birds we fired at. "Done," says Jemmy. Presently we heard his gun go bang, bang, and saw the birds flying away. He was furious, and swore we had drawn his charge, but we did not let him know that we had done so, or we might not have been safe ourselves. "By the holy Moses," says Jemmy, "it was a dirty trick, and a dangerous one too. By my faith, I'd not shoot in such company, if I knew it. Och! but only suppose a "ferry' had come and asked me for *me* gun, what 'ud I ha' done, and no shot in *me barr'ls*. Och sure, it was not right!" And so went on Jemmy till he got his grog in the smoking-room in the evening. This was the only grouse-shooting I had there, killing twenty-three grouse in four days' shooting.

I got leave to shoot on the O'Moore's bogs, near Ballinasloe, and went there for a couple of days, staying at the Hotel. The grouse were very wild and scarce; I only bagged seven birds, and returned disgusted with the sport.

September 13th. We got the route for Killaloe.

KILLALOE

THE scenery about Killaloe is very fine, particularly up Lough Dearg to Scariff and Dromanier. Above these places it becomes tamer as you proceed towards Portumna, the other extremity of the lake. The Craig mountain and others are lofty and bold, rising immediately behind the town, which is itself built on the side of a very steep hill. The main street is so steep that all carts are obliged to go round the town to get to the upper part.

There is a very good Hotel here, where may be had comfortable beds, and." entertainment for man and horse."

A steamer plies up and down Lough Dearg, between Killaloe and Portumna, daily, which gives an excellent opportunity of viewing the beauties which surround the Lake, and the Company to which this steamer belongs are kind enough to give the officers a free passage whenever they like to take a trip.

We had some nice society here. The Bishop of Killaloe was very hospitable and kind. There were also the Maynes, Gonigs of Broadford, and others, and my old friends of Portumna and Walshe Park were comparatively near by steamer.

The shooting around Killaloe is very poor. It is necessary for the sportsman here to be well armed, and to have his wits about him, while shooting in the neighbourhood, for a man is never safe unless he has a brace of pistols to protect himself and gun, when he has fired both barrels. I always carried a brace of pistols when out shooting, but I never had to use them, partly because it was pretty well known that I had them, and that I should not hesitate to use them if occasion required. As a general rule in Ireland, never allow any countryman or farmer to follow or attend you *on any pretence whatever*, when shooting.

I was followed one day when out shooting with Simon

Purdon, at Bird Hill, by five men, all armed. They concealed themselves so well, and dodged us so quietly, that neither of us knew of the circumstance till the evening, long after we returned home. They had never had a chance of attacking us when unloaded, as we seldom both fired at the same time, there being but few snipe.

Colonel Purefoy's sportsman, an Englishman, had bragged that he would defy any set of *Irishmen* to take his gun from him. He carried a brace of pistols. One day he was out on the Bird Hill Ground, when two respectable looking farmers entered into conversation with him, and offered to shew him lots of snipe. They were in company all day, and when he gave up shooting, they bade him good night, but *accidentally discovered* they were all going the same road. They had not proceeded far when one of the rascals dropped to the rear, felled the keeper with a stroke of a stick on the head, and taking his gun, took to their heels. Here his pistols were of no use, as he had not time to use them.

A boy of sixteen or seventeen was shooting at O'Brien's Bridge in November. He was watched by a scoundrel, and when he had fired one barrel, and was reloading, this villain rushed at him. The boy fired in a hurry, and unfortunately missed the fellow, who took the gun, and absconded. I used to say the chances were even whether I shot an Irishman or not, any day that I went out with my gun.

On the 21st of September, we were all in Church, when I got a requisition from Mr. Mayne, the Magistrate, for my Detachment, to quell a riot in Balling. I immediately turned all the men out of Church, went down with fixed bayonets at the "double," and took possession of the bridge in front of the Roman Catholic Chapel, where the service was just finished. The riot was caused by two "factions," who agreed to fight it out like Christians. On leaving the Chapel after Mass, they began in good earnest, but my glittering steel, and forming up

167

in front of them at double time, turned their attention from their private quarrel. The Police then rushed in, and made prisoners of the ringleaders; so finished the row without my interference.

My horse having dropped lame again, in taking a gallop through some fields, I determined to send him to Ballinasloe Fair, where I sold him to Mr. Byrne, V.S. I was now on the look out for another hunter, and went to look at one belonging to a Mr. Biggs with Barry Yelverton. I did not like him, he Was too much screwed; however, I heard he was the best screw in the country, and that no horse in the Ormond Hunt could go across a stone wall country like him. On hearing such a character of him, and his price being only £25, I deputed my friend N—, of the Royals, to get me a trial of the horse with the Ormond Hounds. He wrote, asking me to breakfast with him at Nenagh, and saying the horse would be ready for me at Kilcoleman. I went over accordingly, but found Mr. Biggs had not sent him *for trial.* I therefore said I would have nothing to do with him, and ordered him back to Mr. Biggs, who immediately returned him, saying he had *sold* the horse. As I had not deputed N— to buy the horse, I would have nothing to say to him, and told N— he might do as he pleased about him, so Master N— had to pay the money. We found out that he had requested Lloyd to get the horse for me, and they between them, in misunderstanding one another after dinner, *bought* the animal. However, as he had got the horse on his hands in trying to do me a service, said I would take him and sell him for what I could. I sent him his £25, and rode the horse (which I called Archimedes) on the 18th with the Ormond, when I found he went blind in half-an-hour, and gave me an awful roll by galloping into a ditch. His eyes could not stand the oats. I afterwards sold him for £10.

One day Going of Broadford sent to say he had a brother who wanted just such a horse to drive about, and asked me to send him over to look at. I rode there with

Galway, of the Police, and having put the horses in the stable, we proceeded to luncheon, after which we all went to look at Archimedes, when, to my dismay, he had kicked down the stall, and cleared the place of all the grooms!! I rode him home again.

The state of the country about this time was very disturbed. Mr. Philips, a magistrate, from Bird Hill, was attacked by two ruffians in the middle of the day, on the road to Limerick; he wounded one, and took *both* prisoners. Mr. Philips was always armed with pistols to the amount of eight barrels. Threatening notices were posted on Ogonolue Chapel, etc. I visited the house in which a woman and child were blown up by gunpowder in a piece of turf exploding in the fire. A Patrol of Police was attacked on the night of the 8th of December, and one man shot through both arms.

Five hundred Terry Alts assembled at Newport, half of them in arms. Three policemen were shot; many houses attacked and robbed of arms.

I was now ordered to escort Pat Hogan, alias Ned Hogan, (*who had been on the run for a long time*, but was at last captured by the Police,) half-way to Nenagh with the whole of my Company, 72 *men*, and then to send him on under charge of Hawkes and 35 men. The country was in such a state that the authorities thought a rescue would be attempted; however, although the town was crowded, and the people all came in from the fields to console and con. dole with him, they did not attempt to interfere with the escort. He was supposed to be implicated in several murders and other crimes. He afterwards turned approver or King's Evidence, by which he hung and transported several of his friends, and saved his own neck. After his capture, above 200 people left the Counties of Tipperary and Clare, in fear of being peached on by him, and the country was comparatively quiet. After his release from gaol, he enlisted in the 73rd, at Clare Castle. On one occasion he was sent on escort duty to Nenagh, when he was recognized by the people, and it was with great difficulty he was protected from being murdered.

The almost universal failure of the potato-crop caused the greatest distress all over Ireland, particularly in the South.

Having been at Killaloe for four months, which was the period fixed for Detachments to be absent from Head Quarters, and finding it rather dull, I applied to be relieved; consequently, on the 30th of January we were relieved, and marched through Tulla to rejoin Head Quarters at Clare Castle.

CLARE CASTLE

CLARE Castle we found a dull place, and as long as I was quartered in the Castle, we received very little hospitality.

My only amusement was shooting, which was not good.

My game list this last season, 1845 and 1846, was very poor, having been in bad stations for sport. Total head, 227. Days out, 53.

As to the fishing here, I thought the Castle Fergus river in the tide was the best: it was dirty work, the mud being knee deep, and the best time for fishing when the tide begins to back water; I have risen several salmon there and caught trout weighing 2 lbs. I caught a salmon in Banatyne's meadow, in Ennis, weighing 11 lbs. In this same meadow are large pike, also tolerable pike and perch fishing up the river about the mill.

There is nothing wonderful to see in this part of Clare. Quin Abbey, three miles from Ennis, is a very beautiful ruin, and in a good state of preservation. It was a custom there to throw out the skulls and bones found when digging graves in the burying ground and to place them in a mass against the old ruin. I saw there a heap of heads, arm and leg bones eight or nine feet high. I believe they have since been buried.

February 24th. It being Ennis Assizes, and the magistrates and judges thinking it not safe to bring in the police from the rural districts on account of the disturbed state of the country, I was ordered down with Hawkes and my Company to Ennis where we were billeted, the men being put up in the jail. We furnished a guard at the court house every day during the time that the judges sat; frequently from 9.0 a.m. to 7.0 p.m., or sometimes 8.30 or 9.0 o'clock p.m. We were both obliged to be in attendance, and had to escort the prisoners to and from their van; however, on the 2nd of March old judge Lefroy sentenced the prisoners, and we marched back to Clare Castle.

The distress was very great at this time, and the people had but little to live on; subscriptions were opened, and public works begun, such as mending roads, lowering hills on them, and making new roads to give employment. The Roman Catholic Priest and the Protestant Clergyman worked hand in hand to alleviate the sufferings of their flocks, and superintended them at their works without regard to their different creeds. Colonel Goldie also gave great assistance in their plans and attended the meetings of the magistrates and guardians to give his advice and superintend the works that were going on. He did a great deal of good, and in many cases urged the gentry to *act* instead of *talk* which they were inclined to do. He was afterwards presented with a handsome snuff box and a vote of thanks for his services. Meal was sent round from Limerick in vessels, but they were so often plundered that a war steamer was obliged to be sent to protect them. There were thousands that had nothing but what was given them, as their own potatoes had failed; and these behaved much better than could be expected from starving people, namely, they did not rob the farmers of their sheep and cattle. Many cattle were slaughtered and their flesh carried off, but in no instance I believe by the *really* destitute, but by those who wanted to profit by the general distress of the country. However, they were mostly all found out and received their deserts.

On the 17th of March, Mr. Carrig, a magistrate, who lived about three miles in the country, had been attending one of the meetings for the relief of the poor, and on his return home in the evening he was shot from behind a wall at Tureen and died next day. In consequence of this murder, and the disturbed state of the public mind in Ennis, I was ordered down there with Bell and 40 men.

ENNIS

LORD DOWNS commanded the Limerick District, and inspected the Depot at Clare and my Detachment at Ennis on the 5th of May.

I passed a very pleasant time at Ennis, and received a great deal of hospitality from the Johnstone of Willow Bank, William and Tom Keane, William O'Brien, and J. Crowe. Wainwright Crowe was a very good fellow.

May 25th. I went with the Johnstone to see the Cliffs of Maher which are 900 feet high. The day turned out foggy, which prevented our seeing much of the Cliffs, yet we spent it very pleasantly. Billy Taylor, 66th Regiment, went there a few days before we did, and on inquiring if there were any eggs on the cliffs, (as he saw such thousands of *puffins*,) he was told there were plenty, upon which he set a lot of boys to collect them, as he said they were the best eggs laid. He collected a great number and brought them home. When he arrived he was asked what he intended doing with them? "Eating them, to be sure? They would bring a lot of money in London. Did you never hear of *puffin's* eggs being rarities?" "*Never*, Billy," was the reply; "but we all have heard of *plovers*." "What a fool I am," he said; "I meant Plovers, and have been at all this bother about these confounded things."

What a laugh we had at him! This was much the same sort of thing as occurred once in Ireland. Two men who had been in the Mediterranean were conversing at a dinner party, when the one, telling of the wonders fie had seen in that climate, stated that he had seen *anchovies* grow there on the bushes in great abundance. The other man said he must be mistaken; however, he persisted in his statement and called his friend out for contradicting him. On the signal, each fired, when the positive man's ball took effect in his adversary's heart. The shot man sprang convulsively in the air and fell, when the other, slapping his thigh, exclaimed, "By— ! it was *capers* I meant! "

The month of June this year was the hottest I ever experienced in England or Ireland. The thermometer on the 16th was at 111° in the sun, and on the 17th 112°.

June 18th. To our great regret we left Ennis. The heat of the weather being so tremendous, I marched off my men at 4.30 a.m. for Tulla, en route for Templemore.

23rd. I went to Limerick, picked up Daniell, late 66th, and proceeded to Ennis for the purpose of attending Spaniel Hill Fair on the following day. At this fair I bought a horse for £40, the only one there up to my weight. Having got settled down at Templemore, I obtained a few days' fishing at Castle Connell, on the Shannon, through the good offices of Captain Trench.

July 6th. I was up at two o'clock in the morning to meet the mail by which I arrived at Castle Connell about eight. I commenced fishing in Lord Charles Kerr's and Mr. Thacker's waters, which are considered the best, at eleven o'clock and flogged away till eight o'clock in the evening, only catching three peal and rising none. My fishing guide who lived there told me it was no use trying before eleven o'clock, so I was green enough to believe him, (the rascal,) thinking he must know better than I. I did not begin fishing in consequence till that hour. On the 7th I fished all day, till nine o'clock p.m., and killed four peal weighing severally 5 lbs., 5½, and 6 lbs. The water was low and the fish not inclined to take. I saw a large number of salmon rolling about but they were not in a playful humour. The fish not taking at all, I returned to Templemore.

About the 10th of August I made an application for leave of absence to go to Scotland, which having succeeded, I sent off my dogs by canal boat to Dublin.

I arrived at Fort William, per steamer, on the 17th of August. Met Lord Abinger on board and made acquaintance with Lord Hatherton and Mr. Lyttleton.

I went on to Inch. Here I enjoyed myself as much as I have always done when receiving the hospitality and kindness of my friends: passing the days in walking, riding, and shooting, and the nights in dancing, laughing, and talking till near the small hours. Oh! for the Highlands! *that* is the place to laugh and enjoy yourself. One's spirits get raised by the pure air and the people one associates with, so that in a very short time one scarcely knows one's self.

August 19th. Took out my gun for the first time, and after breakfasting at Blarour, I and B— North trotted off tor the Tulloch beat, where I bagged 14 brace of grouse.

August 25th. Went again to Blarour to shoot with North, but found they had changed the amusement of the day into a picnic where the ladies were to accompany the gentlemen shooting. I was not to be done so easily, and went up to Roughburn with Duncan Mc Kay. I bagged 10½ brace, he 5½ brace. We returned to Blarour where we danced till two o'clock in the morning.

August 27th. Went down to Fort William, and shot with Fraser and Crichton, to Loch Ailt, (Fraser's shooting box,) accompanied by the ladies on their ponies on the road. We arrived at Loch Ailt at eight o'clock well done up. I bagged 5½ brace.

There is a nice little lake in front of the Box where the ladies amused themselves by catching small trout whilst we were shooting. The scenery is as wild as it can possibly be; for the last ten miles of the way there is a track used by the shepherds only, and very difficult to ride. On the 28th our total bag, between five guns, was 63 brace of grouse, and one brace of hares.

29th. We all left the Box, and I shot, on my return, to Larrick Moor, about half way, killing 4J brace. Here my dogs got quite done up, so I joined the ladies on the road, and returned to Inch.

September 1st. Went out shooting with North's friend up Roughburn. Did not begin till twelve o'clock. I killed 71 brace, he 51 brace of grouse. I had the satisfaction of "wiping his eye" three times, at about 70 or 80 yards.

TEMPLEMORE

I REJOINED the Depot at Templemore on the 8th of September.

October 26th. The country getting disturbed again, all leave was cancelled in Ireland. A mob arose in the town of Templemore, attacked the bakers' shops and cleared them. Our Depot were ordered out to the rescue, but the mob had dispersed, and eaten the bread by the time they got to the scene of action.

Prince George of Cambridge, commanding the Limerick District, came over and inspected us, and the 10th Depot. We were brigaded in the Barrack Square, Colonel Goldie commanding. I commanded the 66th Depot, and got on famously. Colonel Goldie, Trench, and myself met H. R. Highness at dinner at the 70th Mess, when he did me the honour of *twice* asking me to take wine with him.

There were a number of gentry living round Templemore, principally retired officers of the Army, but not one of them had the generous feeling even to leave a card on the mess, or on any individual.

Most of the families around are in some way connected either by marriage or cousinship, and it is said the military are kept at a distance in consequence of two elopements having taken place from here. But why should their sins be visited upon whole Regiments and Depots who come after them?

As to the hunting, we had but little. There was a pack of wretched harriers kept by a Mr. L—, just outside the gate of the Barracks; I went with them once to train my horse, but nothing more. The Ormond Hounds and the Ossory came within distance, and I went with the Kilkenny a few times from Templemore. The Ossory are a well appointed pack, in good order.

November 18th. Went with Bigge, 70th, to meet the Kilkenny hounds at Balief Castle, having sent on our horses to Johnston, twenty miles, the previous night. These hounds are the crack pack in Ireland, under the superintendence of Sir John Power; they are certainly in splendid condition, well appointed and turned out. The Bitch pack are the quickest and fastest pack I ever saw. We had a bad day's work, and rode home, 19 miles.

28th November. I got leave and went to England, where we had a hard frost all December, and January, 1847.

I stayed at Davenport, where our principal amusement was in shooting and playing billiards. I shall record one or two days' sport out of the lot.

December 4th. Beat the Pool covert and Cranmere bog with the Squire and Campbell. Total bag, 24 hares, 13 pheasants, 11 rabbits, and one woodcock, out of which I killed 14 hares, 4 pheasants, and 5 rabbits. Home to luncheon at three o'clock.

December 11th. I shot at Coton with Edward Gatacre, Charlton Whitmore, and General Davidson. There had been a great fall of snow in the night, and the bushes and twigs had it half-an-inch thick lying on them, which prevented our seeing any distance in the coverts. The hares were running back as well as to the front. Edward Gatacre therefore requested we should keep in line up the dingles, as then no accident could happen by shooting to the rear. We started Edward Gatacre on the right, C. Whitmore and myself in the centre, and the General on the left. After we had beaten half-way up the dingle, the General not liking his pocket filled with snow at every step, went outside the coverts, and got on in front of our guns, as he said, "to stop the hares at the end," leaving us to imagine he was in his proper position. A hare crossed before me, whose hind legs I broke, but as she was scrambling into the bushes, I let fly the other barrel to finish her. Presently we came to the end of the covert, go yards further, when the General's attendant met me, saying, "You've shot the General, Sir." Here we found him bleeding profusely from the face. My two shots at the hare were the ones that had peppered him. They had carried on through the bushes; two went through his upper lip, and lodged in the gum, one went through his ear, and two lodged in his thigh. I dare say they were very painful, and sharp too, as it was a frosty day, but they were not dangerous wounds. It was entirely his own fault for getting on to the dingle without letting us know where he was. It was an old trick of his, I heard, and he had been often cautioned before that he would get shot.

The total bag of the day was 47 pheasants, 37 hares, 23 rabbits, 2 moorhens, 1 woodcock, 1 wild duck. Total, 111 head, of which I killed 20 pheasants and 9 hares, and wounded a General.

January 5th, 1847, I went up to London, and on the 31st returned to Templemore.

On going down a hill between Abeyleix and Templemore, where one half of the road had been cut away to lower it, (more for the sake of giving employment to the poor than anything else,) the mail upset into the ditch, and fell against the bank. After breaking two traces, we had to take out the horses, unload the coach, and *force* a fat elderly gentleman to get out, then put our shoulders to the wheel before we could get it right again. Several countrymen were looking on, but could not be prevailed upon to assist for a long time, as they said the Guard would not give them a ride when he *met* them, (i.e., overtook them on the road,) but always made them get off the steps of the mail.

THURLES

FEBRUARY 8th, 1847. I marched out of Templemore with Kendall, my subaltern, and 58 rank and file, to Thurles. We found the Barracks little better than a barn, in a very tumble down state, and the town itself a miserable place, but we were soon reconciled to it by the hospitality we received from several of the gentlemen around, Nick Maher of Tertulla in particular. He wanted me to take up my abode altogether in his house, and when I told him I could not do that as I should be a mile from my men, he said, "Oh, as for that, you can have them paraded up here on the drive every morning, so that need not prevent you."

"But," I replied, "suppose anything was to happen in the town and I and my men were wanted?" "Why, a man could run up here in ten minutes and let you know; so now, you understand, you will live here, and you shall have a room to yourself." "I am much obliged to you, but I really must decline your kind offer on the score of duty alone, which will not permit me to accept it." He was nearly being angry with me for not taking a bed after dining there. It was only a mile from my own and I preferred sleeping at home.

Mrs. Maher was a particularly agreeable, nice person, and handsome. Her sister who always lived there was a nice person also. They both sang and played splendidly, and Lablache said they were his best lady pupils. They always had somebody staying there. I found it the most pleasant house to be at of any I ever saw in England or Ireland. The comfort of everything, the pleasant evenings, the beautiful singing, etc.

One evening, after dinner, I was playing billiards with Prendergast, the ladies looking on. Mrs. Maher said she would back my play. "Done," said Prendergast, "for £5." I won it, won another and another, until the stake on me, by betting double or quits, and an odd bet or two, amounted to £48. I lost the last game, and the £48 for

Mrs. Maher.

Another evening a party sat down to loo and continued playing till the pool amounted to £152, when they got frightened and gave up the game; Mrs. Maher winning £115 from her cousin Prendergast, which I dare say she never intended to receive. We went to supper at six o'clock, a.m., after which I went home. The ladies did not go to bed at all, but walked to the post for their letters.

We used to dine there twice or three times a week, and sometimes I have dined there five out of the seven days in the week! Mr. Wilson of Raheen Park called on us, and we experienced great kindness from him and his family. We visited also Major Armstrong's family at Farney Castle.

March 22nd. I was confined to the town most of the day in consequence of the peasantry being riotously inclined and threatening to attack the shops. The magistrates called out my Company and we chewed ourselves in the town for an hour, when there being no riot we returned to our Barracks. For several days the town was crowded with discontented and starving people in consequence of the Public Works being stopped for want of funds. They came in in great numbers one afternoon about four o'clock when I was at Portulla. We had a Ball there; the 70th Band in attendance after dinner. The mob heard there was a party at Maher's and decided upon marching up to the supper, but fortunately they had no one to head them, and did not come. However, if they had I am sure a few words from Maher (who is supposed to be a Repealer) would have quieted them at once and dispersed the mob.

The 28th of March was a Fast Day by order of the Queen in consequence of the famine in the country.

My game list has a greater variety in it this season as I had shooting in Scotland, Ireland, and England. It shows the average sport to have been 9 head a day.

The fishing at Thurles is not good. There is the river Suir in which *are* salmon if you could only catch them. We had the Archerstown Hounds belonging to Mr. Langley only two miles from us—the Tipperary and the Kilkenny occasionally within distance.

February 22nd. Met Langley's hounds at Killaskean, which we drew blank, but the hounds took a hare away to the "Devil's Bit" about three miles, no one following them, thinking they would return. We waited till one o'clock when they were collected. Drew Raelhasty, found between two and three o'clock, and ran through Fishmoyne round to the back of Burros-o-leigh, turned off for Killaskean, was headed up the hills and went right over to the top of Clanbreda, where we flogged off in sight of Castle Otway, being the only check in one hour; Langley and myself being the only ones up. — 70th Regiment, went to within a mile of the finish when he pulled up; none of the rest of the field within miles. We three were riding fifteen stone each!

March 10th. Met the Tipperary Hounds at Kilcooly, having sent my horse on to Lloyd's of Fennar the night previous. Had a run of one hour and three quarters to the Devil's Punch Bowl, near Freshford. Drew Waterloo and had a very good fast ring of twenty minutes. This was the last of the season for me. *Woohoop*!

I now, to my sorrow, got my orders to "move on" accordingly on the 6th of April we were relieved by Captains Reynolds and Wellington of the 70th and marched to Cashel.

April 7th. I writ on my Company under Holmes to Cahir, and after visiting the celebrated Rock of Cashel, on which are the remains of a fine old Abbey, I followed, and reported our arrival to Colonel Sewel, 8th Hussars, who were quartered there, and with whom we dined.

April 8th. We left Cahir at nine in the morning, arriving at Clogheen at twelve. Here we found a troop of the Greys, quartered under the command of Captains Sullivan and Hibbert. Clogheen is a miserable little town situated in a wild, bleak, and barren tract. It was described to us as a good quarter; there being very tolerable fishing, snipe, woodcock, wild duck, and other shooting to be had. Next morning I marched again at half-past eight, and after a wet walk over the Kilworth Hills, arrived in Fermoy, having passed through the village of Ballyporeen, so celebrated in the song of the "Wedding of Ballyporeen." I noticed two sign boards over the beer shops; the one was the "Wedding," the other the "Christening" of Ballyporeen.

FERMOY

HERE we found the 16th and 82nd Depots quartered, also a Squadron of the Scots Greys, under Major (alias Darby) Griffiths, Captain Grant, Scobell, and Hozier.

There are Barracks at Fermoy capable of holding three or four Regiments, but the new Barracks were let or leased to the town Corporation for a Hospital, and never was it more wanted for that purpose than just at this time, for the "fever" was raging through the country; what fever it was, was not known; it was not scarlet, typhus, putrid, or any that had hitherto had a name. It came with the potato failure and consequent famine, and took off hundreds of hundreds. During the time I was there the poor were dying in that Hospital at the rate of 25 a day on an average. It had very peculiar features, namely, two out of three of the lower class who were attacked *might* recover, but scarcely *one* in six of the higher order ever got over it —it took them off in one or two days. Another peculiar thing was this, that when the fever made its appearance in a town all the lodging-house keepers turned their lodgers into the street, and no one would take them in. These unfortunates, therefore, had to live under the hedges and rocks in the open air, ex. posed to all weathers, and consequently were not long in being attacked with fever, and with nothing to support them. I knew of about a dozen of them all in fever, living among the rocks near Lismore. Some of their friends used to get them a little soup from the public soup kitchen, and I have often when fishing there pitched them a shilling a piece. All these recovered; *not one died*. It was the case everywhere, that the people who had fever and were exposed to the open air all recovered. Starvation and famine were now very great, particularly at Schull and Skibbereen on the south coast, but everything was exaggerated and magnified tenfold. I had a £5 note sent me to distribute to worthy objects, but so many impostors were there that it took me a month to distribute it in half-crowns and shillings. One day the

Cork Mail came into Fermoy, I happened to be looking on at the men changing horses, when a woman came up to the passengers and stated that she had not tasted food for three days, that she was starving like all the rest, and did not know how she should get a bit of bread. About an hour afterwards this same woman came into a stationer's shop with the same story. I then reminded her that I had given her half-a-crown at the Post Office *just before* the Mail arrived. I detected two men at different times and places begging for means to *bury their only sons*, who were lying dead in their cabins. These men kept up the same story for a month or more, and not recollecting me, asked alms of me several times.

None of the soldiers caught the fever of the time, except the Sergeant Major of the 16th Depot, who died under the treatment of their Assistant Surgeon. — .

On the 1st of May Lord M— applied to Colonel Goldie for troops to march to Kilworth, in aid of the civil power, as he apprehended there would be some riot, and excesses committed, even if the people did

not attack the house of M— in consequence of their being struck off the Public Works.

The morning was one of those lowering, dark, drizzly ones that indicate a regular wet day, and so it turned out—a thorough soaker. Two Companies of the 66th Regiment, two of the 16th, and half a troop of the Scots Greys, paraded at nine o'clock, a.m., and at half-past ten arrived in front of M— House. His Lordship walked past us (giving us a bow as he did so) to attend a meeting just outside his gate. We had piled arms, and were standing in groups grumbling at the weather, and were allowed to do so, for Lord M— had not even the politeness to ask us into his house, or tell us where we might get shelter from the pouring rain, which was coming down incessantly. About one o'clock some of us got very hungry and obtained leave to go, a few at a time, to the Public-house, where we got some eggs and bacon and whiskey, after which we returned to the park and lighted our cigars.

Lady M. is a good soul I believe; and at four o'clock p.m. she took compassion on us, by sending her compliments and saying luncheon was prepared for us, and hoped we would go in, but the invitation came so late, and all were in such a sulky humour at being allowed to remain outside all the day, that only two or three went in and had some wine.

As it turned out, there was no disposition whatever on the part of the people to make a disturbance, so we returned to our Barracks at 6 o'clock.

CASTLETOWN ROACH

ON the 12th of June I went out to Castletown Roach to relieve Biscoe, taking over his detachment of Kendall and his men.

Castletown Roach was 10 miles from Fermoy, nevertheless I had to go frequently in to preside at Courts Martial, and sit on Boards. This was not so inconvenient as it would appear, for one of us was obliged to go to market once or twice a week and get things from the Mess, as we could get nothing at all, not even tea and sugar in the small village of Castletown Roach. Hozier of the Scots Greys very kindly lent me his dog-cart for as long a time as they remained at Fermoy, and I found my horse an excellent one in harness'

We had but little society, though there were numbers of landed gentry living around us, not one of whom did us the honour of calling upon us, although we were sent into that out of the way place for the protection of their property.

One of the few places we visited was at the Smythes' of Castle Widenham. They very kindly gave us leave to shoot rooks, rabbits, or any thing else, and fish in the domain. We used to meet there the Creaghs of Doneraile, Smythes of Ballinatray near Youghal, the Mountcashel family, &c., and used to have some fun occasionally.

June 28th. I drove Kendall to Killdollery Fair as he called it, to try to get a horse and sell Colonel Goldie's old chestnut, which we did not succeed in doing. We returned through Doneraile, and lunched at Castle Creagh. In returning from thence we had to pass down a hill, one half of which had been cut away to the depth of six feet, leaving only just room for the wheels of a cart to go down the side that was left. To prevent accidents they had put up a parapet of loose stones about two feet high on the verge of the pit which they had cut. When we began to descend, my horse did not like the heavy weight pressing so much on him, and sidled a little, which caused the wheels to touch one of the loose stones on the parapet. The noise of this rattling made him start, the wheel caught the wall, and twisted the horse over it into the chasm, and of course the cart followed. Just as it was on the topple, I told Kendall and my groom to look out for themselves, and I jumped out with the reins in my hand, and landed all right on my feet. They in their alarm cleared the six or seven feet of road that had been cut away, and lit in the hedge. The cart turned topsy-turvy, and the horse I managed to keep down till we got assistance. However at last we got him up and into harness again, and found neither the horse hurt nor the cart much damaged.

This was the second upset I had *into* the "*Public Improvements.*"

On the 29th June, I was ordered into Fermoy to take command of the Depot during Biscoe's absence.

FERMOY

We had but little society here, and should have found it dull enough if we had not exerted ourselves more than is usually the case. The country round is pretty, and there are some nice rides through Castle Hyde, Moorpark, Ballyhooly and to the vale of the Bride, and all along the banks of the Blackwater. The fishing near Fermoy is not good. The Blackwater which runs through the town has salmon in it in plenty, but it is always either too muddy or too low, and it is seldom one hears of any being caught above Lismore.

I used to drive down there frequently to fish, (19 miles,) put up at the Hotel which is very good, and fish the river below the bridge from five o'clock to nine o'clock, p.m., and from three to seven o'clock, a.m. Here you see hundreds of salmon leaping clean out of the water as they come up the rapids. Only a very few people are allowed to fish here. I obtained leave from Mr. Cliff who had charge of the weirs. I found one or two fishermen there flogging away, who had had no sport for a week. They were fishing with very small flies as the water was low and clear. In general this is the rule of fishing, but I tried the exception by putting on large Spring, flies, and on the 2nd of July, between half-past seven and ten, p.m., I hooked one large salmon, (which I lost through having last year's gut on my line,) and rose three others.

The next morning I fished from four-till eight o'clock, a.m., when I killed one salmon of 8½-lbs. and rose another. As soon as I hooked the 8½-lb. fish, it ran up the stream, accompanied by another, and whichever way it turned, the other stuck to its side, and continued to do so, till I brought my victim close to the bank to be gaffed. It was a question whether this was its mate, or whether it accompanied it in consequence of its being in distress. I have often seen the same thing occur, in St. Vincent, West Indies, when catching the river mullet.

July 9th. I went again to Lismore, and used large spring flies, and between half-past eight and half-past nine o'clock, p.m., I rose four fish and hooked two, both of which I *lost by using last year's tackle*! For trout fishing I do not recommend the Blackwater. That impostor "Ephemera" who writes epistles in the Times on fishing, recommends the Funcheon as one of the best rivers in the South of Ireland, and advises Englishmen to go over and try it. I know it much better than Ephemera, and know that it would not be worth while wasting your time there if you had the option of going anywhere else. Unfortunately I was tied by the leg, and for amusement more than to kill fish, I used to flog this *"most excellent stream,"* and never did I see a trout therein as large as a herring, but I have seen six or seven cross lines worked on it every evening that I have been there, with 18 to 20 flies each, which took out all the fish from sprat size to half-a-pound. The river Bride suffers the same treatment, and nothing larger than a herring is to be taken. So much for the fishing of Fermoy.

The shooting is very poor. There is a bog on the Cork road where I have seen snipe and killed a few. From there to Castle Lyons is the home heat, but it is *preserved* by Mr. Somebody in Cork. His keeper lives on the Cork road, just above the bog. The first shot I fired, brought him down on me and Ducie of the 16th. He was armed with an immense horse pistol and a bludgeon, and told us we could not shoot there. I chewed him a shilling, when the pistol was returned to his pocket, and he, said he would chew our *honours* the very best of shooting if we would come another day. The shilling made him our friend—and—easily purchased!

I drove Hozier over to Michelstown to see the "Caves" about six miles further on. They are well worth seeing, and are of very great extent. The people there *say* they reach nearly to Cork, (*only about* 36 *or* 40 *miles*!) It is necessary for the visitor to take at least seven or eight wax candles to be able to see them properly; each candle to be carried by an attendant, and these attendants must be dispersed to different parts with the lights. It is a labyrinth where a person may lose himself in a minute, and not find his way out again if he once leaves his guides. Some part of the caves are very lofty; and from the top hang stalactites of all shapes and sizes: others that have reached the ground are formed into magnificent pillars, (for one of which a gentleman offered £40!) Then again are seen large festoons as of drapery. Some of the passages are so narrow that one is obliged to creep almost on hands and knees, and squeeze oneself into the smallest compass. The guides there are the greatest impostors I ever met with at any show place. They will demand from five to ten shillings each for accompanying you. Hozier and I gave them 1s. each, and 2s. 6d. to the man at the house where the visitors' book is kept. In this book where we were asked to enter our names and state how satisfied we were with the civility, etc., etc. of our guides, I wrote their real characters, as being the most vile set of imposing rascals I had ever met with. These caves were discovered only a few years ago, by some men who were blasting a lime rock, and suddenly blew open an entrance.

On our return we called on Lord Kingstown at the Castle, who sheaved us all over his garden and conservatory. He has one of the largest in Ireland. Here we saw a single vine which had then on it 500 bunches of grapes after being trimmed of the superfluous ones.

July 26th. I drove Hozier down to Cappoquin, and from thence went in the steamer down the Black-water, through beautiful scenery, to Youghal, which is the most filthy, stinking town I ever was in, not excepting even Greenock.

The next day we had a bathe in the sea before breakfast, and afterwards inspected the old Cathedral, (in which is a fine Tomb of the Earls of Cork,) and Sir Walter Raleigh's house, which is not worth seeing, although it is a show place. Visitors are allowed to go all through it, even into the occupied sitting rooms, much to the inconvenience of the residents, and the confusion of the visitor, who is conducted so unceremoniously (as we were) into the presence of two or three ladies in the drawing-room, for the purpose of seeing some old carved oak on the mantel-piece.

August 19th, I went to stay at Nick Maher's, of Tertulla, for the grouse shooting on the morrow.

20th. We divided into parties; Captain Steele, 83rd, and I only bagged four brace. P— and L— served us all a dirty trick by being on the ground before daylight, and shot over all our beats before we commenced.

21st. I went out with Henry Herbert to Ballybeg Bog. I only got one shot at grouse, and came home disgusted. I gave up the shooting as a bad job, and returned to Fermoy.

24th. The Bachelors of the Garrison (i.e., of the 16th and 95th Depots, and my Detachment, Kendall and myself,) gave a splendid picnic to all the surrounding neighbourhood in Castle Hyde Park. About 110 people sat down to luncheon under shade of the large trees.

In the evening we all retired to the 95th Mess-room, where we held a capital Ball. The rooms were very nicely got up, and the avenues of laurels, etc., which led from the Ball-room to the supper rooms were excellently contrived, but were near being the cause of great alarm and accident. I had been standing in this avenue as a cool place, talking to a lady for about five minutes, when we suddenly heard a great crackling, and on turning round, discovered that the laurels were in a blaze; however, I soon managed to put it out without its being known.

We kept up the dancing till half-past four, a.m., when we handed the guests to their carriages, excepting one family. The mother being taken suddenly ill, was obliged to remain, attended by her two daughters, and Major Raines gave up his quarters for their accommodation. They remained there for a week or more before Mrs. M.

was able to remove to her residence near Cork.

On the 27th of August Sir Edward Blakeney inspected the Garrison.

Sir Edward said he would inspect the troops at eleven o'clock, but did not say what manoeuvres he wished to see them execute. Accordingly we were formed up in line to receive him. Scots Greys, (one troop on the right,) 16th, 95th, and two Companies of the 66th Regiment on the left. After presenting arms, we wheeled back in Mass of Battalion columns and marched past, then closed to quarter distance, and wheeled into a line of contiguous columns. Sir Edward then gave some orders, which nobody heard, except his A. D. C., who, like himself, was dismounted, and could not communicate them to the four Commanders at one moment. When the orders were delivered, they were not understood. Major Griffiths (Scots Greys) therefore galloped up to the General to know what the orders were, and having received them, turned his charger round, and dug in his spurs to go and execute them, when the horse let fly his heels at the General's head. Sir Edward became furious, swore like a trooper, and demanded why Major Griffiths rode a kicking horse on parade, ordering him *never* to do so again. The old horse had been a charger for seven or eight years, and never kicked in his life before. We got very unintelligible orders through the A. D. C., and the troops worked well *when* they got orders they could make anything of. However, the old General called us, the Commanding Officers, to the front, told us it was very plain the troops were never practised in Brigade movements, that they worked infamously, and were not half drilled. He ordered that there should be two Brigade field-days a week, under the senior officer, and said he should desire General Turner to come over frequently to inspect us. He left us in a towering rage, and drove off to Cork. This was all in consequence of Darby Griffith's horse's heels!

September 3rd. I went with Hozier to visit the monks

of La Trappe, at Mount Mellory, about three miles up the hills at the back of Cappoquin. These monks were driven out of France a few years ago, and all their property was confiscated. They then came over to Ireland, (only a very few in number,) and obtained a small patch of wild waste mountain land, where they established themselves, and by degrees, with great perseverance, managed to clear part of this rocky ground, upon which they now have a large establishment, with a fine Chapel in the centre. They allow those to join them who wish to do so, provided they can work at some trade, and have sufficient money to pay their entrance. They get up at two o'clock in the morning to work and pray, breakfast at six o'clock on bread and milk, and dine at four o'clock, p.m., on coarse bread, and, I think, vegetables. No meat is allowed at any time in the Monastery. They are *never allowed to speak*!

There is a very jolly fellow as porter to the establishment, who is allowed to speak to any strangers, and explain their rules and customs. He was very talkative with us, and after we had seen everything, he invited us to take some refreshment. He gave us some wine, whiskey, and bread and butter, which were very good, but he explained that they were not allowed to take anything stronger than water. He told us that Dan O'Connell had been there to retire from the world, but was not allowed by the rules to remain longer than a fortnight, without becoming one of them. He was allowed to eat meat, but it was a most extraordinary thing. We left them 2s. 6d. apiece, and drove to Castle View.

Having received a letter to say that poor Ajax had been ill, I made this an excuse to ask for leave, and drove into Cork to get Biscoe to go with me *instanter* to the Adjutant-General with an application for a fortnight, which, with some difficulty, was acceded to. I therefore returned to Fermoy, paid my bills, and left by the two o'clock p. m. mail, arriving at Worfield on the 27th of

September. Here I had some good partridge shooting, though I shot very badly, being "out of sorts," and very weak.

I returned to Cork on the morning of the 21st of October, and joined my Company at Ballincollig, where 8th Hussars were quartered. We found them a particularly nice set of fellows, and their Mess excellent. We had little to do here but ride, or hunt, or shoot.

November 6th. I marched into Cork with my Detachment of 100 men, to rejoin the Depot.

Cork I found much improved since I was quartered there in 1837. The shops are much finer and much larger. It is a good town, and ranks next to Dublin, but we had very little society there. We had a great deal of Garrison duty to do, particularly Courts-Martial, which often prevented me from having a day with the Ballyedmond Hounds when they came within reach. There was a pack of harriers kept by some *squireen*, (worth £150 per annum,) called the "*Cork Sneezers*;" I believe because some snuff manufacturer once kept them. I went out with them one day on the hills opposite Ballincollig; we found a fox laying out, and had a good run of about twenty minutes, when he went to ground.

December 4th. I sent my horse on to Garrane's, (about 12 miles,) to meet the Duhallow Hounds, and drove there in Benson's cart. The day turned out so tremendously wet that they did not throw in the hounds at all. I returned drenched to the skin, and went to bed with influenza, (which was very prevalent,) and I was confined to my room for eight days. Caulfield, Holmes, and Wainwright embarked with a Draft for Gibraltar.

KINSALE

ON the 11th of December the Depot marched out of Cork to Kinsale, where I rejoined, but was not allowed to remain long in the Barracks, as I was ordered to march with Ensign White and 60 men to Charles Fort. It is only two miles from Kinsale, though a separate command from the Barracks. We found the town of Kinsale every much dilapidated, a great number of houses of the first class were in ruins, with roofs off and windows smashed. Since we were quartered here in 1837, forty families had left the place, or died of cholera. It looked quite a deserted town; only two families remained that I had met there ten years before, namely John Heard, called the King of Kinsale, alias the Old Head of Kinsale, with his family, and Dr. Warren with his. I became acquainted with one or two others, the Herricks of Shippool, and Knowles of Oatlands. We might have had more society but for the failure of the potato crop. The famine and badness of the times nearly ruined everybody, and they could not afford to entertain. "The Green," which used to be the fashionable promenade, together with Compass Hill, were quite deserted, except on Sunday afternoons, when a few of the shopkeepers, etc., would appear there.

Being at Charles Fort, and my own master, with White, (who was no sportsman, and never wished to leave the Barracks as long as he had his pipe and Cavendish to smoke,) I had little to do but find amusement for myself, which I was at no loss for, having Benson's dog-cart and horse, besides my own horse to work, so that with shooting, hunting, and in the summer, fishing and boating, I managed to get on. There are six good beats for shooting, which I went over pretty frequently.

As for hunting, there were the Kinsale Club harriers, kept by Mr. Knowles of Oatlands. They were a nice pack and generally had good sport for harriers, but the country was very bad to ride over, all the fences being so very rotten, and in some parts very high. Mr. George

Denn also kept a pack. These were his own property and were of a small size, not much larger than beagles; it was very seldom they killed a hare, but they ran well, and their music was very pretty.

The Innishannon Hounds consisted of about twelve couple, six couple of which were kept by Mr. Sealy, and the remainder kept themselves about the village and were collected on hunting mornings. They are fox-hounds, but are used as harriers; however, they generally draw for a fox some of the Innishannon coverts, which are pretty sure finds; Shippool wood in particular, and when once they get on a fox they will not turn if a hare crosses them! Shippool wood is a favourite haunt for foxes. The summer of 1848, there were two litters there, and in the following winter the hounds had sixteen runs from it.

During January and February, 1848, I hunted often with all the packs. I shot very often, in fact almost every day that I had nothing else to do—frequently with Charles Knowles of Oatlands. I also had cock and partridge shooting with the Herricks of Shippool.

My subaltern, White, remarked one evening to me, "Why you are always hunting or shooting; if you come in from hunting you call your servant and tell him to have your shooting boots well greased for the morrow, and if you come in from shooting you say, I shall want my top boots in the morning."' I believe he was pretty right in what he said.

My game list for the season, from August, 1847, to February, 1848, shews an average of nearly seven head a day. Total 375.

There was an old story that Charles Fort was haunted by a ghost. It was said to be that of a young lady who walked out of her bedroom window one night and broke her neck. The Fort-Major occupied the quarters where the accident occurred, and knowing the legend, and hearing strange noises at night underneath the house, (which were either caused by the sea washing into the caverns below, or probably by smugglers who were detected once or twice in landing on the rocks under the walls,) he fancied the noises were caused by the spirit, and this working on his mind made him believe that the identical lady, or rather her ghost walked past him (one morning in his sitting room) very pretty and beautifully dressed. It so affected him that he fell sick and immediately left the Fort to live in the village of Cove. He therefore implicitly believed that the place was haunted. Some of our men who were superstitious believed it also, and swore they had often seen the ghost in the shape of a white rabbit near the Magazine; the most lonely place for a sentry and quite away from any other in the Fort. The man asserted, and stuck to it, that he was on sentry; that the ghost appeared before him at about midnight, in the shape of a woman that he challenged and came to the charge with his bayonet—that the ghost advanced, and he was not able to resist it, but was quite unwillingly, by some unseen power, forced back, without contact, into the sentry-box, when he bellowed for his life. All the guard turned out to know the cause of the noise. The men talked of these things many of them, I believe, to frighten the young soldiers who had not long joined, and who had but little sense. It had such an effect that some of them asked my Sergeant if I would allow double sentries instead of single ones to be posted at night, to guard each other on their posts.

I thought it now high time to put a stop to such nonsense, and I soon had an opportunity. At about midnight the sentry opposite the guard-room door and on the drawbridge began to bellow and shout for his life. The guard turned out and found this man in a most nervous state. He said the ghost came from under the drawbridge gate; that it rose up gradually till it assumed the shape of a woman dressed in black—then the dress changed to white; and the ghost forced him into the sentry-box without ever touching him, and he could not resist it.

The Corporal confined him at once, and the next day I

blew him up for being a fool, and sentenced him to mount an extra guard and to 14 days' heavy marching drill. Strange to say, the ghost was never seen again.

Since we were at Fermoy Captain Biscoe had been commanding the Depot, till the 29th of February, when Sir William Gordon arrived to take command. Biscoe, not liking to play "second fiddle," packed up his baggage and came down to the Fort without leave or license. Now, he could not remain there as long as I was in the Fort, as there was only one Company to command and that one was mine. He would therefore have been ordered back to the Kinsale Barracks had he not hit upon the expedient of getting me out of his way. He therefore asked me if I did not want to go on leave: that if I did there was the best chance I had of getting it. I replied that the shooting was good and the hunting tolerable, and that I did not want to go on leave till May, when the English fishing would be in its prime. He then said, if I liked to go away, *he* would send in the application for me that day. I, remembering the old adage that "a bird in the hand is worth two in the bush," then said I would go. The application was made out in such a hurry that they did not insert my address, so it was returned to be put in, which being done it was again forwarded. Thus was I sent on leave almost against my will. However, it saved *his* bacon, for he was allowed to take charge at the Fort whilst I was away.

On the 7th of March I embarked in the Sabrina for Bristol with my horse, and had a capital smooth passage, but on entering the River Avon, we went aground on a mud bank, and the weather coming on foggy an anchor was dropped, and immediately parted with the cable which was rotten. Another anchor was then let go, and we had to remain there all night, and did not get up to Bristol till nine o'clock on the morning of the 9th, when I instantly disembarked with my horse, left by the Birmingham railway, and arrived at Worfield at seven, p.m. When I embarked my horse in Cork he was in good hunting condition, but a little too fat—on his arrival at Wolverhampton he was as thin as a herring, and so weak that he could scarcely hold his nose out of his manger. Although I hunted him on the 13th which was not fair, he did not recover his voyage and railway journey for two months.

March 13th. Met the Albrighton Hounds. My horse carried me well. There were an immense number of falls, and I got one by my horse getting restive and falling on his side in a dingle over a lot of bushes. I took him home lame behind, but could not make out where until a fortnight afterwards, when one day in leaving his stall I put my hand over his rump and the joint called the whirlbone. I discovered this to be the seat of lameness. He must have fallen on the stump of a tree and destroyed the synosia (joint-oil bag). He was never any use to me afterwards, and eventually I got only £21 for him—he was worth at least £70.

March 15th. I attended the Leamington Steeple Chases. My leave having expired, I returned to Ireland.

During my absence on leave, Biscoe was sent to Bantry on detachment. He had written to say there was tolerable fishing there, and asked me to go down and see him. I got on the Bantry coach in Cork, on the 24th of April, and arrived at my destination in the evening, having travelled at the rate of 6¾ miles an hour over the most bleak and desolate country.

Next day I accompanied Biscoe to Dumbro' Lake, and after flogging the water all day we returned with about a dozen trout each, of 1-lb. weight.

The next day we fished Patterson's Lake and Dumbro', and returned with 30 sprat-sized trout.

27th. Captain Newburgh drove us to Loch Buy (pronounced Booey), about nine miles into the mountains. We found it bitterly cold with snow-storms. We did but little with our rods, but managed to get the number increased to two dozen with a cross line.

April 28th. Braddel, 70th Regiment, came over from Skibbereen, and went with us to Glengariff, which is very beautiful mountain scenery. Lord Bantry's place, a little cottage, is a nice shooting box. The grounds are beautiful and wild, very much in the style of the Trossachs on Loch Katturin. The deer amongst the wooded rocks add much to the picturesque, and the idea of the capital cock shooting that must be there in the winter adds also to the interest of a sportsman.

On the 29th I left Bantry and rejoined my detachment at Charles Fort.

May 3rd. Willis and Buchanan, 70th Regiment, who came over from Dunmanway on a visit to the Depot, joined Downman, Peel, Benson, and myself in shooting a lot of pigeons we had procured from Cork.

I shot a match with Downman, giving him one bird in six. I killed three out of five. He killed four out of six, thereby winning. I shot another with Peel, giving him one out of six birds. I killed my five birds. Peel only killed three out of his six and lost.

I said to Willis, "I will shoot you a match, and give you one bird." "Thank you," he said, "I will take it back with me to Dunmanway."

Downman, Peel, Benson, myself, and Buchanan then shot for a sweepstakes of 5s. each, which was won by Downman. I killed in all 9 out of 13 birds.

May 6th. I drove Benson over to meet John Meade of Ballintubber, and Tom Herrick at Ship-pool to hunt otters. We had two capital sandy wiry terriers of Meade's as hounds. We found an old bitch otter immediately in an old wall close to the boat-house. The terriers bolted her in no time, when she took to the river and dived, escaping a charge of shot from Tom Benson. We chased her up and down the river and rocks, (bolting her several times,) for an hour; Herrick and myself having each a shot with ball at her but missing. She then took up the river towards Collier's Quay, diving and just raising her nose occasionally for air. She had got near to the ford, when I ran up and got alongside, and to within 25 yards of her. She here just showed her head in the shallow water, when I sent a bullet through her eye, and killed her. We then tried back, and found in the same hold two cubs about half grown. After a great fight between them and the dogs one bolted, when I hooked it with my salmon gaff. The second one after a great tussle bundled out; this I pulled over also with the gaff, but the point did not enter the skin, and Tom Herrick knocked it on the head with a stick, and the terriers finished it.

May 12th. Accompanied Tom and William Herrick in their whale boat, with Perrin to the Sovereign Islands, where we dined on the rocks. These Islands or rather rocks are *covered* with beautiful spinach which continues green and good all the year round; nothing else grows there. The only inhabitants are the gulls and cormorants which frequent them in great numbers. We shot round the rocks and caves on going and returning, and saw a good many blue rock pigeons, which build in the caverns all along that coast.

May 13th. General Turner inspected my Depot, called me out to drill, and after I had done a few manoeuvres, he paid me the compliment of saying I had done very well. He expressed himself highly pleased with the Depot and all concerned.

May 16th. Tom Benson drove me to Shippool to fish, but the tide beat us, and spoilt our chance, so we had some young rook shooting in Herrick's domain. I killed with ball 10 out of 21 with my double-barrelled gun.

I heard of a nice boat, a four-oared gig, that I thought would suit us, and to be got cheap. It belonged to a Mr. Newman, who built her at the expense of £40, but soon becoming a bankrupt, he left Kinsale, and gave the boat to a relation to be sold.

I bought her from him for nine pounds. She was in tolerable repair, never having been much used, and only required four new oars. Downman, Benson, Peel, and

Perrin went shares in her with me, and she afforded us, and me in particular, a great deal of amusement all the summer and autumn.

May 26th. I received the melancholy intelligence of poor Joe's death, which took place at Worfield, at the age of 34 years.

* * * * * * * * *

June. Most of this month was spent boating, going out almost every day, either to row up or down the river to certain points in a given time, or to go out with the "spiller lines," sea fishing.

A spiller line is one about 300 or 400 yards long, with hooks attached by droppers a foot in length, and two yards apart. These hooks are baited with bits of fish about an inch square. The spiller is then coiled up in the boat, with the hooks over the side, all separate and ready to go. The anchor is now attached to the end, and a buoy line to the anchor. The ground being selected, the anchor is let go, taking with it the line and buoy. Having found the bottom, the boat is rowed along till all the line is out, when another anchor and buoy are attached to that end and let go. Several. of these lines being set either at low or high water, (the former is best,) they are allowed to remain for two hours down, when they must be hauled, and every kind of fish that frequents the sea is pulled in, viz., cod, haddock, splendid whiting, (some weighing 1½ pound to 2 pounds,) bream, turbot, soles, skate, conger-eels, red mullet, red Burnet, plaice, brill, *cum multis aliis.*

June 12th. I accompanied John Heard, Major Warren, etc. to the Old Head of Kinsale, where we shot the spiller lines. Whilst doing so, a species of whale, about 4o feet long, followed our boat, within ten yards of us, for about five minutes, and then disappeared. On our returning, in two hours to take up the lines, he reappeared, but much closer, and followed for ten minutes or more, with his great back fin sticking out of the water, when he gave a wheel, and lay about two feet underneath the keel of our boat. Some cried out, "Hit him with the oars!" Others, "Stick him with the boat-hook!" But I called out lustily, "Leave him alone! if you touch him, he will send us all to the bottom with the slightest motion of his tail." John Heard was of my opinion, so he was unmolested, and gradually sank out of our sight. After hauling the lines, the best of the fish were cut up, (some yet alive,) and put into the pot which was ready to receive them, on a fire made on the rocks. The potatoes were boiling also in salt water. All things being ready, we sat down under cover of a sail made into a tent, and such feeding on fish I never had. No one has any conception what fish is, till they have tasted it in this way.

Although we all dined on the produce of the lines, there were plenty of other eatables, in the shape of cold pie, fowls, etc. Here we enjoyed ourselves with our pipes and cigars till about eight o'clock, when we returned to town in Mr. Green's yacht, "The Colleen."

June 17th. Peel and I went after luncheon to have a quiet row up the river, but by degrees resolving to pull to one point further up, and so on, we at last reached Innishannon Bridge, eleven miles, which we accomplished in two hours. We remained there about half-an-hour to get a drink, and pulled back the eleven miles in two hours. The tide was against us half-way both going and returning.

June 30th. Peel and I rowed down to Sandy Cove; on returning, a strong head wind sprang up, which, with a strong tide against us, prevented our making much way. When crossing the broad part of the harbour, my oar broke, and we had none in the boat to replace it, consequently, we were left to the mercy of the wind and tide, which were carrying us towards the mouth of the harbour. However, after a time, a boat from the Old Head appeared, when we made signals, and held up the broken oar. They took us in tow up to Kinsale.

July 5th- I went spillering with young Warren and Perrin. We had about 500 hooks down, but as usual in the harbour we had but little sport. Whilst our lines were down, we rowed ashore in the Banjo to see the herring nets hauled. One of these had landed a Monk fish, *alias* "The Angler." It was about 4½ feet long, with an enormous head and mouth, which latter was sufficiently large to take in a man's head and shoulders. When I saw it, its heart and inside had been cut out, and several slices had been taken out of its back, yet it caught, and held tight with its enormous teeth, a rope that was put into its mouth. Dr. Warren afterwards divided its spine, and even after this operation, it closed its jaws upon the rope and held it fast. It had a long fibre or bone about 24 inches long, at the end of which was attached a pure white substance, which it could move at its will. This was then lying backwards down the back, but was so attached to the head a little above the nose, that it could be thrown forwards, and I have no doubt this was the Angler's bait to attract its prey, and from which it derived its name. The fish in shape was that of the small river fish, called the Bull-head, or Miller's Thumb.

July 12th. Perrin and I went spillering to the Old Head of Kinsale, where we had about 1000 hooks down. We pulled in ten different kinds of fish, and sixty in all. One of these was a cod about 27 pounds weight; he had taken our bait, which was half a sprat, at the same time having a bream of a pound weight sticking in his throat, which he could not swallow. We dined on the rocks as usual, and returned in the cool of the evening.

After the fish which we cooked had been cleaned, a good deal of the entrails had been left on the rocks in the little creek we ran the boat into, and whilst the cooking was going on, I was sitting at the water's edge, when suddenly a large conger-eel came up and took the inside of a fish off the rock just opposite to me. This garbage must have been at least half-afoot out of the water. I gave the alarm, and a man jumped into the boat with a gaff to try and catch this bold fellow, but although he did not catch that one, he gaffed four others, weighing from 3 to 5 pounds each.

July 18th. We hired spiller lines. Peel, Perrin, and I went outside the harbour, and shot about goo hooks. We caught 50 fish of all sorts, one of them called a Dennyhound. Its length was 21 feet; it was spotted all over like a leopard, and with a rough scaly skin like a sole. As soon as it was caught, it curled itself up like a dog, putting its tail over its head and eyes, nor could we get it to lie in any other position till we killed it.

Sir William Gordon returned from leave on the 14th, and took the command.

Smith O'Brien was supposed to have an Army of 10,000 men amongst the mountains, and all officers were ordered to rejoin their Regiments, but the generally disturbed state of the country did not affect us in peaceable Kinsale, and did not interfere with our amusements. I began to shoot a little in August, and having on the 1st of the month discovered that the snipe were fit to kill, went out with John Meade and Peel to Ballymartle. I killed 1 snipe, 2 moorhens, 3 rabbits. Peel killed 1 snipe, 1 duck, and 1 rabbit.

On the 5th I went with Tom Herrick to Ballymartle, and took the same beat to Tureen bog, killed 6½ couple of snipe and 3 moorhens. Tom killed 4 couple of snipe.

17th August. We rowed down to Lower Cove to see the herring nets hauled. *One net* at one haul enclosed such numbers, that when laded into the boats with baskets, they filled fifteen boats to the gunwale; each of these boat-loads was worth about ten pounds. The same net on the 4th of August took thirteen boats full at one haul, and cleared £160 by it. Another net took 17 boats full, but because the 15th was a holiday with the Roman Catholics, they would not draw their nets, and this in the time of great want and scarcity of food September 2nd. We got up a fishing party for the Old Head. I, with Rye, Peel, Downman, and Perrin, rowed down in the Banjo:

Sir William Gordon, his brother, Tom Herrick, and Rutherford, went in Rye's hooker. We shot the lines, with about 1500 hooks, one of them across Hole-open Bay, and the other three in "The Race." We took up those in "Hole-open" first, and caught a turbot, a lot of fine whiting and red gurnet, which we had for dinner on board the hooker. After enjoying them much, we proceeded to take up the lines in "the Race," when we caught two more turbot, besides some skate, whiting, and gurnet. The day was a dead calm, and the sea like oil. As there was very little chance of the hooker getting home that night, I got into the Banjo about nine o'clock with Rye, Peel, and Downman. We rowed up the nine miles, and landed at Scilly, and then they took it into their heads to row back to meet the hooker, and bring off the rest of the party, who did not land till about one o'clock in the morning.

September 8th. I, with Perrin, Tom and William Herrick, got into the Banjo with the Spillers. As they were not baited, Perrin and William rowed down the Harbour, while Tom and I baited the hooks. It was a little rough when we started, but we were so engaged with our heads down, that we did not notice the weather or the sea. When we got opposite Sandy Cove, the lines were ready to let go, but the sea got so rough, that I said it would be a chance if we got them down; however, we would try. We threw over the anchor and buoy, and about 20 hooks, when the sea rose so much and so suddenly, with each wave crested, that I cut the line, and took my oar, much doubting if the boat could live in such a sea as was coming on. We put about and pulled for our lives, making the four oars bend again. For two miles we were in a very critical position, several heavy seas breaking very near to us, but at last we got into a sheltered part. If we had been five minutes later in running in, we should have been swamped, and all lost.

We afterwards got a whale boat and recovered the lines.

KILLARNEY

SEPTEMBER 26th. Robert Gordon started with me for Killarney, where we arrived at 3.30, p.m., and put up at Roche's Hotel at Muckross.

We then went to inspect Muckross Abbey, the cloisters of, which are as perfect as when first built. In the centre is a very fine yew tree, (said to be 13 ft. in circumference,) whose stem is perfectly straight and boughless until it reaches the height of the surrounding walls, when it branches out and overtops them. The trees all round have a shining appearance on their leaves and bark as if they had been varnished. Muckross Abbey is the burial place of "The O'Donoghue." We then walked down to the edge of the Lake, and had a fine view of Glenah Mountain and the Lower Lake with Ross Island and its Castle on the right.

We continued our walk up the avenue to Mr. Herbert's of Muckross about a mile, where we had a view of the house, which is good and built in the Elizabethan style. It looks very snug lying at the East end of Tork Lake, with Tork and Mangerton Mountains towering in its rear. We then proceeded along an almost interminable avenue, which is cut close, the boughs meeting overhead much like a long bower. After two miles walk, we found ourselves at Brickeen Bridge, under which Tork Lake empties itself into the Lower Lake. From this point, although it was raining hard, we got a capital view. Up Tork Lake with Tork and the Drooping Mountain at the opposite side, also to the right of it, we had the Eagle's nest, Glenah and several other mountains to back up with, in all it was a fine view. It was then getting dark, so we retraced our steps, and on arriving at the Park Gates, found ourselves locked in. We tried to climb over, but in that we failed, and it was a long time before we made ourselves heard, and were let out.

On the 27th we breakfasted at seven, and having procured a guide with a bugle, (without which you cannot experience half the wonders of Killarney,) we started on a car through the village of Killarney to the Gap of Dunloe. We were very unfortunate in the weather which was heavy, and the tops of the hills enveloped in mist.

On 7 entering the Gap, the scenery is very wild and beautiful, but I have seen *many passes* in Scotland quite equal to this, if not finer by far. The echoes of the bugle from rock to rock, as they reverberate along, are most astonishing. The sound of one note on the bugle echoing and re-echoing a thousand times, is exactly like the sound of an organ in a cathedral. Half-way up the road we met a man with a small cannon about a foot long, which he discharges for the benefit of travellers, charging *only* a shilling a shot. The echoes from this are like a tremendous thunder crash, which rolls away, re-echoing from hill to hill, till out of hearing. After this we met a man in a hole in a rock fiddling to the hill opposite; the echoes of this were quite supernatural and had a most curious effect. This man, as also every one who spoke to us, begged from us, saying it was the custom to give him something.

The girls selling whiskey and milk almost forced us to buy from them. The Gap of Dunloe is about ten miles from the village of Killarney. A Scotch parson went to see it a few days before we were there, and being a charitable man wished to give to the poor, but thought a bag of half-pence would be inconvenient to carry, so he bought a small bag full of Queen's head postage stamps to carry with him. Whenever he met a ragged boy or girl he pulled out a stamp, telling them that if they would take it to the village, (*only* ten miles,) they would get a penny for it. The children not knowing what they were, threw them away before the parson's face. He soon came to an intelligent looking girl whom he questioned. "My good girl, can you read?" "I can." "Well do you know what this picture is, on this red bit of paper?"

"I do *nat*," "Well, what is it like?" "It's like a *baste*."

The poor parson was obliged to laugh out, and give up the hopeless task of giving charity in Queen's head postage stamps to people who perhaps never heard that there was such a person as the Queen.

At the top of the Pass which is about two miles long, a very fine view is obtained of an immense valley, well studded with natural wood and bold rocks. On the right is a fine glen, in which are seen two small lakes, with a river running from them, (a capital stream for salmon and trout,) and emptying itself into the Upper Lake. The head and right of this glen is formed by the McGillicuddy Reeks.

We descended from the top of the Gap, and followed the course of the stream to the head of the Upper Lake, where, according to previous directions given, we found a boat with lunch awaiting us. We embarked and rowed to one of the islands where we picnicked, and afterwards went down this lake, (which can boast the finest scenery of the three,) passing through the "Long Reach "till we came suddenly upon the cliff called "The Eagle's Nest." Just on entering the Long Reach, the boatman called "*Paddy Carey*," which means he held a conversation with Paddy, *i.e.*, the echo, on shore at the base of the Drooping Mountain.

The echo was so very distinct, one could hardly be persuaded some one was not posted there to repeat the words uttered by the boatman. After a long talk he sat down in the boat saying, "If I was to be blackguarding him all day, he'd have the last word wid me."

All the echoes on the shore of this lake are very clear and distinct, many of them repeated twice or three times; besides those which, running from chink to chink, sound as an organ.

At the Eagle's Nest we fell on another set of whiskey and milk girls, who haunt the lakes, and who had not now much difficulty in making us buy some. The boatmen here fired a cannon which caused splendid echoes.

Having perpetrated a sketch at this point, we continued our trip down under Old Weir Bridge, which is exceedingly pretty, and where we came upon another relay of whiskey and milk girls, who were very pretty also, but passing them and Dinas Island we entered Tork Lake, and from that through Brackeen Bridge into the Lower Lake. Here we took a look at Glenah Cottage at the foot of the mountain, which Lady Kenmare built and fitted up for the accommodation of visitors who choose to picnic there. The mist having cleared off, Glenah Mountain looked the finest and wildest of any of them.

We rowed on down the Lake to Ross Island, where we found the Nursery Garden in beautiful order, although there were several rabbits running about the borders. We then ascended the ruins of the Castle, and from thence had a fine view of Innisfallen Island with Glenah and Tomies Mountain to back it up. This is the best view on the Lower Lake. Here we saw hundreds of water-hens and bald coots, and a few wild ducks which are never allowed to be shot at.

We looked into Mr. Herbert's kennel to see the celebrated Killarney hounds, but only saw three couple, the remainder having been disposed of on account of the famine in the land. These were fine large hounds, much of the blood-hound breed, but they were in wretched condition. They occupied a large and good kennel, big enough to hold a pack, and were only there to keep the red deer, (of which there are a good number on Tork and the other mountains,) out of the gardens and low grounds of Muckross. During the famine, Mr. Herbert had a great number killed to feed the poor with.

September 28th. I was up at six o'clock intending, as we had arranged the previous night, to go to McGillicuddy's Reeks which are said to be better worth seeing than anything about Killarney. The highest point of these is 3410 feet, whilst Mangerton is only 2693, Purple Mountain 2793, and Tonries 2413 feet high.

However I was much disappointed when my

companion Gordon came down to breakfast, for he had fully made up his mind to go straight off to Scotland that day, to a place where he owned he had not a soul to speak to, and his only companion a monkey! His excuse was that he had business. It was no use talking to him. He had made up his mind; and I a wilfu' man *wull* hae his own way.' The morning turned out cloudy, and Mangerton Mountain was capped. Our hotel-keeper told us it was no use attempting either that or the Reeks, which really was some consolation to me. We therefore paid our bill, which was very moderate: Gordon went on his way, and I got on the mail car at half-past twelve o'clock, and reached Kenmare at half-past three (21 miles). The Tork Cascade about two miles on the road is worth seeing. The car stopped for me whilst I ran to look at it. (It is only about 300 yards from the road side). As I was running up the path a hind came trotting down, and we nearly ran up against one another. She gave a good bound out of my way, and disappeared with a grunt, but on my return I was examining her track where we met, and where she nearly slipped down. In her turn I saw her examining me at about 50 yards, as if she could not make out what I was. I gave a whistle and a shout but she remained motionless still gazing on me until I stirred, when she went off, much alarmed.

The drive along the foot of Tork Mountain up to the Police Station and a little way beyond that, is magnificent scenery, with all the lakes, Glenah, Eagles' Nest, and other mountains on your right—the lakes far beneath you. On your left Tork Mountain, which is beautifully wooded, and Drooping Mount very wild and naturally wooded, with fine bold cliffs of immense height sheaving here and there.

Verily that drive is finer than anything of the kind I have seen in Scotland. Certainly Glen Coe is wilder and more *grand*, but not half so beautiful. After passing the Police Station we drove on, keeping Black Valley on the right, (which they say, but I don't believe them, the sun only enters two months in the year,) to the summit of the road. We then descended the hill to Kenmare (10 miles). The scenery from this summit is fine but not beautiful, and much adapted to sheep farming, being all grass hills: in fact an amphitheatre with a morass at the bottom.

I remained only about ten minutes in Kenmare to lunch and change horses, and started in a car for Glengariff, and although half the road is against the collar to the height of 1000 feet, I arrived at Glengariff, doing the 21 miles in two hours and ten minutes, and this with a small horse that was so primed in his joints, he could not step out more than half the usual step of a pony, and could not get his hind feet to reach the track of his fore feet. The Lansdowne Suspension Bridge at Kenmare is talked of as a grand affair, but it is no great things and no lion except that it is the first of the kind ever attempted in Ireland. The drive up the hill to the tunnel is through a wild mountain country studded with small farms, on which white-washed stone houses have succeeded the old dirty mud cabins. They are the property of Lord Lansdowne.

There is nothing fine to see until you arrive at the summit, when the view towards Kenmare is beautiful, looking down the valley for six to ten miles, and surrounded by lofty black hills. The road passes through three small tunnels on the summit at a distance of about half a mile from each other. One of these is not much more than a long arch, the next is about 40 yards, and the third zoo in length. The view on coming out of the latter where the road begins to descend is magnificent. There is the Glengariff wooded, and full of streams, and a small lake or two surrounded by very high and rugged hills, immediately under you on the right, with an extensive view of Glengariff and Bantry Bays with their islands in front, and backed by the Bantry hills. This is one of the most magnificent views I ever saw.

From this point the road winds, twists, and turns round every little glen and corrie, but so beautifully engineered that the descent is only 150 feet in the mile, till it finds a level at the lodge of Lord Bantry's domain, and from there to the pretty and comfortable little inn is only another mile.

September 29th. I was up with the lark, intending to visit Hungary Hill, but found the morning lowering and the mountains capped. I therefore contented myself with making some sketches of Cromwell's Bridge, and walking up the glen, where I amused myself by watching the deer with my telescope, and by committing Lord Bantry's house and back hills to my book. The glen is very beautiful, and the mountains grand.

Arbutus here shews off the natural wood—more so than at Killarney.

I left Glengariff at twelve o'clock for Macroom, walking on my way through Mr. White's of Glengariff Castle, having ordered my car to meet me at the far end of the grounds. I was much amused by my guide, an old woman from the lodge, who said, "Well, Sir! it is most *extraordinary* what can make all the English Quality come all this way to see them *divils* of mountains. As for me, I would rather see a good green field than all the blackguard mountains in the country."

Many of the views from these grounds are fine, but none so fine as the one at the top of the hill on the Bantry side of Glengariff. From here we have Hungary Hill, the Sugar Loaf, the glen itself, and all Bantry, Berehaven, and Glengariff Bays, which put together form a splendid and grand scene.

After mounting my car, I drove off towards Macroom, having a good view of the Bay all the way to Ballylickey, where the road turns off towards Keimaneigh. From this turn for several miles nothing of interest is to be seen, until we enter Keimaneigh Pass, where it is said an action was fought which lasted from six a.m. till six p.m., between the White Boys under Captain Rock, and a Company of the 39th Regiment under Lord Bantry, (with a lot of his tenantry,) in which the White Boys lost six killed and eight prisoners, one of whom was after-wards hung; and on the other side were three killed. This was in 1822.

The Pass is talked of as beautiful scenery, but I confess I saw nothing beautiful in it, as the cliffs on each side are of no height.

The Lake of Gaugane Barra, about a mile beyond this, is well worth seeing, the hills surrounding it being wild and precipitous. In the centre of the lake are the remains of an old Abbey on a small island, now only used as a place of penance. There is one Square in it. In each wall of the Square are two cells in which the penitents have to say five Pater Nosters, the Creed and confession in the first; 10 ditto, ditto in the second; 15 ditto, ditto in the third; and so on all round. They then have to go into the next building, which was last used as a place of worship in A.D. 1700, and say forty more Pater Nosters, Creeds, and confessions, and notch the number said on a stick as they go on, to make sure they miss none. I saw some twenty or thirty of these sticks lying about, and I and my guide, who was a Roman Catholic, counted the notches on several of them. They had most of them the right number, but one had a double score and ten more into the bargain, at which my guide exclaimed, "Well! that must have been the Divil's Boy to have made all them."

There is a very fine echo amongst these hills around the lake which reverberates six times.

When I had taken my sketch of Gaugane Barra Lake and got up to go away, my guide said very earnestly, "Did yer honer put in the Holy Well?" "Oh yes, of course," I said. "But his Riverence's tomb, yer honer, you did not forget that, did ye?" "Why, I did not put it in my sketch because I cannot see it from here, as it is behind the brow of that hill," I replied. "But sure, yer honer, you'll be putting it in. Yer honer knows well what it is *without seeing it from here*, it's just like them cells in the Abbey, and so yer honer might put it into yer sketch well enough, or at least a *round circle* to shew the place"!!

At the Posting House at Keimaneigh, of which house with a mud cabin Keimaneigh consists, I changed my car, having travelled 21 miles, and continued my route along the River Lea which rises up in this quarter, and runs through some lakes about seven miles in length, which lakes are said to be full of very large pike.

These lakes continue almost to Inchigeela, a dirty, miserable little village. The scenery from Keimaneigh to Macroom is not worth seeing, in fact there is none, but on leaving Inchigeela, I had the luck to see the most splendid sunset I ever witnessed in this country. The sun was just hiding behind the mountains of Keimaneigh, which had on all of them a most beautiful purple hue; the clouds indescribably and beautifully tinged and coloured by the setting sun. I then descended the hill towards Macroom, got amongst the low grounds and swamps, with the dew rising in almost a heavy cloud. I got a chilly feel, felt low in spirits after leaving the grandness of Nature in which I had been living for a week, and did not get into that most miserable place called Macroom till half-past seven, p.m. I drove up to the Hotel, (where of course I was surrounded by beggars before I could get off the car.) Here I found a carriage at the door which had been benighted on its way to Killarney, with a party who engrossed the whole attention of the house. I ran- the bell most assiduously for nearly half an hour, and was allowed to do so without interruption for my amusement, in a room without any fire, and by the light of a farthing dip. I did eventually get a bedroom allotted to me which was all in confusion with women's dresses, men's shirts, and the like, and happy I was to get out of it again.

I then took to the bell-rope once more, and kept the wires warm until a very dirty woman, covered with coal-dust or the like, promised to get me some dinner. This at last came, and it consisted of herrings, and the remains of the benighted party's dinner. I drank a quantity of porter as a sleeping draught and some punch, then retired to my bed to drown my misery in sleep.

September 30th. After breakfast I walked up to Mount Massey, formerly the seat of the Hutchinsons, but now belonging to Mr. Massey. It has for the last two years been used as a barrack, having had a Company quartered in the house. It was once a fine establishment with fine rooms—capital house, with stabling for 25 to 30 horses, all loose boxes, with the exception of one stable of six most excellent stalls—a large kennel for two packs of hounds and large coach houses—but since the time I am writing of it has come still lower in the scale of mansions. It has been converted into a poor-house!

"Sic transit gloria mundi."

I returned to Cork, and from thence to Kinsale that evening.

KINSALE

OCTOBER 5th. General Turner came from Bandon (where he had been staying with Lord Bernard) to inspect us. The morning was very wet, but it turned out fine in the afternoon for the Review. The General expressed himself much pleased with the appearance of the men, cleanliness of the Barracks, and the general interior economy of the Depot.

I bought a horse from John Heard's groom for the sum of twelve pounds. Heard could do nothing with him, could not get any work out of him at all, and he got an idea into his head that his horse could not eat hay! He said it was an extraordinary thing that all his horses were broken-winded, his stable was a bad one he was sure, and he must build another. I thought that the management and not the stable must be in fault, so I inquired how it was. His horses seldom got any hay. They had a bucket or as much water as they could drink in the morning, and the same in the evening. They had two feeds of oats, and the remainder of their food was carrots. Upon this diet he expected them to do quick work, such as being driven in a car eight or nine miles an hour.

I wonder they were *not all* broken-winded with such treatment. This particular horse he had driven one day to Kilbrittan, where he had some hay and a lot of water given him, and when coming home the horse almost choked with repletion. He then told his groom the horse was broken-winded, and to get rid of him in any way, even to send him for a jingle horse in Cork. Luckily the man brought him up to the Barracks to sell for £15. I rode him, galloped him, and leapt him. He coughed, but I thought I could manage that, and paid £12. That evening Heard wrote to me, saying he heard I had bought the horse in his absence, which he regretted, and offered to relieve me of him, as he said he should be sorry any friend of his should be taken in. He said it was fair to let me know the horse was *broken-winded* and *could not* eat hay, for which reason he was anxious to part with him, but that if I did *not* repent of my bargain and decided upon keeping him, he would send me a cart-load of carrots on which food only the horse could thrive. I told him I was much obliged for his kindness, but that I would keep the horse and accept the carrots. I put the horse through a course of alternatives and a dose of physic, stopped his carrots by degrees, gave him as much oats as he could possibly eat, and a little hay at night, and in the day time kept a muzzle on him to prevent him from eating his bed.

His cough left him in a month, and he carried me beautifully for the winter, with my hounds, which I shall hereafter have to notice.

November 3rd. On returning from hunting in the evening I got the route to march the following morning with my Company for Newcastle, in the county of Limerick. I accordingly left "Auld Kinsale" the next morning at eight o'clock with Lieut. Webster Gordon and 85 rank and file, and marched into Cork, where we halted that and the following day, the latter being a Sunday.

November 6th. Marched from Cork to Mallow, 20 miles. Here we found a party of the officers of the 41st Regiment, who had come over from Buttevant and invited us to dine with them, which we did. I found an old acquaintance amongst them in Handcock, late 24th Regiment, son of Lord Castlemaine.

November 7th. Our March was only from Mallow to Buttevant, (7 miles), where the head quarters of the 41st Regiment were stationed. They sent their band out to meet us and play us into town. We lunched and dined at their mess, and were favoured by having their string-band, which was a very good one, to play after mess. We received every civility and hospitality from them.

Buttevant is a small miserable town with only one street; so small indeed that I had difficulty in getting billets for my men. The Barracks seemed good.

November 8th. Marched from Buttevant to Drumcollogher, 14 miles. This place is far worse than Buttevant. I got a pretty good billet, but Gordon could scarcely get a place to sleep in. He did eventually get a bed made for him in a large garret-looking room, but could get neither basin nor tub, and had to perform his ablutions in a *pie dish*!!

Next day we reached Newcastle, where I relieved Major Goold and a Company of the 88th Regiment.

NEWCASTLE

NEWCASTLE is a better kind of small Irish town than is generally met with. It has four streets irregularly built, a large Square, where the market is held, a Church, a large Roman Catholic Chapel, a meat market, which is well supplied, and an Hotel.

"*The Castle*" (Lord Devon's) is a large house, with some nice grounds round it, but nothing like a Castle. Lord Devon's agent, Captain Kennedy, occupied the house, and Colonel Clarke, late Scots Greys, who commanded that small district, also had apartments in it. Lord Aluskerry lived about eight miles out of the town, and was very hospitable to us. Other than the above we had no society.

The shooting about there is most excellent, the best in Ireland I should say; and the snipe, particularly within three miles of the town, are very large, nearly half as big again as the snipe are in general in Ireland.

November 13th. Went shooting. Saw millions of snipe in the grass fields, but they lay badly. I bagged 16 couple.

14th. Went out after two o'clock for an hour and a half, bagged 31 couple of snipe at the back of the Poor-House.

15th. I saw an immense quantity of snipe, but all very wild. I bagged 12 couple of snipe, 2½ couple of plover, 1 wild duck, and 1 water rail.

16th. Went out for an hour's walk with my gun; bagged 2½ couple of snipe.

10th. Blowing a gale of wind. I expected to get a bag full of golden plover towards Fehanah. The rain came down in torrents. I only bagged 7 couple of snipe and 3 plover.

22nd. Went shooting on the mountains to beat the little glens. Bagged 21 couple of woodcocks, and 2½ couple of snipe. 23rd. Shot at the back of Mr. Shea's, of

Maine. Birds very wild. Only bagged 9½ couple of snipe, and 1 couple of plover.

28th. Having received an invitation with Colonel Clarke to spend a day or two at Lord Muskerry's, we returned an answer that we should be happy to dine there on this day, but that we could not make a longer stay. Colonel Clarke borrowed a carriage, and ordered posters from the Hotel, but there was a doubt as to whether these said unfortunates would be home in time enough from some journey they were on; however, they did return in time, and were accordingly "put to" the carriage at half-past five o'clock, allowing them an hour and a half to do the seven miles in. We started off at a pace between a trot and a canter, which I thought was too good to last, but before we had gone half a mile, we dropped into a walk, and from this nothing could make the wretched animals go faster; they were completely knocked up and starved. The night was pitch dark, and one lamp went out, whilst the other only just flickered, and the rain came down heavily, beating against the windows. In this miserable plight we crawled along till we reached Fehanah, having twice been nearly upset into the deep ditch which runs along the side of this road. In Fehanah we halted to inquire the way, as none of us knew it, nor did our driver. We here discovered it was seven o'clock, and we were not much more than half-way to His Lordship's. However, we proceeded at a snail's pace (but stopping to consult at every lane or turn) into a field to discover whether that was the entrance to the grounds, our postilion having several times to dismount, and go to cabins off the road to inquire the way. At last we reached a small village consisting of a few cabins, where we were directed to turn to the right, and in about a mile we should find a turn to the left, which would take us to the entrance gate. It was now *eight* o'clock. Away we went, and to our joy found the turn; the postilion lashed the horses, and we went up in grand style till we found ourselves — in the middle of a small farm-yard from which there was no outlet! Here we were brought up all standing. After some time shouting to the natives who lived there, they told us we had taken the wrong turn, and they were kind enough to help to back the carriage and turn the horses, which was not so easily done. The master then took hold of the horses' heads, and led us about half-a-mile up to Lord Muskerry's Castle, where we arrived at half-past eight o'clock, having been three hours doing the 7 miles. We found the ladies had just retired from the dining-room, and the gentlemen quietly sitting over their claret, having waited dinner an hour for us, and then given us up. However, we had dinner brought up on a side table, and did very well. At half-past eleven we ordered our carriage again. Lord Muskerry insisted on our staying all night, and used every argument he could to induce us to remain, telling us it was impossible our horses could take us back, but we had made up our minds, and start we did, at about the same pace that we came. On arriving at Fehanah, the horses made a rush at a house where I dare say they had stopped at some time or other, and crammed the pole of the carriage against the wall. It was with the greatest difficulty we got them away, and when we did, it was only to let them drive across the street against the opposite cabin. In trying to get straight on the road, the driver got the wheels into a deep dirt pit which was at the side of one of the doors, and there we stuck. There was nothing for it but to get out in our patent-leather boots and full dress, to put our shoulders to the wheels, and lift the carriage out of the hole. At last we made another start. I became quite resigned to my fate, went to sleep in a corner, and awoke on entering Newcastle at half-past two o'clock, a.m., having been three hours in returning.

November 30th. It being marching out day, Colonel Clarke requested me to march in the Drumcollogher direction, as we might be required to assist the civil power in that quarter, and sure enough we were wanted. The stock and hay, etc. of a farmer who was in arrear of rent were to be sold on the farm that day, but he obtained assistance from the country people, who carried most of the hay away on to another farm, and drove off the stock. They were hard at work at this laudable *trick*, when they were detected by the man who was going to sell the property, and whose party attempted to stop the removal of the things. The Police were there. Both parties of natives got very furious, and were going to rush upon one another with pitchforks, sticks, stones, etc. Colonel Clarke, being a Magistrate, called us up as soon as the row commenced, and we helped the Police in stopping the removal of the property, and taking charge of their prisoners. After we had the ringleaders, and Colonel Clarke had made the others promise not to fight, we marched back with the prisoners.

At three o'clock I went shooting behind the Poor-House, and bagged 4 couple of snipe. I could not have been out an hour.

I dined at Captain Kennedy's to meet Sir Charles Napier, the hero of Scinde. He is a very affable, plain-spoken, straightforward man, without any humbug about him, and exactly what the prints of him represent in appearance. He told us the following story:— "I was on one occasion dining with a Native Chief in India, when as usual there was a juggler in attendance, who was the most expert swordsman I ever saw. I saw him place a lime on the palm of a man's hand, and after giving one or two flourishes with his sword, he cut the lime in half horizontally. I also saw him cut a clove into two pieces (a green one, of course) with his sword, the clove being placed on the tip of a man's tongue, which he stuck out of his mouth. I believed it was all humbug, and told the juggler that he could not cut a lime into two pieces on *my* hand. The fellow said he could, and the lime was accordingly placed on my palm, but my thumb was a little higher than the level, and he was afraid of cutting it off, and several times before he attempted the cut, pressed my thumb down. He at last cut and partially divided the lime, but knocked it on the ground, giving as an excuse that he was afraid of cutting my thumb off. He then said he would not cut a lime in two horizontally on my hand, for he was afraid of injuring me, but he would divide one on my palm by cutting straight downwards. I was in a great funk at this proposition, for I believed my hand *must* be cut in two. However, as there were a lot of Chiefs, my own Staff, and an immense number of people looking on, I screwed up my courage, and let the man go on. He placed a lime in my palm, cut straight down and divided it, without even ruffling or leaving the least mark on the skin, although I distinctly felt the edge of the sword on my hand. The cut was made without "drawing."

December 4th. I received an order to proceed to Tralee to take command of the Depot.

TRALEE

I ARRIVED at Tralee on the 6th of December, 1848, and took over the command of the Depot from Captain Trench.

Tralee Barracks are very good, with a large grass square in front of them, and are about three quarters of a mile out of the town. The town itself is a very dirty hole, consisting of five or six streets, which are generally in a state of shish nearly over one's shoe tops. When they are cleaned the heaps are put into the middle of the street, so that in an hour it is all trampled out again to where it came from.

There is not much society at Tralee. The only people I knew were the Fairfields, Mr. Neiligan, and Richard Chute of Blennerville. It is a most bleak and desolate looking country around, and presents a very striking contrast to its neighbouring county of Limerick. There is very good shooting to be had from Tralee, and as facts are the best arguments I shall record a few.

SHOOTING AT TRALEE

December 12th. I left Tralee at one o'clock with Downman and Peel to shoot at O'Doheny, 7 miles off. We saw lots of snipe on the red bogs. I bagged 7½ couple snipe and 1 teal, Downman 6 couple, and Peel 3½ couple snipe. Total, 17 couple snipe and 1 teal in 24 hours.

13th. Went with Downman to Castle Island, we found no snipe till half-past two o'clock, when we left the fields and got on to the red bog. Here I killed 9 couple snipe and one hare. Downman only killed 3 couple snipe.

16th. I accompanied Downman and Peel to shoot at O'Doheny. I killed 13 couple snipe, Downman killed 6½ couple, and Peel 7½ couple. Total, 27 couple snipe.

19th. Went shooting to Castle Island with Peel, where Downman joined us at two o'clock. I killed 9½ couple snipe, Peel 2½ and 1 hare, Downman 1 couple snipe.

29th. Went shooting to Castlemaine with Downman and Peel, (11 miles,) saw but few snipe. I killed 7 couple of snipe and 1 teal, Downham 4 couple, and Peel 3 couple and 1 moorhen. Total, 14 couple, 1 moorhen.

January 4th, 1849. Shot at Ardfort with Peel. It was a hard frost, and all the snipes at the springs. I killed 74 couple snipe, 2 plover, 2 moorhens, and a widgeon, which latter was pointed by "Ned" and I picked it up in its lair. Peel only killed 1 snipe.

5th. Shot with Downman and Peel at O'Doheny; snipe wild, and I shot badly. I killed only 6 couple snipe and 1 teal, Downham killed 7 couple snipe and 2 teal, Peel 3 couple snipe and 1 teal. Total, 16 couple snipe and 2 couple teal.

Woodcock shooting all on the mountains and little glens. Lord Ventry gave me leave to shoot on his mountains at Dingle, where the woodcocks abound. I was told I could kill a cart-load, (Hibernice,) Anglice a game bag full, at any time I would go, but especially when there is a little snow on the hills.

16th. I killed 13 couple snipe and 1 moorhen, Downman 5 couple, at O'Doheny.

20th. Went on the mountain with Downman, and beat Blennerhassett glen. I killed 8 hares, 3 woodcocks, and 3 snipe; Downman 2 woodcocks and 5 snipe.

My game list for the past season of 1848 and 1849 is as under, and averages 12 head per diem.

1 partridge	4 hares	2 quail
536 snipe	9 rabbits	17 woodcocks
10 wild ducks	26 plover	
16 moorhens	6 pigeon or tag rag	
Total, 627.	Number of days out, 52.	

Christmas Day, 1848. We received the melancholy news of the death of officers from 'yellow fever at Barbadoes. In three months, 7 officers and 72 men of four Companies of the 66th Regiment, 6 officers and 98 men of the 72nd Regiment, 1 officer, R.A., and 1 staff surgeon.

December list. I met the Blennerville hounds (a kind of heavy stag hound, or something of the old southern harrier kind) at the Kerries, where a stag was enlarged and gave a very fast run of about 25 minutes. I lost a fore shoe after the first ten minutes and had to pull up, but I saw the run from a distance. I was much pleased with my "*broken-winded*" horse; he carried me beautifully till I pulled up.

Mr. Richard Chute, the owner of these hounds, called on me and offered me the sole management of them, for he said he seldom went out with them himself, and that I was quite welcome to take them and do as I pleased. He said he should give his huntsman directions to obey my orders, and go where I wished. The huntsman was well mounted, he said, and if he lamed his horse there were others in the stable for him. Of course I was much obliged to Mr. Chute for his kindness in giving me his hounds for the time I might remain in Tralee and bearing all the expenses himself.

For some time I did not take advantage of Mr. Chute's offer, but contented myself with going out to look at them hunting hares *when they could find any*, but I found during my shooting excursions that there were plenty of coverts round the country that were likely to hold foxes. I therefore undertook the management of the pack, raised them a few pegs by turning them into fox-hounds, and instead of their going out at one o'clock to suit the lazy buckeens of Tralee, my meet always took place at half-past ten, and generally from 10 to 14 miles from town. This arrangement did not meet with the approbation of the Tralee *gents*. "It was too early" — "The meets were too far off" — "There was no sport in a fox-hunt" — "and it was assuming a great deal too much on the part of the officer to take the hounds away in that way" — which were the views and observations of these snobs, but they affected me but little. They sent messengers to the huntsman telling him the meets were too early, and I returned an answer that if they were not at the meets to the moment, I should wait for none.

Under these circumstances we were not often favoured with their company. We had one or two runs which in Irish mouths do not decrease in telling, and none of the Buckeens had been out. The ladies of Tralee heard this and taunted the unfortunates most unmercifully, telling them that they were very fond of riding up and down the town to shew off on hunting days, and talked very large about their exploits when at a hare hunt, yet it seemed that they could not "ride a fox hunt." This put their pluck up, and on the 12th of February they came out strong, and were all vanquished as I shall presently show.

The meet was Castlemaine at eleven o'clock. We drew Castlemaine Wood blank; Miltown, Sir Edward Godfrey's, blank also; but some of these snobs started a drag at the bottom of the wood back to Castlemaine. I saw it was a drag at once, so kept to the road as there was no stopping the hounds. The three miles they went over was very deep, and the hounds flew, consequently there were innumerable falls and most of the horses puffed. As soon as I collected the hounds I went off at a brisk trot over a deep country to Lon-field Wood, and no sooner were the hounds thrown in than away went Reynard, right along the track we had just made—ran back to Castlemaine Wood, (82 acres,) where we could do nothing with him. Time 45 minutes at a good slapping pace. Peel, Sanderson, and Gordon, each got two falls, and the snobs plenty. The country was very deep, and my "broken-winded" one carried me beautifully. None of the Tralee horses could chew again for a fortnight, and I was told many of them were very ill. My horse was not at all done.

The Magistrates were constantly in the habit of sending for troops in aid of the civil power when they had no right to do so, and I was determined to stop it.

January 2nd. It was an intensely cold day. I was

passing the Poor-house at one o'clock, when I noticed about 150 poor miserable wretched creatures crouched round the gate, waiting to receive relief. There were old men, women, and children.

On entering the Barracks, I received a requisition for troops in aid of the civil power at the Poor-house. I knew there was no necessity for their presence, therefore sent none, but went myself to remonstrate with the Magistrates and Board of Guardians there assembled. On entering the gate, I found a policeman sitting down in the sentry box half asleep, behind the larger iron gates which were shut—I then counted five other policemen who were there doing nothing, and I walked up to the Board Room, introduced myself as commanding at Tralee, and asked where the police were as they had sent for troops. "Oh, the police are all here, said Mr. Fairfield the President, and we want some of your men." I replied, "I beg leave to say there are only six policemen now on duty, and those seem to have nothing to do, one of them being half asleep in his sentry box, I therefore decline complying with the requisition of the Magistrates, and shall send no troops."

"You will, then, be responsible for anything that may happen, for we apprehend that the Poor-house will be attacked."

"Then why don't you send for your police," I said, "I am not going to do police duty for you."

"We have not a sufficient number of police to bring them up here from the town; if we did bring more up here the people would attack the shops and rob them."

"Why not apply for a larger force from the head quarters, if you have not sufficient? "

"Because we should have to pay for them if we did, and we don't want them so long as there are soldiers in the Barrack."

"Under these circumstances I shall apply for them for you, and by the next post, as you wont do it yourselves."

I went on to say that their requisition was not made out in form: it did not state that the police were inadequate to perform the duty required, neither was there a Magistrate to accompany the troops, under which circumstances I should still decline sending any men whatever. They then asked if I would comply if the requisition was properly worded? I said, provided a Magistrate went to the Barracks to accompany the troops I would, but not without.

"But," they said, "we cannot spare a Magistrate, we require them all here."

"Then I shall send no troops," I replied.

After a consultation amongst themselves, the spokesman. said, "Well Sir, you are the most strict officer and certainly stick to the letter of the law more than any officer we ever had here."

"Very likely," I replied, "and I can tell you Gentlemen that I *intend to be so*, and that I do not intend that my men shall do your police duty: moreover I shall apply for police for you, and report the whole of the circumstances to the General commanding in Limerick."

At last a regular worded requisition was made out, and a Magistrate- accompanied me to the Barracks, where I paraded a party of about 35 men under the command of Perrin. I then gave him orders to return to the Barracks the very moment the Magistrate left him, and I warned the Magistrate that the order would be carried out. Of course there was no disturbance, and the party returned in the course of the evening.

I reported *the whole* of the circumstances to General Napier commanding in Limerick, who replied I had acted quite right, and that the soldiers were not to do police duty. The Magistrates never called on us for assistance again, but one day Saunderson was in the Club House in the town, when some chimney took fire. Two or three voices exclaimed immediately "Send for the troops." But a Magistrate said to Saunderson "I suppose Captain

Davenport would not send them without a requisition, and a Magistrate to accompany them?" "*Certainly not*," was the reply. We were never bothered again for aid to the civil power.

There was an order at this time that troops were not to turn out in case of fires, as they might be caused only to attract the troops from their position while that position was attacked by the disaffected mobs in their absence.

February 21st. To my utter surprise I received orders to proceed to Barbadoes with as little delay as possible. To this I demurred as Trench returned from Canada a year before I did, and had consequently been at home longer than I. I wrote to the authorities about it, and it was decided in Dublin that when a Regiment goes abroad after home service a fresh roster commences, without reference to former services. Therefore that I, being the senior, must go out.

I packed up my traps, gave my dogs, "Bonnie and "Shot" to Peel; the latter to be returned to me in Canada, and "Ned" I gave to Downman. I sold my horse to Benson.

March 1st was my last day at Tralee. I dined as a guest at the 'Mess, where my health was drank with three times three. It was very gratifying to me to find that although whilst in command I had always the duty carried on *most strictly*, allowing no laxity, I had been all through a great favourite. Every one, I must say, seemed to feel my departure deeply. They were all very low in spirits, and one or two nearly sheaved that weakness which women sometimes do on the departure of a sincere friend.

March 3rd. I arranged all my affairs at Newcastle, gave over my Company to Tom Benson, and was just leaving, when the men of my old Company sent to say they hoped I would not have any objection to their seeing me off by the coach, and giving me a cheer at parting. However not liking any public demonstration, I went to bid them adieu in their Barracks, and told them that I was much obliged to them for the compliment they intended to pay me, which was much more than I expected. I said I had commanded the Company now for a long time, for more than five years, with a great deal of satisfaction to myself. I dare say many of them would think I had acted very harshly and severely in giving heavy punishments for offences committed by them, (cries of "No, no, Sir, you did not,") but I only did that which I conceived to be my duty and nothing more, (cries of "We hope yer honer will soon command us again, we were always satisfied to be under you.") I was sorry to leave them, and hoped always to hear of their welfare. I would now wish them all good-bye in the barrack-room instead of in the street, as I thought their all turning out and cheering on the turning departure of the coach would only collect a crowd and cause inconvenience. "Well, good-bye Sir, may luck attend *yer*, and we hope Sir we'll soon meet again. Three cheers for the Captain."

Three cheers were accordingly given, and one cheer more. The whole Company did come to see me off, but stood mute at a distance from the coach.

On the 8th of March I went up to London, reported myself at the Horse Guards, and applied for a month's leave of absence, which was granted. I was ordered to proceed per the packet of the 17th of April from Southampton to Barbadoes. I left London for Worfield. During March, and at the beginning of April, I had some very good trout and greyling fishing in the Worfe.

April 3rd being my birthday was kept with the bells ringing morning and evening. I received presents in numbers.

VOYAGE TO THE WEST INDIES

I EMBARKED on board the Royal Mail Steam Ship Avon, 500 horse power and 880 tons, on the 17th of April, at about one o'clock, when a very heavy snow storm came on, and appeared to lie thick all over the country. It certainly looked like Old England giving me the "cold shoulder" at parting, the wind was intensely cold.

About 60 or 70 passengers and their friends who came to see them off sat down to a sumptuous luncheon. At three o'clock the mails came on board, the friends parted, got into the steam-tug alongside, and gave us three cheers as we wore round and steamed off, which was returned from the Avon. Amongst the passengers were Sir Joshua Rowe, Chief Justice of Jamaica, and Lady Rowe. The remainder were a motley set, chiefly foreigners, for the different West Indian Islands. I found Mr. Wm. Stewart and Tony Hobson of St. Vincent very good fellow-passengers. There were also a number for California of all nations: Germans, French, Peruvians, Mexicans, English, Irish, and Scotch. I had a very comfortable cabin, about 6 feet square clear of the berth, with plenty of light and air, (thanks to Mr. Colville, Director Steam Packet Company, for that same.) We had a capital run down the English Channel, and no one ill; but the 19th saw us in the Bay of Biscay, when it blew a double gale of wind with good sea on. Great was the smash of crockery. Several heavy seas struck the ship making her stagger again, and broke heavily over her. The fore part of the paddle-box was carried away, as also the pig-house. Fortunately the pigs had been removed beforehand. The ship rolled terrifically. I was so ill I could not get out of my berth, but lay rolling from side to side with the motion of the vessel.

On the loth the gale moderated, the sea was smoother, and in the evening it became beautiful. My sickness left me, and having managed a breakfast off curry I became quite well. We passed Cape Finisterre, and were off Oporto on the 21st, with splendid smooth weather. Here I noticed the reflection of two stars in the water to be quite as large and strong as the moon in England.

Sunday, 22nd, the Rev. Dr. McGrath read prayers to the ship's company and passengers in the cabin, and gave us a capital extempore sermon afterwards. The weather was so hot I was obliged to put on summer clothing. We were somewhere off Lisbon, and the following day the Captain had the awning put up, reaching from the mainmast to the stern of the ship.

23rd. We were south of Gibraltar, going at the average rate of 200 miles a day.

24th. We sighted Porto Santo at six o'clock, a.m., Madeira at eight o'clock, and dropped anchor in Funchal at ten o'clock. Here we were put in quarantine in consequence of a few cases of cholera having occurred in England, which was a great nuisance to us all, but particularly to a few. "Tony" Hobson had come purposely by the Avon on his way to St. Vincent, (because it touched here,) to see his sister who lived at Funchal, but he was not allowed to leave the ship, nor her boat to come near it, so they had to bawl out their conversation for the benefit of the curious passengers who, of course, rushed to the side on seeing a boat. Another man, a merchant, who had been the rounds of the West Indies, America and England, and who of course was most anxious to see his friends immediately, was taken in a boat, and towed by another boat to the lazaretto to have five days' fumigation. Another came with all anxiety from London to see his wife, who he had heard was on the point of death, he also was sent off for five days to the same place.

From what I could make out of Funchal from the ship through the telescope, it was built on and at the foot of a beautiful mountain; the houses or rather cottages scattered two-thirds of the way up the hill with vineyards and gardens running between them have a very pretty effect.

The mountain which is green to the top, with a dark glen on each side of it, is very beautiful. The houses seem to be built chiefly of wood, and look like boxes with windows in them more than any thing else, as they have no chimneys.

The principal objects are the church, the Fort over the town, the Fort at the entrance of the bay, the English Burying Ground, the Governor's house, and the house our Queen Dowager lived in.

From the cool position I was in on the water, it seemed like looking out of early Spring into a very hot Summer, for the people were all lounging about and idling in the shade with umbrellas over their heads; the mules and horses swishing their tails and kicking at the flies. There appeared to be some nice avenues in the streets and along the shore affording delightful shade.

Having taken on board a supply of coals, some bullocks and other provisions, consisting of new potatoes, green peas, French beans, guavas, plantains, greengages, &c., &c., we steamed out of the Bay at 7 o'clock, p.m.

We crossed the tropical line at 4 o'clock, a.m., on the 30th of April. The weather on the 4th and 5th of May became excessively hot, the thermometer standing at 85° in the shade. The old West Indians suffered much from it and looked quite done up. I did not feel it much, it did not oppress me, as it seemed to do others. On telling Dr. Magrath this, he said, "Ah! you'll be lucky if you don't feel it next year."

We made land at 10 o'clock, a.m., on the 6th of May, and anchored at 2.25, after a most beautiful passage of 19 days. I disembarked immediately, Biscoe, Perrin, Kendall, Dunbar, 66th Regiment, and Paddy Stewart, D.A.Q. General, having come on board to meet me. I was much struck by the beautiful bright green colours of the water in the Bay.

BARBADOES

ON landing, I found our men and the 72nd Regiment under canvass, as the Barracks were not allowed to be entered since the raging of the yellow fever in them, with the exception of our Mess room in the brick Barracks in the Savanha. The officers were allowed to live in lodgings or private houses, except the one on duty who had to remain in camp during his tour. Our Mess was the worst one I ever saw, and the cooking was done by an infamously bad cook.

For the first three or four days I thought the climate good and felt very well. The thermometer was at 76° to 78°, in the shade and 108° to 112° in the sun, with a cool breeze during the day. The island generally was healthy, no fever or other sickness prevalent, but there were constant heavy showers which lasted for ten minutes: then the sky cleared, and the sun drew up the steam from the ground as it would rise from a boiler. I went out in the sun as others did, and felt no inconvenience from it at first, but about the fourth day after landing I became quite sick and languid, all energy left me: even the act of dressing in the morning completely knocked me up, and I was obliged to lie on the sofa most of the day, till the evening when I would take a ride for a couple of hours before Mess time. I found Barbadoes anything but pleasant, and longed to be out of the low, flat, burnt up dreary island.

I took a house with Dunbar at Hastings, in which we had one sitting-room and two bed-rooms, but in a most dilapidated state, and overrun with ants, bugs, cockroaches, fleas, flies, and jack-spaniards, (the latter are a kind of large red hornet, and build their nests, which have the appearance of a bunch of chrysalis, on the ceiling of the rooms. Their sting is worse than a hornet's.) There were also lizards of all colours. For this we paid at the rate of £60 per annum, but that was better than living in tents with the men. The musquitoes, flies, and bugs were quite awful, and fed most ravenously on me nightly.

One morning I was lying in bed, I detected a villanous land-crab hustling across my room, however as soon as he saw I had noticed him, he took shelter under an old glove which was on the floor, so I immediately ejected him through the window. The land-crabs are very active, and run as fast as a mouse, and if attacked, will turn up and fight most vigorously with their claws.

May 16th. I was invited with Perrin to dine with the General Sir — Berkeley. Colonel Johnston ordered a full-dress parade at half-past four o'clock, p.m., for drill, and to read the articles of war. I asked leave from it for myself and Perrin, as we were to dine with the General, but the Colonel refused us, saying he would dismiss us in plenty of time to go afterwards. We first had drill, then were formed into square under a broiling sun to hear the articles of war read. In the middle of this, I became very sick, the men seemed to get into a confused mass before me, then total darkness came over me, and I fell back against the men behind me. As soon as I unbuttoned my coat and got a little breeze, I recovered but went to my quarters. I wrote to the General stating that I had been taken ill on parade, and made my excuse for not dining with him. Perrin with the Regiment was kept on parade till half-past seven. He of course was an hour late for the General's dinner, and gave his reasons.

The next day an order came out that no Regiment was to be kept on parade for more than one hour from the time of its turning out till its dismissal. The General said he had asked two officers to dine with him; he had to wait dinner half-an-hour for them; that one could not come, being taken ill on parade from the carelessness of his Commanding Officer, and the other did not arrive till half-an-hour after he had sat down to dinner. In fact he was furious.

Having been only a very short time in Barbadoes, I found the climate did not suit me at all. I was subject to constant headaches, which I could not get rid of. The

237

glare of the white roads with the sun on them added, no doubt, to the headaches. When out riding, I could scarcely open my eyes on account of it.

The wind, which is always from the North-East, rises with the sun, and goes down at sunset.

Although our Mess was a very bad one, we had a splendid Mess-room; the windows without glass, but with jalousies on two sides, and large folding doors opening on to a gallery or balcony. Bridgetown, the of the Island, was close to the Barracks, and a most miserable, dirty, beastly place it was; all the houses being built of wood, looked like a lot of deal boxes packed together rather than houses.

As to society, there never was any at all that I heard of, nor did I ever see a lady or gentleman about, excepting those belonging to the military establishment.

I was much struck by the beauty of the trees, all of them, even the largest mahogany, having blossoms to their very tops, like flowers in England. We had one great luxury here in the shape of ice, which we could get in Bridgetown at 1½d. per pound. Four pounds would last two people a whole day, where we consumed such a lot of iced cup, consisting of claret, soda-water, and sugar.

The beef and mutton in Barbadoes is the most miserable stuff imaginable. It is only surprising how the poor animals manage to live until they are wanted. The only food I tasted that was good was the guinea-fowl. These are nearly wild, and are obliged to be shot as the only way of catching them.

On the 30th of May I got my orders to proceed in charge of two Companies to Demerara.

June 3rd, I embarked on board the "Flying Fish" Schooner, with Sorrocold and 80 men of my own Company. I was glad to get out of Barbadoes, for I was quite sick of it, and disgusted with everything there; my zeal for soldiering oozed out of the ends of my fingers, and I would have sold out and quitted the Service altogether, if I had only some employment to fall back upon at home, but knowing the misery of having nothing to do, and leading an idle life, I resolved to stay until something offered itself, so I embarked for Demerara, but I would not have taken a Lieutenant-Colonelcy if it was offered me to remain long in the country.

VOYAGE: BARBADOES TO DEMERARA

The "Flying Fish" was well named, for she dived through the tops of most of the waves she met, even when not blowing hard, the water on the lee-side washing half the deck through the scuppers. She was a miserable schooner for troops, with no accommodation whatever. She had been employed in the cattle trade, and fitted up to carry bullocks. She was *cleansed*? by burning sulphur, etc. in her for this particular trip, to get rid of lice, etc., nevertheless she was full of cockroaches, ants, fleas, etc., and was as black as pitch from the smoke of the sulphur. We had no beds to lie upon, or chair or table in the cabin, and only two berths (for three of us) in the vessel. We were four days at sea, and not once able to take off our clothes or wash ourselves the whole time. It was lucky we ever arrived, for the Captain, who was a most uncivil brute, steered entirely by compass, and had no sextant or anything to make out his whereabouts with, if we had been caught in a gale of wind, and it was quite a miracle that he hit the entrance of the Demerara River.

The men were as badly off as we were, or worse, for the water washed down into the hold of the vessel.

They were wet through during the whole voyage, and lying in the wet decks. The arms and accoutrements were much damaged by the salt water.

* * * * * * * * *

All this I reported to the General at Barbadoes through Colonel Johnston, and concluded my report by saying that "the vessel was totally unfit for the conveyance of Her Majesty's troops, and whoever the officer was that reported her fit knew nothing about it, nor could he have ever been on board of her; and I left the case for the consideration of those in higher authority."

June 6th. We got in sight of land, about 30 miles off. Here we stuck, for the wind chopped round so often that we were steering all the points in the compass. All our provisions having failed us, we were compelled to fall back upon our salt rations for food. We at last entered the river with the tide, and anchored at twelve o'clock that night opposite Georgetown. The land of Demerara is so very low, that for miles before seeing it, we could see, what I first thought were a lot of steamers, but which really were the tall chimneys of the sugar-mills on shore.

On the morning of the 7th of June I reported my arrival to Colonel Mills, 3rd W. I. Regiment, but from the perverseness of our uncivil Captain, who would not bring the Flying Fish alongside the Wharf, we did not disembark till four o'clock p.m., although the authorities did all they could to assist us.

DEMERARA

ON arriving here we were immediately made honorary members of the 3rd W. I. Regiment. When we first went to Demerara, the Quarter-Master of that Regiment was dying; his room was within three of the mess-room, in the same balcony. On the night of his death the Band was playing at mess close to his door till ten o'clock, and he died at eleven!!

Georgetown is a curiously and very prettily built place; it is large; all the houses separated from each other by small gardens, in which are cocoa-nut, cabbage-palm tree, (or mountain cabbage,) bamboos, and quantities of different kinds of shrubs. The streets are very wide, a canal of water being in the centre, with roads on each side.

The country did not appear to me to be nearly so hot as Barbadoes at first, having the recollection of the strong sun on the white glaring roads there. Here it was always cloudy, with tremendous showers of heavy rain, (such as is never seen anywhere else, I should think,) which make it cooler. Here it rains from ten o'clock at night in successive showers till about two o'clock in the afternoon, when it clears up, and out comes the sun, draws the steam out of the ground in an incredible way, and causes the atmosphere to be muggy and damp. The land is all low, indeed, six feet lower than -the level of the sea, which is kept out by high embankments, formed by the Dutch when they had the country

The climate suited me better than Barbadoes, and I almost enjoyed myself.

Most people have fever and ague here, and many times over, but it only lasts a few days, and the patient recovers till another periodical attack.

The sun here when out is considerably hotter than at Barbadoes. On Christmas Eve this year the thermometer stood at goo in the shade at noon: on Christmas Day at 90°, and on the 27th, 128° in the sun at three p.m. Our

Barracks in Demerara were very good, two stories high, built upon pillars six feet high, and with a verandah of about eight feet wide all round; but being built of wood, the upper story got so hot from the sun about four o'clock, that I was always obliged to leave my room at that hour, for it was like being in a gradually heated oven. All the bricks used for building in Georgetown are imported from England and Scotland, although there is beautiful clay in the country, but no labourers to make it up.

The streets of Georgetown are gravelled from Scotland, and macadamized from the Penal settlement, 140 miles up the Essiquibo River. Gangs of convicted felons, 50 or 60 in number, all armed with a cutlass and long shovel each, parade the streets to clear them of grass, under charge of *one policeman*, with a walking stick or umbrella. The coolies who have been imported from India as labourers, (but many of whom turn beggars,) go about naked, with the exception of a cloth round the middle, and between the legs.

Many of the Negro women (Africans) who are in this colony wear the string of beads round the waist as a charm.

"The Bucks," the Indians of these parts, who come into town occasionally, only wear a slight lappet of cloth or leather in front, attached to their waist-belt of beads.

The negroes carry everything upon their heads instead of in their hands, a bottle, a cup, a tumbler, a piece of fruit, or even a letter; in the latter case they put a stone on the top of it to keep it from blowing off. This habit causes them to be extremely upright, and gives them a very free carriage. They have all remarkably fine figures, both women and men; the latter are more like statues of Hercules than actual men, the development of muscle is so enormous.

June 29th. I find a letter written by me to England at this date, saying, "1 continue to like Demerara much, and it agrees with me very well."

"I find that I dine out somewhere or other three days in the week or more. Yesterday I dined at the Governor's where we sat down 26 to dinner. There were all the bigwigs in the colony, and such a lot of grey heads that I was almost ashamed of my own brown one."

I started into "the bush," having collected five guns and as many dogs, (half hound, half anything,) to look for deer, tiger, tiger-cat, or pig. The huntsman was armed with an old gun, a cutlass, and an old key-bugle. The cutlass I could not make out the use of at first, but afterwards found that it would have been impossible for him to get through the bush, which is matted and intertwined with bush-rope, without cutting his way in several places.

This bush-rope is like a kind of vine which runs from the bottom to the very tops of the trees, and entwines itself amongst the boughs like woodbine. It grows as thick as a man's leg, and is of enormous strength. The key-bugle my huntsman had was both to make a noise, I suppose, and call the dogs. The parts of the bush we drew were some it *"abandoned* estates" which had been grown over with shrubs, bush-rope, etc., and some standing sugar-cane fields.

The plan was, for the huntsman to go on with his pack, and for the sportsmen to run on and place themselves at corners of the cane Areas (where two sides of the trench which surrounded them could be commanded) to get a shot as the deer bounded out.

We drew all morning and found nothing but a crab-dog, (an animal something between a racoon and a fox,) to which the pack gave chase through the caves and were called off. We saw the tracks of deer innumerable, but that was our share.

I was, however, struck by the various birds of beautiful plumage, and numerous reptiles and fruits which were new to me. Amongst the latter I found the orange and lime trees bearing the blossom, the unripe, and the perfectly ripe fruit, all at the same time, which they do all the year round. The orange here is *green* when ripe, and not *orange colour*. The pine-apples in Demerara look very fine but are not equal to the English grown ones. Indeed none of the West Indian fruit is equal to what we get at home.

June 30th. Lieuts. White and Perrin arrived in the schooner "Flying Fish" from Barbadoes, with the B. Company.

By this time I had formed a pretty large acquaintance in Georgetown. Craig, the Solicitor-General, became my greatest friend and ally.

July 7th. I breakfasted with Craig, and started with him, Johnson R. A., Captain Travers, 3rd W. I. Regiment, and Van Waterschoodt, the Police Inspector General, in the carriage of the latter, in which we put police horses, and drove up to Victoria, Jack Alt's country farm, to shoot.

The roads were so bad (in some places under water) that the carriage stuck fast. We all had to get out and lift the wheels with levers out of the holes, getting up to our middles in water ourselves; however, we arrived at Alt's at four o'clock, p.m., and went into the Bush to look for ducks, red or brown, and other game, such as wipipi, muscovy ducks, curry curry or flamingo, of which there are red and brown. We got eaten up with musquitoes and sand-flies, and did not get a shot, so we retired to Alt's, where we found that excellent fellow Alt had come all the way from Georgetown, between 18 and 20 miles, to entertain us, which he did in grand style. We each had our hammock with us, an indispensable thing in the country, and turned in about ten o'clock to be up early the next morning. Much against my will, we were all out by six o'clock excepting Vanderschoodt, and having put three police horses in the carriage, we drove up to Mahaica Barracks, (then deserted and over-grown with bush,) and went down the Creek in a boat. Amongst us we killed 5 curry curry, and 5 wipipi ducks. We lost 5 other ducks that fell into the water. The sand-flies were so thick that I could not remain on the shore to re-load my gun after shooting the wipipi.

Having been devoured by the musquitoes and sand-flies, we returned by the sea-shore (where we saw lots of ducks) to Jack Alt's to a lunch breakfast at eleven o'clock, and left again for Georgetown at two, p.m.

We had to wade through parts of the road that were under water, and when within half a mile of our journey's end, close to our Barracks, the axle-tree bent, the springs broke, and we were just running off the road into the trench when we were pulled up, and found the sand of the road had got into the boxes of the wheels and had set them on fire! We had to walk the rest of the way, and I sent a fatigue party out to bring in the carriage.

July 19th. My detachment joined the 3rd W. I. Regiment in giving a Ball to the Governor and Mrs. Barklay, which was attended by about 160 people.

July 21st. A party of us, viz., Vanderschoodt, Johnson R. A., Mills, 3rd W. I. Regiment, Dennis, the Governor's Private Secretary, and myself, left Georgetown in the police schooner, a vessel of 20 tons on a trip to the Arabian Coast. As the wind and tide were against us, the Captain of the Ferry Steamer towed us out of the river, and then left us to sail away with little or no wind at two o'clock, p.m.,

Our steersman was one of the police who knew nothing about his work, or scarcely the way we were to go. The water during most of our voyage was very shallow; the soundings were taken by a black boy with a seven foot pole, who kept constantly at his post, exclaiming, as he thrust the pole into the sea, "Plenty water dare, plenty water dare; five foot water—hard sand. Plenty water no dare;" and bump went the schooner on a sand bank. After getting off into deep water again, the nigger would go on in the same strain, occasionally varying his monotonous cry with, "Six feet water—soft mud;" after which he would change again to, "Plenty water dare, plenty water no dare," and bump again we went.

In this way we went on, sometimes scraping, sometimes bumping, on these sand banks, until about ten o'clock p.m., when we struck heavily on Zimmerman's Bank, a very dangerous place. Here we were left by the tide high and dry, till its return, six hours afterwards, when it came with a heavy surf, which washed right over us, and struck us so heavily that the schooner shivered again, and would have broken up had she not been got into deep water in about twenty minutes after the return tide. As it was, our rudder was unshipped, and we were at the mercies of the surf, three miles at sea. We, however, managed to get into Essiquibo River, and landed at Spring Gardens at five a.m., bathed and breakfasted on the side of the River, and afterwards dropped down five miles to Pomona, a Police Station. Here we slung our hammocks all in a row, in a dilapidated old house, which had once been a nice place; took a walk out to the church, and much admired the splendid trees, fruits and shrubs. We dined off our provisions from the schooner, to which we added some chickens, and after sundry glasses of cold rum punch, turned into our hammocks, well tired. The next morning we were up at five a.m., why, I can't say. Johnson, &c., went up the Pomona Creek in a boat, with their guns, but returned without having a shot; however, they captured an Ai, or three-toed sloth, which they brought home.

I drove with Vanderschoodt 12 miles down the coast to Cossony, and went over the convict prison there. I was much pleased with the drive, though the roads were bad. We all dined with a Doctor Stark, near the Church, where we met some ladies.

We were told there were *no musquitoes* there. The ladies appeared in low dresses, with bare arms! The musquitoes were in millions; and I never heard such a slapping and tapping as went on amongst the fair sex. Poor Dennis had a pair of thin white trowsers on, and unfortunately sat on a cane-bottomed chair. He was excessively restless for some time, and at last rushed away to a sofa, feeling as if he had sat down in a bed of nettles. The dinner went off as well as could be expected in an atmosphere of musquitoes and sand flies; and after a slow evening, we returned to our hammocks. I had a musquito netting tent over mine, so was free from the annoyance of bites, but the rest of the party got half eaten alive.

Next day we embarked again, at seven a.m., having repaired the schooner and got out to sea on our return to Georgetown, but were becalmed off some Island, and did not get back till four o'clock the following morning. The 3rd W. I. Regiment had a good billiard table, which was a great source of amusement. The general business of the day with me was to breakfast at the Mess breakfast at nine o'clock, play a couple of games of billiards, settle with the prisoners, get into my hammock, which swung in the verandah, and read; lunch at two o'clock, read or write, or play billiards till four o'clock, then get on my horse (which I was allowed forage for, as acting Paymaster and Quartermaster of the Detachment) and if possible get Craig out to take a ride with me. I generally, then, finished the day by dining with Craig, or McNulty, or J. Cooper; and on Mess guest days, at Mess with two or three dining with me. On the latter occasions, after the Band had done playing, speeches were the order of the evening. The American Consul would get up and propose the health of his distinguished friend, the Attorney General, (Craig was then Acting Attorney General,) and would not sit down under a ten minutes' speech, which, however, was the same on each occasion. The Attorney. General would then rise, return thanks, and make a most clever sarcastic speech in return, which would bring the Consul on his legs again. With this and other people's health being drank, and thanks returned in long speeches, the evenings were got through.

On the 12th of August Sergeant Kinahan died in Hospital, of yellow fever, after four days illness. This was the first case of "yellow" that had occurred, but the common fever and ague now became very prevalent. The average number of cases monthly treated in hospital during the Autumn, was 135 out of 152 men; but some of these men were treated two, or sometimes three times in the month. August and September were considered to be the most sickly months there. The dry season sets in in August. In former years, before this fever was understood, the old planters never ordered a new suit of clothes till October, as they. were uncertain who would wear them next.

August 18th. I joined Craig, Dr. Bunyon, and Armitage, and proceeded up the Demerary River to visit the Camooney Creek, 20 miles above Georgetown. We halted our boats, and dined with Mr. Henderson at Vive Ja Force, and he persuaded us to remain all night. The house is situated close to the river in a regular swamp, and goes by the name of Fever Hall, from the circumstances of every one's getting fever who stays there. It was in a most dilapidated state, nevertheless we slung our hammocks in some empty rooms and slept the night through, till four o'clock the next morning, without any incident occurring, except that one of our boat's crew had his toes bitten and sucked by vampire bats in his sleep.

We left Vive la Force at 5 a.m. after getting some coffee, and rowed up the river about 6 miles before we reached the entrance to the Creek. On arriving there we rowed a little way up against a regular sluice water, then halted, bathed, lunched, and remained to rest for two or three hours. The rain now came down in torrents, and continued the whole evening. We were obliged to keep constantly baling out the boat, but as it was, we were ankle deep in water the whole time. Craig and Bunyon, who had been up there some years before, thought that Mount Pleasant (only a sand-hill in the dreary track) was about *three* miles from the entrance of the Creek. This was the place we were to land and sleep at. However the crew pulled for hours. We passed another Creek when some doubt arose as to which was the proper one to pursue, and we resolved to keep to the right. The crew got disheartened and tired, the sun began to set, or rather it began to get very dark, and the whole bush was under-water. We saw no prospect of a landing-place. I then took an oar to encourage the crew, and we plied our oars vigorously for another hour, till the Creek got so narrow that it was not wide enough to use them; our passage was obstructed by fallen trees as well as by those that threw their branches across; however we persevered, pushing, the boat along for some time after dark, and were just consulting what to do where we were till daylight, when we gave a few halloas as a chance of being heard. Our shout was answered, and presently we saw a light through the trees. We then pushed up to the place, and found the sand-hill (Mount Pleasant?) where a negro was living in a hut for the purpose of cutting shingles or wooden tiles.

On reaching this place, we found Craig and Armitage, who had been sick all evening, so ill that we had to carry them out of the boat, up to a deserted hut of a shed. Here we slung the hammocks, which with everything else we had were wet through. We deposited Craig on an old kind of seat made into a sofa, Armitage we put into his hammock, and after getting up our provisions and attending to the sick, Bunyon and I pitched into a piece of corned beef, smoked our pipes, and turned in.

About twelve o'clock everything was as still as death. I lay awake, not being able to sleep, when presently I heard a noise; *pit, pat, pit, pat, pit, pat.* I suddenly held my breath for a few seconds, and glad I was to breathe freely once more. Craig was awake also, and cried out, "By God, Davenport, that's a tiger."

"I know that too well, old fellow," I replied, "but *how* did he get in here?" for I believed he was under the hammocks, and only choosing which of us he would take.

I had matches in my flannel-jacket pocket, which I had on, and struck a light. I looked out and all round the hut, but saw no tiger, and if he had been there he had left through the open window-frame. The crew of the boats I found lying on the floor, and they had not been disturbed.

Next morning I tracked the tiger along the sand, to where he jumped on to the top of our hut and off again.

The shingle-man told us that there were several of them about, and that his comrade was taken by one of them in the middle of the day, about a fortnight before. I suppose he smelt us out, but did not like attacking so many at once.

After we had put our guns in order that morning, (for they had been under-water the previous evening in the boats,) I took a walk out into the bush to see if I could get a shot at our friend, but saw no traces after he got amongst the trees.

Afterwards we borrowed the negro's canoe, and paddled up to a marshy savannah, to see some "Bucks," who had a quantity of preserved bird-skins, together with tiger and other skins. We then, finding little to shoot at, amused ourselves by bathing, eating, and drinking, till the "night-hawk" or "goat-sucker" came out; when we sheaved what a difficult thing it is to kill them, as they dart and twist about, catching the flies at night-fall.

The following day we left these "*pleasant*" quarters at seven o'clock, a.m., intending to visit another Buck" settlement up the other creek, to see a camoody snake or boa which they had captured, and which was said to be 40 feet long. They took it while stretched out ill a sleepy state, digesting a wild pig which it had swallowed. We found, however, we had not time for that, so pushed on down the creek, shooting at any curious birds we saw on the way, such as the toucan, &c. On entering the Demerary River we discovered a troop of black monkeys rushing along the tops of the trees, alongside the river. We put in Is close to the bank as we could, to get a few shots at them, but some very thorny bushes prevented our landing. We got into a lot of long rushes close in, and awaited the troop. When they passed we fired several shots and floored a couple of them, but found we could not get on shore to pick them up, much to our annoyance. After firing these shots someone told me to look under my feet in the rushes, and there I saw a great snake coiled up asleep. Craig shot him and he measured six feet. We then continued our journey to Vive la Force, where we arrived and dined at four o'clock. We left again at eight and returned to Georgetown at ten o'clock, p.m.

September 13th. A good deal of fever amongst the troops at this time, I generally had from 40 to 45 men in hospital daily, out of my 150. Three or four of the officers had had it for a week or so but recovered.

Poor Colonel Mills, 3rd W. I. Regiment, the Commandant of the Garrison, was taken ill about two o'clock this morning with purging and vomiting, and fainted in trying to get to Dr. Simpson's room, in the same verandah, where he lay for some time, and at last crawled back to his bed, where he had to wait until his servant came at six o'clock, as he had no means of calling for assistance. The doctors physicked him instead of giving him something soothing and nourishing (for he had eaten nothing for two days previous) and at ten o'clock a.m. he was in a collapsed state. They *then* sent from Dr. Blair from town, who said he was too late: that he ought to have been sent for before. The Colonel remained in this state till seven o'clock in the evening when he died. We buried him the following afternoon with military honours, after having the funeral service read over him in the Cathedral. All the judges and principal people of Georgetown attended the funeral. I had the command of the firing party, consisting of 320 of his own Regiment, with my Detachment added.

I never was so disgusted as with the common negroes here, men, women, boys, and girls, at the funeral, dancing, shouting, yelling, and singing all round the procession as it moved along.

September 11th. I went out golden plover shooting

with Craig and Travers, within three miles of Victoria. We fired away about 2 lbs. of shot each and only bagged nine plover.

17th- Van Waterschoodt sent Craig and myself With Police horses about ten miles up the coast to Annandale, when in two hours I bagged twenty plover, and Craig fourteen do. Total 17 couple. We had the sun at 128°.

A TRIP UP THE ESSIQUIBO RIVER

SEPTEMBER 19th, 1849. I left Georgetown with Imlach in a schooner to join Armitage and Bunyon at Ampa, and go up to the Falls on the Essiquibo.

We took the precaution of bringing a quantity of provisions with us, and I took my canteen, with a breakfast service for three in it, also my cooking tin, which had three tin plates and a teakettle in it. I likewise took tea, sugar, coffee, spirits, etc. I found my companion Imlach a good fellow, so we got on well.

We got becalmed at night, and dropped anchor near to Hog Island. We were still becalmed most of the next day in the river, but got up at last to Mr. Baird's, of Ampa, where we were hospitably received, and met Bunyon and Armitage. We all slung our hammocks in one room, five in a row, at half-past ten o'clock, after the tables were cleared away, and the ladies had retired to their rest.

On coming, up the river we saw a large snake of various colours swimming along; he made for the schooner with his head erect, but not being able to get up the side, he swam over to an Island in the river half-a-mile from where he must have taken the water.

September 21st. We were roused out of our hammocks, much against my will, at six o'clock. We got some coffee, then went to the river and bathed for an hour. I was rather put out by not getting breakfast until half-past ten o'clock. The day was passed in superintending Armitage and Bunyon's canoes and boats, being prepared by having awnings of rushes put up, and places for their cargoes arranged for their expedition. They intended to go a long way up the Essiquibo, nearly to its source, then cross to some branch of the Demerary, and return by that river. This might occupy two months. They undertook this, attended by a lot of Bucks as crew, for the purpose of collecting specimens of all kinds of plants, and bird and animal skins of the country.

Bunyon was busily engaged in making bullets for an old rifle of Armitage's. I took a shot with this article, when the nipple fled over my head, and the bullet remained in the barrel. I therefore recommended them to abandon the rifle, if they valued their own lives, which they did. Their gun was just such another article, but that they persisted in taking with them. We dined principally on mine and Imlach's provisions, for there was little else at Port Ampa. We passed most of the evening in the garden-house on the hill behind the house with books and pipes.

September 22nd. Roused out again at six o'clock! We bathed for an hour as usual in the river, where there is a beautiful sandy place, surrounded by rocks. Here we had again nothing to do all the livelong day, not being able to start on the trip, as the canoes were not ready, nor many of the crews assembled, so most of the time was passed in the summer-house reading Natural History. Our kind hostess, Mrs. Baird, was taken suddenly ill

I was awoke in the night by hearing an old cock crying out in great distress. I fancied a snake had hold of him, for his cries at first were very loud, but by degrees became fainter and fainter, till they totally ceased, when I knew *his* life was up. I reported the circumstance in the morning to Mr. Baird, and on looking into the hen-house, there was my friend dead enough on the floor. He had been attacked and killed by a vampire bat.

Craig and Spencer Hackett joined us from Georgetown, which in some way made up for the *ennui* of the two last dreadfully stupid days. We passed a jolly evening, and tried Brumenhausen[11] by jury for amusement. We kicked up a great row, I am afraid more than we ought to have done, considering Mrs. Baird was in the house ill.

---

[11] A settler up the river, who had arrived that day.

On the following morning we were all awoke at 3-40 by Brumenhausen (or as we nicknamed him Brummagem) hammering at the door with his villanous high-heeled shoe as hard as he could, for which he got "pretty considerably" abused by us all.

The canoes having now arrived at a state of perfection for the expedition, and most of the crew being assembled, we left Ampa. The party consisted of Armitage, Bunyon, Craig, Spencer Hackett, Imlach, Doctor Ward, and myself. We touched at "the Grove," about five miles up the river, to breakfast and pick up the rest of the Indian crew. We then proceeded 25 miles, or nine hours' paddling, up to Ouyha, (pronounced who are you,) where there were a few Buck huts, one of which belonged to Herman Patterson, the Captain of our crew. Here we slung our hammocks in an empty house, and remained the night. On roaming about amongst these people I found one cooking the leg of an alligator, and the shoulders of a large red monkey. I tasted the alligator, but it was uncommonly tough, and had something the flavour of an old cock. The monkey looked too much like part of a child for me to try it.

The next day we left Ouyha at six o'clock a.m., and paddled up the river, four Indians paddling in the bow, and four or six in the stern of each canoe. The centre of the canoes was arched over with rushes to protect us from the sun, but I found it such stupid work, and hot into the bargain, lying inside, that I took a paddle and worked most of the day. Armitage and Bunyon had invited us all as their guests, and of course provided the food and liquor; however, they trusted too much to the resources of the country they were to pass through, expecting to shoot all kinds of game, deer, wild pig, etc., and laid in little or no stock, except some flour, salt fish, and spirits. Luckily Craig and S. Hackett had brought up a supply of salt beef, tongues, preserved salmon, etc., for their own expedition. These things and a barrel of biscuits lasted till this day, when we found Bunyon dealing out the biscuits very sparingly, and when it came out that we had no provisions for ourselves or crew, with the exception of salt fish, a few plantains, and the flour, which latter we were not to touch, as it would be required by the botanists and geologists when far beyond the regions of the Indians.

Our prospects of starving (for no provisions could be got nearer than Georgetown, and we were going daily farther from it) were so bad, that Craig hired a Macousi Indian as a hunter, to go daily into the bush for game. However, it appeared that the country was quite destitute of anything of the kind, and the Macousis themselves were nearly starving, but as luck would have it, in the middle of the day, a wild pig was discovered swimming across the river at a distance from us. Both the canoe and the boat gave instant chase, and prevented his gaining the land.

The Captain of the crew shot an arrow into his shoulder, and Craig finished him with a charge of shot. We dragged him into the boats with joy, and directly to a landing place, where we cut him up, and put him into a "*pepper pot*," and found him uncommonly good, with some cassava (or cassada) bread, which we got from some Macousis.

"Pepper-pot" is made by boiling up pork or chickens, or in fact any meat, in an earthen pot, (which is never emptied, but all scraps constantly put in and warmed up afresh,) with hot peppers, green and red, and with about a pint of cassareip added to it, and a capital thing it is. cassareip is made from the cassada (pronounced cassarda) root, which is taken up and grated on tin graters into a pulp; this pulp is then put into a basket-work strainer, and hung up to strain. The juice that drops from it is caught in a vessel for the purpose, and is the most deadly poison. This liquid is then boiled for a certain time, during which process the poisonous matter escapes, and the liquor, which becomes like treacle, is called cassareip, and is used in making many of the sauces, under the names of Harvey, Soy, etc., and is always put into pepper-pot. The pulp of the cassada is washed and strained, and then laid on a griddle, formed into cakes, similar to the oat-cake of Scotland. This is the only bread used by the Indians, and, it is also much used in the towns.

The bows and arrows used by these Indians are very fine, and of immense strength, the arrows formed of a reed about five feet long, at the point of which is inserted about half a foot of some very hard and heavy wood, and well whipped in with twine. The point of this is burnt to harden it, and make it sharp; it is then made to fit into an iron hollow point, which has in some cases a double barb, or in others five or six barbs. This point is not a fixture, but is attached to the arrow by a string a few inches from the end. When shot from the bow, the iron head is put on the point of the arrow, and after entering the object comes off, so that in case of shooting a fish, the arrow would act as a float. From the place where the iron head is attached there is a long string, which runs up the side of it, and which the Indian puts round his thumb, so that he may pull away at the fish without injuring the arrow. It was this arrangement which saved our pig for us in the river, for it would have sunk directly it was killed, if the Indian had not got the barb of his arrow in its shoulder, and the string round his thumb.

These Indians don't know the use of the gun or rifle, and entirely live by their bows and arrows in killing both fish and animals. They sometimes use the blow-pipe and darts, a long hollow tube of about six or eight feet, through which they blow darts, (like a boy with a pea-shooter,) which are poisoned with the Wourali, a poison they make by extracts from the fangs of some kind of snake, and different herbs. It is so deadly that a bird, or even a large animal, struck with the point of one of these, dies almost on the spot, but this does not render the flesh unwholesome in any way. The Indians are capital shots with these things, and scarcely ever miss their object.

After cooking our pepper-pot with the pig, and making a good meal, we started afresh, and got up to Arratacka Rapids by four p.m. We got over these without any very great difficulty, and slung hammocks in a deserted -Buck's logic" just above them for the night. At this point there was only one inhabited "logis," which was occupied by a starving Buck and his wife.

After cooking, bathing, etc., till it was dark, we turned in, all our hammocks slung under the shed, which had no sides to it. In the middle of the night Craig awoke me by shouting out that he heard a tiger roar in the bush once or twice, and as we, were all lying at the edge of it, it was not comfortable. The starving old Macousi heard the roar also, and immediately blew up his fire. Our fires had gone out, and all my shouting to our crew could not awaken them.

It was no use lying there to be attacked, so I jumped out to look for the Indian crew. I saw by a few sparks that they were about a hundred yards away from us in the bush, and all fast asleep. I dashed into the underwood, and got to them, not without the almost certain conviction that I should be nabbed on my way. I found them slung in their hammocks amongst the trees, and very soon made them blow up our fires afresh. We were then all secure, for no wild animal will approach a blaze.

For all this trouble I got the abuse of Bunyon and Armitage for awakening them and making a noise!

We all turned out at five o'clock, and sent the huntsman away to hunt fish. Bunyon and Armitage went away in another canoe, for the same purpose, for we became very sensible that we had no provisions left. They came back about eight o'clock without any success. We then proceeded up the river, expecting to- find our huntsman had shot some "Pacco" fish. These are peculiar to the Essiquibo, are much of the shape of a John Dorie, but grow to the size of 8 or 10 lbs. weight. They feed entirely upon a kind of mossy weed which grows upon the rocks under water, at the rapids, the leaf of which is something similar to lettuce. It is at the time these fish are *grazing* (their mouth and front teeth being like a sheep's or any other grazing animal), that they are shot with the bow and arrow by the Indians; there being no other way of taking them except by poisoning the river, which is often done, when hundreds float to the surface quite stupified but none the worse for food. The wourali is the poison used by the Indians for this purpose. On our overtaking our huntsman we found he had been unsuccessful himself, but had bought a pacco about 7 lbs. weight from some Carribee he met with. This was cut up and shared the fate of the pig, by being put into the pepper-pot, and was very good indeed. Hunger makes a good sauce.

We left Arrataka at eight a.m. and passed up Arrasaw, Tamunado, Marrahi, Carra-carrahoo, Haboniabanaro rapids, (or *falls*, as they are called) and arrived at Harroo, a Carribee Indian Settlement, about the Ittabally rapids, which we also passed up. This we found a different tribe. They were the Carribees or Red Feet, had woolly heads, (so different from the long lank hair of the Maconsis), and were quite naked with the exception of a small flap in front. They wear a naked knife in the string which they have round their naked waists, and paint their feet and ankles red. The women, in addition, wear a long common pin stuck through the under lip, with the point outwards. They received us civilly, and allowed us to sling the hammocks in an empty logis amongst them. We got some cassada bread and dined upon the pacco, leaving the Indian crew to look out amongst their countrymen for their suppers. The manner of getting the boat up the rapids was very extraordinary. As soon as we came to the foot of the Falls, and paddling was useless, the Maconsis would all jump out, the first one with the end of a rope in his mouth, dive right under the current, and appear far up on the other side of it. As soon as he had gone down a few yards another would dive, laying hold of the rope with his teeth, and so on a good many of them, and would follow the first till they all came up in the same place. They then hauled up the boats by this rope. This operation had to be gone through several times in each rapid, before the thing was accomplished. These men and boys could not have stemmed the current if they had attempted to swim over it, so they dived beneath its force, and rose far up the stream.

They are like otters or fish in the water. I saw one remain quite stationary for a long time in a very rapid stream, he then sunk his head and appeared in the middle of the same stream, but much higher up.

Harroo was the highest point of the river that I went to, and much as I had heard of the grandeur of the "Falls" of the Essiquibo and the magnificent scenery, I could not see it myself. The broad placid river studded with islands covered with thick foliage, below the rapids, was fine scenery, but there was nothing *magnificent* about it. The rapids themselves, running between rocky and wooded islands, were pretty, but as to calling these streams "Falls," it is preposterous. They are nothing in comparison to the rapids on the St. Lawrence, which really are fine, though they do not even get the name of Falls. I could, *by myself*, easily steer a canoe down the Essequibo streams, although the Carribees and Maconsis call them dangerous. The Fraquoi or Huron Indians of North America would laugh at their brethren of the bush for even thinking as they do of them.

We left Harroo on the 27th of September, on our return, Bunyon and Armitage accompanying us,, as they found they had not sufficient provisions nor even common utensils for cooking, knives or forks, spoons or plates, or anything to drink out of belonging to them; though to give them their due, I must say they seemed perfectly content to eat their salt fish, or anything else, with their fingers, in which they seemed by far to surpass the Indians in their barbarity.

Lucky it was for the rest of us that I had my canteen,

which provided us with knives, forks, spoons, plates, glasses, coffee, &c., &c. The knives and forks I gave out at each meal, on the condition that they were returned to me *clean*, to put up again. As for any of the party, not one had the slightest idea of arrangement or management. This day we shot the Itabally rapids and got to Carracarrahoo at eleven o'clock, where we landed and found some Carribees cooking a baboon and others manufacturing the rouge with which they paint themselves and use for dyeing. We embarked again, I took a paddle and worked down the rapids, which we shot at an awful pace, and arrived at the Arataeka at one o'clock. We halted to bathe; (here it was that we were disturbed by the tiger's roar, on going up.) We saw a few Macaws flying about and a flock of Muscovy ducks, which we tried to stalk. We got behind a rock within fifty yards of them, and tried Armitage's gun, but both barrels snapped and away went the ducks much to our disgust, as we were hard up for food.

We then went, on our return, and called at Morabally (where Brumenhausen lived,) for Mr. Baird, who had gone up the river to assist him in surveying some land, but in doing which they both got lost in the bush, the night being very dark and wet. We sent out people in the canoes to look for them with lights up the creeks, and they did not get back till ten o'clock, having managed to hit upon them by a mere chance. We punished old Brummagem's cellar for the detention. Having picked up what we could here we crossed the river to our old resting-place Ouyha and slung hammocks for the night, though as it turned out, not to sleep, for the baboons, of which there seemed to be a large colony, kept up such a howling till daylight that sleep was out of the question. In addition to these howling brutes, the razor-grinders were hard at work, and would defy any one to sleep whilst they were awake. These are large brown beetles with beaks exactly like the large claw of a lobster, with which they take hold of a bough of a tree and spin themselves round and round it till they saw it off. The noise occasioned by the operation is exactly like a fellow grinding a razor, hence the name.

Next morning one of the crew was taken ill with cholera; his cries might have been heard a couple of miles in the bush. I sent him some spirits which relieved him a little, but neither Dr. Bunyon nor Dr. Warde had anything to give him, and we were obliged to leave him to his fate in the tender hands of some Maconsis who were there.

We all left for Ampa; Armitage then went back to the Penal Settlement up the Cayuna River to make arrangements for a passage back to Georgetown for myself, Craig, Imlach, and Spencer Hackett, in a schooner that was there taking in stone. This vessel picked us up at Ampa where we got becalmed and lay all night, but got down the river by degrees, and to Georgetown at half-past two on the 30th September, after a very uninteresting, badly arranged, and disgustingly stupid trip as any one could conceive.

After all my precautions not to touch the ground with my naked feet I found that two jiggers had got into my toes, which the cabin-boy on board the schooner extracted for me, and the next morning my servant picked out three more. The jigger is a kind of small worm that gets under the skin and breeds if let alone, and in time causes the place to fester and become very sore. Although mosquitoes are in *myriads near* the *sea*, yet there are none twenty miles up the rivers in the bush.

GEORGETOWN, DEMERARA

October 2nd. I took a ride up a "side line," on the East Coast, where I met with an alligator, about three and a half feet long. He ran into the middle of the road, and stopped until I galloped at him, when he retreated into some long grass. I pointed him out to a "nigger," who killed him with a rail.

October 4th. I went with Birch and Craig to Hagg's Bush, about seven miles up the Demerara River, to shoot parrots, which fly across between four and six o'clock, to their roosting places, after feeding on the berries of some large trees in the bush near there. We saw about 400 or 500, but only bagged three birds. They take very heavy shot to bring them down.

December 17th. I was going down to the Men's Barracks, across the Parade Ground, where they play cricket, when I saw two snipe walking about. Wainwright was with me; we got our guns and beat *the Parade*. I killed one snipe and wounded the other, which flew into a cane piece close by. We followed and found several others. I bagged five couple myself, Wainwright killed one and a half couple and a snake, six feet long. We were out about two hours, when I was completely knocked up and sick.

October 14th. I was dining with Craig, but was obliged to go home and go to bed at eight o'clock, with something very like fever. The English Mail had arrived that day, and I walked down to the Post Office for my letters (about a mile) when I was suddenly taken so ill that I could scarcely walk back; however, I did not give in, but dined at Craig's. I was in great pain with spasms all night. The next day also, I continued suffering much from spasms all over my body, and very seedy besides. I did not lay up at once, which was foolish, but went out and sat with Craig, who was then laid up with fever and ague. I was obliged, however, to take to bed again at eight o'clock and physic myself, but I got no rest from the continued spasms. The next day I was regularly *hors de combat*, —in high fever, and vomiting excessively. Simpson attended me and gave me twenty pills (sixty grains) of quinine, morphine, and calomel, in five hours. I continued dreadfully ill all night, retching every five minutes, till I fell back exhausted on my pillow. Major Abbott happened to hear me as he walked in the verandah, and remarked, as he afterwards told me, that I would not live till daylight next morning. This prophecy did not turn out correct, for next day I was considerably better, though suffering great pain in my stomach from the vomiting and quantity of quinine I had taken. Simpson put a mustard plaster on my stomach, to stop the irritation, or rather to bring it out, which it certainly did. Whether there was cayenne in it or not, I can't tell; but I suffered the tortures of the — for the time it was on. I have often had blisters, but they were fleabites in comparison to this. On the fourth day of the fever, the 17th, I got up, and in three days more was pretty well again.

October 22nd. I was invited by the Colonists to a public dinner, given to the Hon. Mr. Stanley, who was making a tour through the West Indies for his own information, with respect to those Colonies. He was young man, about twenty-two years of age, rather ugly, spoke as if he had no palate in his mouth, and was almost inaudible through this defect; but he made a most excellent speech after dinner. This month the thermometer stood higher than any other; for, on the 28th and 29th, it was up to 96° in the shade, at half-past three o'clock, p.m., 1st November, 97° at a quarter past three p.m.

November 9th. A grand Ball was given at Government House, to which the whole Garrison was invited. The Officers of the 3rd W. I. Regiment considered that they had been *slighted* by the Governor, because they had not been asked to join his parties to Berbiee and Essiquibo, and because he had not got up a dinner for some Major of theirs, who arrived to take command of the Regiment.

In consequence of this idea which they had got into their heads, they went to the Ball in a body, made their bow to the Governor and Mrs. Barkley, and walked straight out of the room, with the exception of Major Abbott. They went to their mess room, which was in the town, got excessively drunk, and kicked up such a noise that they were heard by most of the houses in the neighbourhood.

It was lucky for them the Governor was as mild a man as he was, or they might all have been tried by Court-Martial for disrespect; however, he took no notice of it, and Mrs. Barkley merely remarked it was just the conduct that might have been expected from the 3rd West India Regiment.

I got more disgusted every day with the set of the 3rd West; and as I so often dined with Craig, I resolved to leave their Mess, as a regular member, and only be on the books as an honorary one.

Craig persuaded me to dine with him every day that I was otherwise disengaged. He tried hard to make me take up my abode in his house, and proposed that I should turn his drawing room into my bedchamber!

The Dry Season now ended—for since the middle of August—we had had no rain, and were put on an allowance of two buckets of water a day each; but as I was allowed a horse by Government, I got three buckets a day more for him, which I appropriated for my bathing purposes, and sent my animal to a pool in the Square for his drink.

There were no wells in Georgetown, and rain water was selling at fourpence a bucket in the town, where there were but few tanks. I have often seen the trenches, which are choked up with weeds and stagnant water, being ladled out with tea cups by the negroes, to get a bucket full from them.

November 13th. Michel came down from Barbadoes to visit us, and dined with me in my own quarters, where I gave a dinner to Craig, Goodman, Schrach, Imlach,

Norton, Johnson, R. A., and Perrin.

Major Abbott left Demerara by the mail of the 5th December, and I being the next Senior Officer, the Command of the troops in Demerara devolved upon me.

December 14th. The Garrison gave a ball to Cowan of the Commissariat, on his leaving Demerara for Barbadoes. Ninety invitations were issued, but the rain came down in such torrents that only about thirty people attended, including the Governor and Mrs. Barkley. Mr. Cowan is a natural son of the Duke of Kent, and upon the accession to the throne of Queen Victoria, she settled £1000 a-year upon her half-brother. He was a universal favourite, and every one was giving him parties.

December 25th, 1849. Christmas Day. What a difference was here from Christmas Day in England The thermometer stood at 86° in the shade at eleven a.m., and at 91° at half-past twelve. No merry bells or cordial greetings of "A happy Christmas to you." No preparations for Christmas cheer, as rounds of beef, mince pies! &c. No blazing logs, but a blazing hot sun, all the people drunk and rolling about the streets, with drunken songs and continual firing of pistols. I dined with Craig *in his own* house for the last time, as he had given it up to Holmes to live in.

One morning I went into Kerr's room, 3rd W. I. Regiment, when I saw a heap of what I thought were nuts on the floor. I asked him where he got them from, when he told me that they were black beetles, which came in a flight into the mess-room the night before during dinner, and that these had been taken off the table and put into the finger-glasses and shades of the candles, and he had had the curiosity to count them and found that there were over 1100 of them.

I had nearly forgotten my friends the ants of this country. First is the house, or black common ant, otherwise called the wild Irish ant, from its quick movements, running to and fro in the most absent manner. Nothing can keep it away from sugar; wherever sugar is, and one ant finds it, immediately the whole nest assemble and carry it off by bits.

When I packed up my baggage to leave Demerara, my servant put a bit of sugar in my large chest, which was filled with all kinds of things. A few days afterwards somebody wanted some shot, I found my man had packed that up also, and on unpacking the chest I found thousands upon thousands of these pests had got down to the sugar, and were making their nest there.

The *little* red ant is a diminutive insect, not larger than a pin's point; it is of a yellowish rather than red colour. It also builds behind the cornice of the rooms, and is a great nuisance in the dressing-room. It delights to feed upon oil, and where there is any kind of grease, there are these little insects found. They get into the hair-brushes, and being so small are not seen, but very soon felt after brushing them into the hair.

The Hunter Ant is a large black fellow, that only appears after dark, when it goes in droves from one end of the building to the other, killing, and eating up all other kinds of insects it finds, such as cockroaches, flies, centipedes, scorpions, &c., in fact it clears the whole place in a night and is never seen; the only sign of their visit being a few dead ones that have met with accidents, or been drowned in their travels.

One morning whilst lying in bed I witnessed a battle between two ants. They fought most vigorously and much like dogs, biting fiercely at each other's legs. The battle lasted several minutes, till the one crippled the other by breaking his legs with his teeth.

The Parasol Ant lives in the country, in a sandy soil; it is a large yellow one. It throws up its nest or mound of sand to the height of a couple of feet. It traces a long way from the nest to its feeding places, in a track made by itself. It will destroy a whole garden in a night, by biting the leaves of the plants off, cutting them to a convenient size to walk off with, and then carrying them away to its nest. They somehow (each one singly) carry the burden the head, or on the side of the head, from which it got the name of the Parasol Ant.

The Wood Ant, which lives in the bush, builds in trees and forms a nest, much like a wasp's, between the forks or attached to a bough. This ant always forms a covered way, from the ground up the tree to its habitation, and frequently has its covered passage along the ground. Another wood ant is a small red one, that eats away dry timber: for instance the wooden pillar of a portico. It will find some little hole at the bottom to begin with, and in a few years the pillar, to all appearance perfectly sound outside, will be as hollow as a quill inside, with the exception of these ants and their nests. When I relieved Buck, at Eve Leary Barracks, on moving the table in the room, one of the legs was found to be quite hollow, having had a nest in it. I one day was leaning against the railing of the verandah near the mess-room, when quite suddenly I felt stung as if with nettles all over. I found my hands covered with these little devils as well as my body. I had shaken the railing in which they had a nest, for this they attacked me, nor could I get rid of them until I got into a bath.

In my room at St. Vincent's, I found a little hole in one of the supporters, as if eaten by a worm, but on poking with a stick, I found three out of four of them were quite hollow, and deserted by the ants.

I recollect a balustrade in St. Vincent, which had only been erected three or four years, falling with a number of people on it, in consequence of its being undermined by the ants. Several of the people were nearly killed by it.

Mischievous as these insects are, the cock-roaches are a greater bore, for they eat every bit of patent leather off a boot in a very short time. They ate for me the leather off my razor strap, the cork in my hair-oil bottle, four large holes as big as a penny piece in the corner of some folded towels that had been starched by accident; and one night I wafered a letter for the Adjutant-General, on the following morning I found it open, the paper and wafer having been destroyed by them.

Amongst the diseases peculiar to Demerara is lockjaw. It is a common malady there, the least thing bringing it on either in the horse or human being.

Now as I have done with Demerara I give the table of Fever and Ague, and cases treated in hospital out of my Detachment of 152 men.

Men in hospital on September 14th	30	98 in one
Admitted from 14th to 30th September	68	month.
Remained in hospital 1st October	43	94 in one
Admitted 1st to 14th October	51	fortnight

Ditto 1st to 30th October a total of 135 cases, 86 men out of the lower Barrack-room, and 49 out of the upper one!!

From 30th Oct. to 15th Nov. cases treated in hospital	76	155 of which
From 15th to 30th November	79	32 remd. in.
From 1st to 15th December	72	156 of which
From 15th to 30th December	84	38 remd. in.

From 1st to 15th January, 1850, 83, of which 38 still remained in.

FRENCH BLACK FISH. — One day when riding with Van Waterschoodt, he pointed out to me the French black fish, which is not much larger than one's thumb. Its peculiarity consists in its building its nest, consisting of mossy weeds, which it carries in its mouth! and in which it deposits its spawn. Van chewed me several of these in the trench near the Race Course.

There is another small fish in Demerara which comes into the trenches from the river or sea, called the "Four Eyes," from its having four optics; it is a small, narrow fish, and of no use.

SNAKES. — The principal snakes in Demerara are,

1st. — The "Bushmaster," which is the only one that always attacks. Its bite is so deadly that its victim dies in an hour after the attack, and the flesh rots from the bones in about six hours afterwards.

2nd. — Is Le Barry, another very deadly snake, whose bite is always fatal, indeed as fatal and venomous as the Bushmasters.

3rd. — The Camoody, both land and water snakes, which are of the boa species; some say they are venomous, others not.

4th. — Brown snakes and white innumerable, but not venomous.

5th. — The deadly rattle snake.

6th. — The rat tail.

7th. — The whip snake.

8th. — The coral snake, all most venomous, besides others innumerable.

BIRDS. — The snipe, golden plover, crane, white stork, curry curry or flamingo, Muscovy ducks, wipipi and brown ducks, hummingbirds, creepers, ortolan, mocking bird, the *qu' est ce qui dit*? man-of-war birds, parrots, and a thousand others.

ANIMALS. — Deer, tigers, tiger-cats, crab-dog, monkey and baboon, agouti, (a breed between a hare and a rat to all appearance,) sloth, opossum or manicou, armadillo.

INSECTS AND REPTILES. — Besides snakes are the lizards, green and brown, the wood slave, the chameleon, the bat and vampire bat, the scorpion, centipede, the locust and grasshopper, the musquito and sand-fly, the firefly, the jigger. Ants—the hunter, parasol, red, yellow, and black, wild Irish and marabunti, or Jack Spaniard, shock shock, razor grinder, frog, etc.

After I returned from the Essequibo, Armitage and Bunyon started afresh on their expedition, with as little arrangement and precaution as before. They had been out about a fortnight when their stock ran short and they lived, their crew and themselves, on *one plantain* a day for *three days*. They got into a district where game of all kinds was innumerable, and could have killed any quantity, but they had no means of preserving it, no salt, etc., so they had a feast for one day, for meat will not keep in that climate. Armitage was attacked by paralysis, and Bunyon had to urge the Indian crew to exert their utmost power to get back to Ampa in the shortest possible time. They got down in three days and three nights constant paddling, without once stopping to cook any provisions, but were stimulated with occasional drams of spirits. Bunyon got him down just in time to save his life, but he, poor fellow, went blind, and never saw again, and became quite a cripple from the paralytic attack.

VOYAGE TO ST. VINCENT

ON the 19th of January, 1850, the Princess Royal transport arrived with two Companies of the 72nd to relieve my Detachment.

Having been very ill for the few days previous to going on board, I was soon very sick, and had to take to my berth and remain there till the following day, when I got up on deck, and was persuaded to have some devilled cheese and a bottle of champagne, which did me a "world of good." I would recommend it to any sea-sick person as the very best cure.

A booby-bird came on board, and allowed Sharpe to catch it in his hand; it was released, but again boarded us, and was retaken by some of the men, who finally let it go.

January 24th. We found ourselves between Trinidad and Tobago, and made Grenada in the afternoon. Several whales round the ship. Dropped our anchor at 8.40 next morning at St. George.

The view from this Bay is very beautiful, surrounded as it is by lofty hills: Fort George on the left, the town of St. George in front, from which rises a hill well wooded, with all kinds of green shrubs and trees, amongst which are the palm and cocoa-nut, and with various pretty residences peeping out here and there, until it is crowned by Fort Matthew, and backed up by some high hills in the distance.

Linton (my old friend) was quartered here on the Staff, and Biscoe and I went on shore and took up our abode with him. We rode up to Fort Matthew, from whence is a splendid view, which one might dwell on for hours; then went through the town, (a very insignificant one,) and visited Fort George, occupied by the Artillery. We (all the officers on board the Princess Royal) were landed to sit on a Court-Martial on some "nigger" for insubordination. Next day we procured hacks at noon, and rode through the most beautiful, wild, and grand scenery, (very like Killarney,) to the Grand):tang, a lake almost at the summit of the highest hill in the island, 700 feet above the level of the sea. Having viewed the lake, and seen La Bay at the other side of the Island, we lunched on some beef-steak, (how it got there I can't tell,) and Sharpe and I galloped down the hill (some parts of which are excessively steep,) to make some sketches. The pony I rode was the exact cut of a mule, but the best animal I ever crossed for mountain work.

January 28th. After breakfasting with Linton, and taking some sketches, we went on board the Princess Royal and sailed, when she was within an ace of running on the St. George's Point in getting under weigh. Mr. Tubby was left on shore, but came on board the ship in the Bay, much to the annoyance of the Admiralty Agent, who swore awfully, and said, - if it was the Angel Gabriel, I would not wait for him."

We got a glimpse of St. Vincent in the afternoon, a long way to windward, and made the Island out clearly, with the wind dead ahead, and a current running five knots against us.

We dropped our anchor in Kingstown Harbour at four o'clock p.m., and got some of the baggage ashore, which was carried up to Fort Charlotte between two mules. The mules are worked thus. The one is placed before the other as if in tandem; they have regular cart-harness, with breast-strap and breeching; two long bamboo poles are then slung from the back-band, (one on each side like the shafts of a cart,) one end through that of the leading mule, the other through that of the hinder one. Between these poles are placed some iron half-hoops, upon which the load is placed, (about 3 cwt.)

We, that is, Biscoe, myself, Perrin, and Storey, disembarked on the morning of the 31st of January, but did not get up into the barracks at Fort Charlotte until after ten o'clock, for the men were so done up from the effects of fever and ague at Demerara, that it was as much as they could do to walk up the hill, indeed, several were left on the road to take their time.

Fort Charlotte is situated one mile out of the town, 700 feet nearly perpendicular above the sea, on the left entrance to Kingstown Harbour. From the Fort is a most magnificent view all round. On the land side is a valley 700 feet below, filled with guava and other trees, and backed up by ridges of hills, which are clothed with green foliage to their very summits. The highest of these may be between 2000 and 3000 feet. There is a beautiful view of the harbour and its shipping immediately beneath, and a most extensive sea-view on two other sides, with all the Grenadines and small islands, and on a fine day, even Grenada, seventy miles off, spews itself distinctly.

ST. VINCENT

DULL as report made out St. Vincent to be, we rather changed the aspect of affairs. A great number of the inhabitants immediately called on us, which we returned. There were constant dinners going on for a long time, until the people seemed to have a surfeit, for we could not get them to go on dining with us as often as we asked them. We had Sir John and Lady Campbell at Government House, Tony Hobson the Provost-Marshal, C. Stewart the Solicitor-General, etc., also many families in the country. Last, though not least, but biggest by far, and the best of all, Barney Jackson, of the Rocks, near Layon.

The Garrison consisted of ourselves, a Detachment of Royal Artillery, Lieutenant Grant, R.E., Daniell, Barrack Master, etc. We got up a pretty good mess, considering the horrid supplies that were to be obtained on the Island. Beef and mutton, (so tough we never could roast or boil it, we were always obliged to mince it or make it into soup.) Fowls about 2s. 6d. and Guinea fowls, the only good birds there, about 3s. or 3s. 6d, per pair. Turkeys, 5$ or 20s. each. Turtle, about 5d. per pound. Limes I have bought 60 for 6d. Kid and goat mutton is far superior to the sheep mutton, which is very poor, thin stuff. The sheep here have hair, not wool, on their backs. Even an English sheep might be landed, and in a year his wool would fall off, and hair grow in its place. They don't thrive at all, in fact, there is very little for them to feed upon in the Island. The cattle are brought in vessels from the Spanish main. They are worked there till they have no flesh on them, are then put on board, are perhaps a week or nine days at sea, with little to eat, then swum on shore, and fed on cane-tops, which only just keep life in them, until the butcher wants them. They are literally nothing but skin and bone.

Whenever an ice-ship came in from New York, we could get tolerable mutton, geese, turkeys, codfish, lobsters, good butter, etc., as long as the cargo lasted.

I generally passed my time in reading, writing, taking sketches of different views about; and in the afternoon riding through the country, and calling on my acquaintance.

February 11th. Was the Carnival at Kingstown, when the people dressed themselves in all kinds of grotesque dresses, wore masques, etc., and paraded the town. The Chief justice Sharpe thought this was foolish and improper in this enlightened age, and calculated to disturb the neighbourhood, so he attempted to stop the amusements, and was in consequence mobbed by the populace when riding through the streets with his two daughters, who with great difficulty were rescued from the crowd. It was expected that the mob would attack his house, and we were in consequence under arms from five o'clock till eight p.m., but we were not called out.

February 13th. Breakfasted at Tony Hobson's to join a Maroon Party. We rode our horses to the Buckamont Valley, (a beautiful ride,) taking our fishing-rods with us. We found the river too low and clear, and caught only a few small mullet, which rise to the fly like trout. We devoured some provisions on Table Rock, and rode home.

16th. Hearing that the ramier or wood-pigeon shooting was first-rate, and the perdrix also, Grant, Biscoe, and I started off with our guns up the mountains opposite the Fort to the Cavalries. The bush was so thick that it was with great difficulty we picked our way along the ridges, which were from three to six feet wide at the top, with precipices on each side. We saw no ramier or perdrix, but if we had, we could not have shot them, as the Bush was so dense. We saw nothing but a large black snake, which crossed us near "The Spa."

This Spa is strongly impregnated with iron, and the fixed air which bubbles up through the water is as sharp as that in Seltzer water. The other Spa at Bellair is also strongly impregnated with iron, but has no disagreeable taste. This Spa is built over with bricks like a well, with an opening at the top, and the fixed air arising through it is so powerful, that a person putting his face close over it would be nearly knocked down.

March 4th. I went with Sir John Campbell and Nanton to visit Jackson at Layon, where he met us on the beach with horses a-piece. One of his horses took a long drink of *salt water*, which Jackson told me he always did when he went to the seaside.

"The Rocks" is situated very prettily, but it was in a most miserable tumbledown condition. However, a hearty welcome compensated for that.

Next day we were up betimes, got into the canoes, and went down to Chateau Bellair, where we had a second breakfast in the Court-House in which Jackson transacted his Magisterial business. I took my fishing-rod to Richmond valley, about a mile, and caught in the midday sun about a dozen nice mullet with the willow, black and red fly. The following morning we returned to our respective homes.

March 7th. Called at Government House and escorted Mrs. Browne, with Sir John Campbell, to a Maroon at Caliagua. Lady Campbell and the rest of the party went by sea.

Dasent came during the afternoon, and finding his horse, which fie had lent to Mrs. Browne, tied to a cocoa-nut tree, flew into a rage, and ordered his lad to tie it to a bush near there, which he (lid, the consequence of which presently. Perrin and I returned with the Government-House people, and spent the remainder of the evening very pleasantly.

The bush which Dasent had his horse tied to in his anger turned out to be a Manchineal, which is a poison. ' The horse in kicking at the flies very likely broke some of the leaves, and probably ate one, for everywhere that the sap touched him was formed into a blister, his head next day was one mass of blisters, he could not see. His chest was swollen enormously, and blisters all over the front of his body. A thick discharge came from his eyes and nostrils, and he was unable to open his mouth to eat or drink for many days afterwards, and was reduced to skin and bone. It was months before the horse came round again.

If a person were to take shelter under a Manchineal tree from rain, every drop that ran off the leaves and touched the skin would blister, and any dropping on one's clothes would burn them like caustic.

I took much to sketching at this time, before my eyes got too much accustomed to the grandeur and beauty of the surrounding scenery to lose the proper effect; but my pencil could never do it justice, nor any other pencil either.

St. Vincent suited me much better than Demerara. I felt very much better for the sea voyage and change of air.

We had not many musquitoes at Fort Charlotte, except at one time a few were bred in the tanks and annoyed us.

I rode with Dasent into the Marriagua Valley to Mesopotamia, where we had a magnificent view of the whole valley, a kind of amphitheatre, (from a ridge called the Vegé) backed up by the fine mountains called the Big Bonhomme, and the Little Bonhomme. Another beautiful ride which I often took was along the precipice of Boyd's Valley (on which the path is only wide enough for one horse to pass, and with a perpendicular fall of about 200 feet) on to the Leeward Road, thence into Buckamont Valley, the upper part of which is very fine scenery. The stream which flows through it affords very fair mullet fishing.

April 11th. I started on a trip round St. Vincent and left Fort Charlotte in a canoe with Storey, but on arriving at Layon the canoe men, being drunk, refused to go any further. We therefore shouldered our bags and walked up to Jackson's to dinner, where we found Judge

Sharpe and his party. They were very nice people, and Mrs. Gillespie a most handsome woman. After spending a very pleasant evening, we got *"shakes down"* on the sofas, &c., for the night.

The next morning, after a bathe in the river and breakfast, at seven o'clock the whole party,, left in canoes for Chateau Bellair, where we arrived in a deluge of rain. That evening we went on to McKenzie's of Richmond, in the Valley of that name, dined and slept, and were hospitably received.

As is the custom in the Island, the River Richmond was poisoned and turned off, as the only way of taking the best fish. It was a curious sight to see some 70 or 80 men *and women* busily engaged catching them, diving completely under water to get under the banks, from whence they always brought out a fish.

After witnessing this sport we walked to Mont Rond, a settlement of the Carrib Indians, where we were entertained with Hollands and water by their chief, Captain John. It was a most difficult and steep ascent to their village, which is situated on a high hill at the foot of La Soufriere, in a very picturesque spot. Here we bought some baskets which are made only by these people, and which are quite waterproof, being lined with the plantain leaf. We returned, well soaked by rain, to dinner at McKenzie's.

We intended to have started early the next morning from Richmond, but it rained so heavily that we were induced to remain there till two o'clock, when Mr. McKenzie got us some mules from the estate, and we ascended the Soufriere, in doing which we got as well soaked by riding along through the bushes and long jungle grass (which was far higher than our heads) as if it had rained all the time in torrents.

The ascent is excessively steep, and the path which runs on the tops of ridges, with a precipice of from 20 to 200 feet on either side, is not more than three to four feet wide. It is so steep that it is as much as a mule can do to climb up with a man on its back, one girth is always buckled across the breast of the animal, the other in its usual place. We saw plenty of ramier, or wood-pigeons, on our way up, sufficient to determine me to go there on a future occasion to shoot. At four o'clock we reached the old crater, which breaks on the view very beautifully, the lake at the bottom of it being about three hundred feet below the top. From here we sent the mules back to Richmond, and walked to the New Crater, which is wilder but not so fine as the other, and has a muddy red pool at the bottom of it.

We left this spot at half-past five, to descend the other side of the mountain to Mr. Cumming's of Lot 14, expecting to find mules sent half-way to meet us, but found none, as we were afterwards told they did not expect us in such bad weather. We got benighted in the wood. The night was pitch dark, we had no guide, and the narrow path was overgrown with long grass and bushes. I had a sort of idea that I knew in what direction Lot 14 lay, so I took the lead, not only for that purpose but to get on quicker than either of the others would have gone. I had to *feel* the path with my feet, through about two miles of bush, on ridges from two to three feet wide, and with precipices of from 20 to 200 feet, nearly perpendicular, on each side, formed by the lava from the eruption in 1812. Once I was persuaded by the others that I must have taken the wrong direction and gave in to their decision, but we soon found they were wrong. I then took my old line again, and once came to a stand-still, as the path seemed to end, but just then a fire-fly crossed between two trees and gave me light enough to re-find my way. Hobson got quite done up, so much so that he lay down and declared he could go no further, and that we must send a mule for him. This however was impossible, for we should never have found him again, and did not know where we were ourselves. We at last got him on his legs again, and by dint of brandy and a little rest got him on, and we arrived at Lot 14 at half-past seven p.m., where we found them all at dinner. My horse arrived from Fort Charlotte to meet me here.

13th April. I joined the Gillespies - and Sharpe party, and rode to the Carrib Settlement of Sandy Bay, along a beautiful path on the sea coast. Here I found the Carribs of more pure blood than at Mont Rond, as they had not intermarried with the negroes. Some of them had their hair as long, black, and silky as ever it was, though some also had hair which partook a little of the woolly nigger. Miss Julia Sharp got a fall in galloping with me along the sandy beach, but luckily was not hurt. Storey and I returned to dinner at Lot 14.

16th April. We rode over to Mr. Browne's, close to Georgetown, and remained there till the 18th, when we rode to the Colonial Election, where Hobson had preceded us. I and Storey fished in the Colonial River, when I caught eight or nine mullet, Storey caught none.

The sport not being good, we returned to see how the Election was proceeding. We found that there were three candidates, and at the close of the poll at three o'clock, one had five votes, another had six, and the third eight votes, these being all the qualified voters in the district. (At the Chateau Bellair Election *two* members were returned by one voter.)

Notwithstanding they were so few there was a good deal of excitement, for they were not at all particular in their language to one another, "Blackguard;" "Liar," "Falsehood," were epithets that were issuing in all directions. Hobson had to turn *three* of these gentlemen out of the room for accusing him of partiality in taking the votes, and I heard more apologies made in that one day than I ever heard in my life before.

It was a joke against Hobson (the Sheriff) that he took *me* with him round the elections to help to fight his battles. If I had been situated as he was, and had the language addressed to me that he had, I certainly should have had a fight or two, but he displayed the most admirable coolness imaginable.

After lunching at the expense of the returned member, we rode on to the "Union," where we were hospitably received, and where we dined and slept; that is, I tried to sleep, but what with a vile little puppy, barking in the rain all night just opposite my window, the chattering of a monkey, and the crying of a peacock, together with heaps of musquitoes in my bed, I had little chance of getting any at all. To add to my discomfort, on getting up in the morning I found the rain had been beating in through the open window, and had wet everything I possessed in my portmanteau.

Mr. C— I found was quite a Yankee in ideas, and not my style of man, and his wife never opened her mouth, so that I was not sorry when we left the next day for Fort Charlotte. We were caught in very rain, so called on the priest, McNamee, for a couple of hours' shelter and to put up the horses, but the priest not being at home we rode on, and got home in time for mess at seven o'clock. So ended my trip round St. Vincent, which all in all was very pleasant. Mr. McNamee, the priest, who was a very good fellow, once asked me to go and stay with him at the "Pastures," saying he had just finished his little country-house there, which was quite delightful. He said he had "capital shooting and excellent fishing; the house was situated on a rock immediately over the sea, and was *very pleasant*. All night you would fancy yourself in a steam-boat at sea from the noise." I inquired of him what shooting he had. "Oh!" he replied, "sea gulls and hawks, which afford excellent sport." As may be supposed, I did not accept the kind offer.

May 5th, Sunday. I walked with Cumming, Perrin, and Storey, up to "The Spa," on the Cavalries, and whilst there found a walnut tree, with plenty of last year's fruit strewed on the ground. A man who was with us told us that they were good to eat, upon which I used four of them. The consequence was that in half an hour I found myself poisoned, and vomiting excessively. I was very ill all night from them. They were called the St. Vincent walnut or hickory.

The tides at St. Vincent do not rise and fall more than one foot, whilst at Guernsey and the Channel Islands, they rise and fall from thirty-five to forty feet.

TRIP TO THE SOUFRIERE

May 10th. Packed up my gun, hammock, a couple of changes of clothes, and my 13 ft. square of oilskin, with my cooking apparatus and gridiron, a ham, some bread and brandy for my own use, and joined Sir John Campbell, McLeod, Browne, and Nanton, and went in a boat to Chateau Bellair, calling on our way at Barrow-a-lee, to pick up Barney Jackson, who was dispensing justice and mercy at his Court there. Here we met Dr. F., who invited us to his house, gave us champagne all round, and then invited himself to join our party. On arriving at Chateau Bellair, Barney Jackson gave us a dinner in the Court House and Police Office, with lots of champagne, which latter had too great an effect on Doctor F—'s already excited brain. He got nearly screwed; and after Sir John left us, to get lodgings, the Police Sergeants made us shakedowns on the floors and benches in the office. Mine was made on two high-backed benches, but as the Doctor had friends in the village, there was none for him, so he said he would sleep with me. To this I positively said, no, that he would not. I hurried in, and immediately the Doctor jumped in, boots, clothes, and all, as he stood; upon which I took him by the collar of his coat and the hinder part of his breeches, and dropped him over the back of the benches on to the floor, on his stomach.

He then set to work to abuse me, calling me all the names his inventive brain could collect together; and when I had settled myself in bed again, he pulled apart the benches, when I told him, if he did not behave himself, I would throw him out of the window, and that he had better leave the room before I turned him out.

A little after this, in pretending to go home, he had to pass the head of my bed. He made a snatch at my throat, but as it was bare, his fingers slipped off. I then took him, body and bones, to the window, which was about twelve feet from the street, and held him out by the legs, with his head down, and swore I would let him drop if he did not promise to go away quietly. In a short time the pain of hanging out in that position made him say he would do so, I then pulled him back, but on gaining his liberty, he became restive again, so I twisted his arm behind his back so tight that he bellowed like a bull. I walked him into the street, whence he serenaded us for half an hour, saying how he would shoot me in the morning, and have his revenge.

The following morning we sent an invitation to the furious doctor to come to breakfast, but he did not make his appearance. I afterwards met him in the street, with his arm in his waistcoat breast, instead of a sling; he declared he thought it was out of the socket. He, however, instead of shooting me as he promised, invited me to a friend's house in the village to have a sangaree! (cold wine negus.)

We could not get our party together for a start to the Soufriere before twelve o'clock; and Jackson, who was to make all the arrangements as to provisions, &c., &c., was obliged to remain in Chateau Bellair, to hold his Court. He, however, told us to go on up to his hut on the mountain, where everything would be ready, and he would join us. I, Sir John Campbell, and Brown, rode mules up. We all arrived about three o'clock p.m., and slung the hammocks, but we found the hut not waterproof, and no provision whatever. There was nothing to cook with, nothing to eat off of or to eat, and nothing to drink or to drink out of. Luckily I had *my own* cooking tin, gridiron, a ham, and some bread and brandy. We commenced to shoot ramier, or wood-pigeons, which take flights across the ridge upon which the hut was built, for two hours in the morning, and return in the evening. They fly like lightning, and are very difficult to find in the brambles and rocky holes they fall into when shot. I went about half-a-mile higher up the mountain, to where the low brush-wood grows, and killed six ramier, but I only could pick up *one*, from the broken state of the ground and bushes. McLeod killed four but only got one. On returning to the hut, about six o'clock, sunset, (in this climate it becomes perfectly dark ten minutes after the sun is down, and there is no twilight,) I found that we had no candles, and were all in the dark. I got the two pigeons plucked, and set to work to cook them, with some of my ham, but could get no assistance whatever from any of the party. They were one and all perfectly helpless, and did not know what do in such a case.

The smoke from the fire was so suffocating that we could neither sit nor stand, and had to lie on the ground to cook and eat, or rather, "pig" in the dark. When I had finished my cooking, I cut up the viands with my knife and fork (the only one there) and distributed to the *helpless*.

About eight o'clock Jackson sent up some fowls, with a ham, knives, forks, and candles, also some brandy and sugar, so that we were then set up. After making a kettle of brandy and water, and putting it by the fire for the night's use, we all turned into our hammocks at nine o'clock. These said hammocks I had to sling myself, or they would never have been put up!

I slept well in my hammock, getting no rain, having placed my canvass upon the plantain thatch of the hut, immediately over my berth. It rained in torrents and blew terrifically all night.

I turned out at six next morning, got some grilled ham and a glass of hot grog, and went up to the low bushes to shoot, when the rain came down in such torrents that I was obliged to return to camp. We got some capital pepper-pot, which I made, for breakfast, after which the party set to work and played cards. I did not, but occasionally got a shot at the door of the hut, and killed three out of four.

We stayed for the evening's shooting and bagged eight ramier between us. Next day we returned to the Fort.

Being Quartermaster (as also Paymaster) to the

Detachment, I found that from the unusually dry weather there was only 18 inches of water in one tank. We were, therefore, necessarily obliged to be put on two gallons a day, which was disagreeable where one requires a bath twice a day.

Having been Paymaster and Quartermaster to the Detachment since we went to Demerara (for which I only got keep for a horse) and as Pilkington took over the Regimental Paymastership at Head Quarters without knowing one bit/babout the business, or even taking the trouble to look into his accounts, or the management of his office, he so bothered me with incorrect abstracts of accounts which I never could get him to attend to when I returned them to be altered, and I so frequently received his balances of accounts from £10 to £98 wrong, that I was nearly driven mad in wading through them and trying to make out his mistakes. Indeed, most of my time latterly was taken up in that way. I therefore gave up the appointment, and handed it over to Perrin on 1st June.

1st to 6th of June. I took a trip with Biscoe to the Soufriere to shoot pigeons.

I killed 39, but only bagged 22 owing to the long grass, brush, and underwood in which they fell. I decided that the proper time for the shooting is from 7.30 a.m. till 9 a.m., and from 3.30 p.m. till 6 p.m. Our Mess at this time went to the bad, under S—'s auspices. To save 2d. a day we scarcely got anything on the table that we could eat.

They broke up our breakfast and lunch mess, S— refusing to cater for either of those meals. The consequence was that I and Nash had to provide our own breakfast in the mess room.

I offered to cater, but would not bind myself to keep their messing down at 2s. 6d. or under 3s. But this they would not allow.

The messing was so very bad that we could not ask people to come and dine, but when Perrin catered we dined, breakfasted, and lunched well, and gave capital dinners to large parties every Friday.

I used to go pretty often to - Buckamont Valley to fish. On the 29th June I caught ten mullet in an hour. 1st of July I went there with Biscoe, when I caught 20 mullet and 1 cro-crow, so called, I should think, from the noise he makes with his mouth when landed. The heat of the sun is so great that it always gave me a head ache in about an hour. On the 2nd of July the thermometer stood at 84° in the shade, 102°, 112° and 114° in the sun, and at 118° on the 3rd July. This excessive heat prevented my going often. I went to dine very often at Government House, alias The Garden. The first time I dined there I was much surprised on entering the drawing-room after dinner to join the ladies, to see Sir John Campbell, McLeod, etc. pull out their cigars and smoke away.

They did not dress for dinner, and the ladies sat down in morning dresses. The servants attended table without neckcloths, collars, or waistcoats!!

The nuisance of little children talking when they are not wanted will be seen from the following dialogue.

Lady C. — "Captain Davenport, this little child has been looking for you all the morning, and talking all day about you."

Child.— "So have you, Lady C."

Lady C.— "Hush, child! We expected you to lunch, Captain Davenport."

Capt. D. — "I am very sorry, but I sent a messenger to say I couldn't come to lunch, and am distressed you should have waited."

Child.— "Oh, yes! Lady C. was talking about you in the carriage, and—"

Lady C.— "Nonsense child, be quiet."

Child.— "Captain Davenport came to see Lady C., and she is so glad!"

Child's Mamma.— "Be still child, and don't talk."

Child again.— "But I've a right to talk, I've got a tongue, and its no use unless I talk."

Now there is nothing in reality in the above, but before a number of people who were present, it was very awkward to say the least of it.

July. St. Vincent became insufferably dull and stupid. Several maroons were attempted as a break, but the rains always prevented their coming off. I got quite tired of riding the only two roads in the Island, and, in fact, got sick of the place. Doctor Clarke, the P. M. O., was suddenly ordered away, and as S— had always breakfasted with him at the Hospital as a guest, and had never had him to dine with him in return for his kindness, I wrote the following letter.

"MY DEAR CLARKE,

"Your being so suddenly ordered away has taken me quite aback, and will leave me no time to return the kindness and hospitality received at your hands, which I ought to have done in some degree long ere this. I have certainly "spunged" to an enormous extent on you, and should most probably have continued to do so had you been allowed-to remain. Your time here is now short; nevertheless may I beg that you will shut up your own establishment and kindly do me the pleasure of living with me until you leave. I promise you capital breakfasts, luncheons, dinners, etc., etc.

"Believe me to remain,

"Yours very sincerely,

"W.S—"

This I directed to Doctor Clarke, P.M.O., enclosed it in another envelope, addressed to Doctor S— , and had it dropped on the road from the Hospital, as if by accident, when S— was coming from it. He picked it up, found Doctor Clarke's note inside, returned with all speed, delivered it himself, and had the satisfaction of seeing his friend read it. Clarke saw it was a joke played off on S—, and laughed at him and it; but poor S— was furious about it for several days.

He never found out, even to this day, who played the trick upon him.

August 11th. Lieutenant-Colonel Johnson retired from the service. The mail which arrived on the 10th brought out the Gazette, in which he goes on half-pay; and Lieutenant-Colonel Grubbe, late 76th Regiment, brought in in his place.

August 16th. Every probability of a hurricane sheaved itself. The Barometer fell considerably; the wind went suddenly round to the South, (the hurricane point) with rain and thick fog.

Grant, R.E., went all round the Fort, closing, bolting, and barring every window, door, and crevice. The ships in harbour lowered and took down their yards, top and top-gallant masts. The people of the town assembled on the beach, expecting to see the vessels come ashore. They pitched and tossed, and dragged their anchors considerably, but did not part with them. The cutter, Vigilant, was not so fortunate, for she came ashore, and was a total wreck in a short time. All the small craft got up their sails and went round to Calliagua for shelter.

The scene was painfully interesting. There was one unfortunate nigger who could not haul up his sail in his cutter himself, to run out of harbour, and nobody would go and help him, the surf was so heavy. He became distracted, danced, swore, shook his fists at those on shore, after imploring their assistance. They only laughed at the unfortunate creature.

All his ropes gave way, and there was no hope for his little vessel: at last he got into his dingey, to come ashore, and was immediately swamped by a heavy surf. He would not let the boat be lost, for he swam about till he got hold of it, and managed to bring it with him, through all the surf, to the shore-. I am happy to say, his little cutter withstood the storm, and I saw him next day putting his rigging in order, to go home to Beguia.

There was not so much wind, but it was the surf that made the vessels drag so heavily, until 12 o'clock at night, when it went round to the East, and blew a regular gale. It always blows from the East or South-East, from which circumstance the sides of the Islands are called the Windward or Leeward.

August 30th. I was taken ill about four o'clock a.m., with dreadful spasms in my stomach, which kept me writhing, with my knees contracted up to my chin, in bed till three o'clock p.m., when I applied hot water for two hours. I took two glasses of essence of ginger, besides brandy and pills, which had some slight effect in relieving the pain; but the fearful spasms came on again at night, when I took opium, castor-oil, and essence of ginger and tea. They continued all next day till evening, when they left me very sick and squeamish, and excessively weak.

Three men in the neighbourhood died this week of Asiatic cholera, and on the 4th September Mulgheeny died of it in the Hospital.

On the 6th September I received accounts of the dangerous illness of my mother, when I immediately applied for six months' leave of absence, which was forwarded by Biscoe to the General at Barbadoes, and I received it on the 25th.

After packing up and selling off all my things, and my horse to Stackpoole for 150$ (20 more than I gave,) I bid adieu to all my friends in St. Vincent.

It was quite time I left, for I had been so weak for several weeks that I could not ride four miles or walk more than two without being completely knocked up. The least exertion caused a fit of vomiting- to come on at any time. On awaking in the morning I was always very sick indeed, in fact I was quite done up.

I embarked on the 28th September, in the packet Eagle, at 6-30 p.m. for Barbadoes, and was accompanied to the beach not only by a number of my old friends, but also by many that I was not aware knew even my name. These latter all wished me a prosperous voyage, and I did not leave St. Vincent without regret.

Before closing this volume of my journal I may as well record the surprising activity of the mules used in the cane fields. It is quite astonishing to see them galloping across these, filled with cane holes, as fast as they can go, and without ever making a mistake.

The enormous muscle of the negro men is amazing. They are beautiful models of strength. The women also have very good figures although they have black ugly faces. On week-days both men and women are very slovenly in their dress, but on holidays and Sundays they come out in all the colours of the rainbow.

You may see three or four beautifully dressed women in silks, satins, and lace, walking about. You go up to look at their pretty faces, and find them as black as night. They have a very good ear for music, and are exceedingly fond of the drum, which they let you know at "Cross over" (answering to our Harvest Home,) when they get together three or four drums, to which with their voices (which are tremendous) as an accompaniment, they "dance all night" and keep it up for three days successively. It is very seldom, even on these occasions, that a drunken negro is seen.

In the Island of Montserrat there are a great number of Irish, and many of the-niggers have assumed Irish names. On the arrival of some emigrants there (a short time ago) who understood it was Irish Colony, one of them asked a native how long he had been there? He replied, "Only two months." By my faith then is it that black you've got already I'll be going back to the ould country," said Pat.

The barbarity of the negro women surpasses any thing one can conceive. On the 23rd of September a woman was brought up before the Magistrates for "*peppering her child*," a girl of ten years of age. This barbarous act was done by cutting one of the hottest peppers and rubbing it into the tenderest parts. A woman at Demerara, when I was there, was convicted of cutting gashes with a knife in her child's flesh, and then rubbing pepper into the wounds.

A girl in St. Vincent was rescued by Mr. Cowie from the lash of her mother, who had tied her to a tree, when the mother said, "Nebber mind! I shall catch her again, and then I'll pepper her."

In Mustique and other of the Grenadine Islands the boughs of the trees hang down into the sea, when the oysters attach themselves to them, and we have the remarkable circumstance of oysters growing on trees.

The fruit and vegetables produced in the West Indies are Grenadillos (similar to pumpkins, but sweet); Sapadillos (shape of apples, but something like sweet medlars); Pomegranates, Sour tops (fit for pigs); Custard Apples (similar to the soft seeds of the sun flower); Guavas, an apple for jelly; Java plums, Mangoes (*alias* turpentine balls, but which make good pickles); Mamme Lapotas, Jamaica plums, Hog plums, Avocado pears, Cashew, an apple (when baked, and the juice squeezed into punch makes it a nice flavour); Otaheite gooseberries, sugar-apples, bread-fruit, cocoa-nut, and sea-side grapes; none of which are good save the Sapadillos, cocoa-nut and pomegranate; also Oranges, Shaddock, Forbidden Fruit, Pine-apples, Banana, and Citron.

Of the vegetables, bread-fruit ought to be one, but is not; sweet potatoes, plantains, Akroes, Pigeon, and Angola pease yams, Tamers, &c.

Of the plants, some are the following:—The Papau, the leaf of which has the effect of rendering the toughest meat tender in an hour or two if wrapped in it, or if the meat is placed on the papaw plant. The Sugar-cane, coffee, and cocoa plants, and the Cassado, from which Cassarcip and the Cassada bread is made.

The Rifles (Berkshire and Wiltshire) Museum
Publications

The Museum is proud to have published many titles relating to the history of its regiments. The following pages list and describe them. Visit the Museum's website, where you can also order on-line, at www.thewardrobe.org.uk or telephone 01722 419419

19th Century Histories

Regimental Histories

    Royal Berkshire Regiment

    The Duke of Edinburgh's Royal Regiment

Illustrated Regimental Histories

First World War Battalion War Diaries

First World War Battalion Histories

    Royal Berkshire Regiment

    Wiltshire Regiment

Second World War

    Battalion War Diaries

    Battalion Histories and Accounts

Post Second World War

Music CDs

19th Century Histories

Soldiering 50 Years Ago – Australia in the 'Forties' is a reprint of the account by Major George De Winton published in 1898 about his service in the 99th Regiment during its service in Australia in the 1840s. It is unusual to have an account of a regiment's activities during peacetime, even more so in this case as it covers a decade early in the development of Australia.

From Calcutta to Pekin is a personal account of Captain J H Dunne of the 99th Regiment from February to September 1860 when a British force invaded China, captured the Taku Forts and sacked Pekin. Dunne served with his regiment and on the Staff, and also raised the British flag over the Taku Forts after capture. He went on to achieve high rank in the Army. Dunne only published the journal on reflection back home. It is all the more informative by being written without the thought of publication.

19th Century Histories

Maiwand – The Last Stand of the 66th (Berkshire) Regiment in Afghanistan 1880 is a well-researched account of the 66th Regiment in the period around the Battle of Maiwand on 27th July 1880. It also covers a brief history of the Regiment, the activities which led to the Second Afghan War and the following months, selected biographies, roll of the Regiment in 1880 and extensive index.

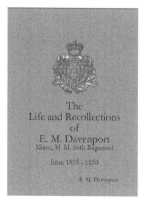

The Life and Recollections of E.M. Davenport, Major H.M. 66th Regiment from 1835-1850. This is a reprint of the book which was first published in 1868. Davenport served with the Regiment and its Depot, which included England, Ireland, Scotland, the West Indies, America and Canada.

Royal Berkshire Regiment Official Histories

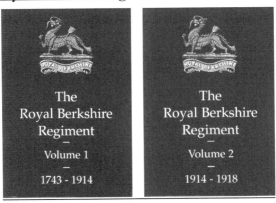

Facsimile editions of the two volumes of the history of the Royal Berkshire Regiment up to the end of The First World War have been published by the Museum, written F. Lorraine Petre.

History of The Duke of Edinburgh's Royal Regiment

The cover says it all. Written by David Stone, this is the story of the Duke of Edinburgh's Royal Regiment, formed on the amalgamation of The Royal Berkshire Regiment and The Wiltshire Regiment in 1959, which itself amalgamated with the Gloucestershire Regiment in 1994.

Illustrated Regimental Histories

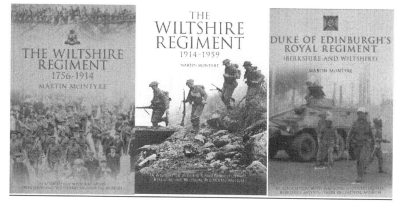

An imaged based history of our regiments in five volumes compiled by regimental historian Martin McIntyre from material in the Museum and elsewhere and published by the History Press.

The volumes are:
- The Royal Berkshire Regiment 1743-1914
- The Royal Berkshire Regiment 1914-1959
- The Wiltshire Regiment 1756-1914
- The Wiltshire Regiment 1914-1959
- The Duke of Edinburgh's Royal Regiment 1959-1994

Each volume contains 200 images with supporting text, depicting people and events in the history of each regiment.

First World War Battalion War Diaries

The First World War saw the introduction of unit war diaries, which have provided a valuable historical record for future generations. The Museum has, through its volunteers, transcribed and published the 14 battalion diaries for the Royal Berkshire Regiment and the Wiltshire Regiment, both as books and on its website. A Second Edition of each has been published and, in addition to the diary transcripts, all have

- The relevant extract from the respective regimental histories
- Battalion Roll of Honour
- Battalion Awards and Decorations
- Organisation of the Division(s) in which the Battalion served
- A comprehensive index

For the Royal Berkshire Regiment the Battalions included are:

- 1st and 2nd (Regular)
- 1st/4th and 2nd/4th (Territorial)
- 5th, 6th, 7th and 8th (Kitchener or Service).

For the Wiltshire Regiments the Battalions are:

- 1st and 2nd (Regular)
- 1st/4th (Territorial)
- 5th, 6th and 7th (Kitchener or Service)

First World War – Battalion Histories
Royal Berkshire Regiment

The China Dragon's Tales – The 1st Battalion of the Royal Berkshire Regiment in the Great War

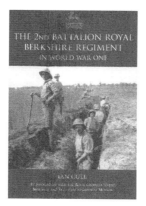

The 2nd Battalion Royal Berkshire Regiment in World War One

Researched and written by the team which had previously published histories on the Royal Berkshire Regiment's 5th, 6th and 8th (Service) Battalions, the two volumes above continue the theme and are the stories of the Regiment's two regular battalions. Each title is based on the battalion, brigade and divisional war diaries, including operational orders and reports, together with personal accounts and diaries which have been brought together to provide a much more personal history than official histories.

First World War – Battalion Histories
Wiltshire Regiment

The 2nd Battalion Wiltshire Regiment, A Record of their Fighting in the Great War 1914-18 by Walter Scott Shepherd M.C.. Originally published in 1927, the Museum is publishing a Second Edition which includes an introduction by Shepherd's son and a full index.

A Journal of the 1st/4th Battalion Wiltshire Regiment 1914-19 –by Sergeant Fred Munday D.C.M.. A Wiltshire schoolteacher, Fred was encouraged to keep a journal of his battalion's activities during the war. The original journal, the basis of the official history battalion by Lieutenant George Blick, was presented to the Museum by Fred's son. This publication is a transcription of the journal, indexed and with many of the maps and images it contained.

First World War – Battalion Histories
Wiltshire Regiment

The 1st Battalion The Wiltshire Regiment in the Great War, by Edwin Astill, is a detailed commentary and analysis of the war diary of the 1st Battalion.

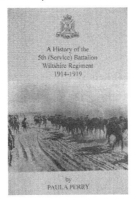

A History of the 5th (Service) Battalion Wiltshire Regiment 1914-1919, by Paula Perry is a comprehensive and well-written story of the Battalion from its formation, through the Gallipoli Campaign and on to cover its war in Mesopotamia (now Iraq). Paula's grandfather served in the Battalion throughout the War and was the inspiration for the book.

Second World War Battalion War Diaries

Of the Battalions of the Royal Berkshire Regiment and the Wiltshire Regiment which fought in The Second World War the Museum has, through its volunteers, transcribed and published all the battalion diaries. Second editions of each have been published which, in addition to the diary transcript contains:

- Relevant extract from the respective regimental histories
- The organisation of the Division in which the Battalion served
- A comprehensive index

For the Royal Berkshire Regiment the Battalions included are: 1st, 2nd, 5th, 10th and 30th.

For the Wiltshire Regiments the Battalions are: 1st, 2nd, 4th and 5th.

A tenth diary, for the 1st and 4th Battalions The Royal Berkshire Regiment and covering the period 1939-1940 has also been published.

Second World War Battalion Histories and Accounts

The Maroon Square is the account of the 4th Battalion Wiltshire Regiment, compiled by three of its officers; Majors Gilson, Parsons and Robbins. This Second Edition includes a full index. Available in paperback and hardback.

The Fifth Battalion Wiltshire Regiment in North-West Europe 1944-45 by Captain J.S. McMath was written for and published by the Wiltshire Regiment in 1949. This Second Edition includes a full index.

Second World War Battalion Histories and Accounts

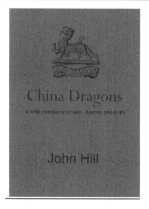

China Dragons a rifle company at war – Burma 1944-45 is the story of B Company of the 2nd Battalion Royal Berkshire Regiment, between November 1944 and June 1945 when it was in close contact with the enemy for 86 days, written by its commander, John Hill.

Private Young's War is the personal account of Geoff Young of his time with the 4th Battalion Wiltshire Regiment from 1939-45, in particular his personal reccolections of the activities of his unit from its landing on the Normandy beaches, the break out and crossing of the Seine, defending The Island at Nijmegen and on into Germany to the end of the war. A4 softback.

Post Second World War

Short History of the Wessex Brigade is a reprint of the booklet, written by Colonel NCE Kenrick, published in 1953 and issued to all recruits when they started training at the Wessex Brigade Depot, Exeter. Softback, 47 pages.

The Last Twelve Years by Major Frederick Myatt M.C. covers the final period of the Royal Berkshire Regiment, from 1948 up to amalgamation with the Wiltshire Regiment in 1959. It follows on from the previous history by Gordon Blight *The History of the Royal Berkshire Regiment 1920-1947* most of which has been incorporated into the respective battalion Second World War histories and diaries covered earlier in this listing.

Music on CD

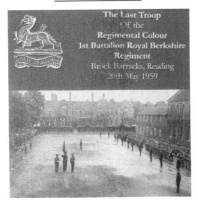

The Last Troop is a live recording of the final troop of the Regimental Colour of the 1st Battalion Royal Berkshire Regiment prior to the laying up of the Colours at Windsor Castle. The parade took place on 20th May 1959 at Brock Barracks, Reading, the Regimental Headquarters. Originally released on vinyl.

"35 Glorious Years" The Duke of Edinburgh's Royal Regiment (Berkshire and Wiltshire) 1959-1994 is a double music CD produced by Music Masters Ltd for the Museum, and is of music by the Regimental Band and the Corps of Drums of the 1st Battalion. It incorporates recordings made at different times, including a rare 1961 recording made for the London Branch of the Regimental Association and never before released. There are 44 tracks plus regimental marches.